Mirrors of Celestial Grace:
Patristic Theology in Spenser's Allegory

Mirrors of
Celestial Grace:
Patristic Theology in
Spenser's Allegory

Harold L. Weatherby

UNIVERSITY OF TORONTO PRESS

Toronto Buffalo London

© University of Toronto Press Incorporated 1994
Toronto Buffalo London
Printed in Canada

ISBN 0-8020-0548-9

Printed on acid-free paper

Canadian Cataloguing in Publication Data

Weatherby, Harold L. (Harold Lerow), 1934–
Mirrors of celestial grace : patristic theology
in Spenser's allegory

Includes bibliographical references and index.
ISBN 0-8020-0548-9

1. Spenser, Edmund, 1552?–1599. Faerie Queene.
2. Spenser, Edmund, 1552?–1599 – Knowledge –
Fathers of the church. I. Title.

PR2358.W43 1994   821'.3   C94-930446-8

For

Ward Sykes Allen

Contents

Contents

Acknowledgments

Parts or earlier versions of chapters 1, 2, 4, 8, and 9 (the last two as a single essay) were published in *Spenser Studies, Studies in Philology,* and *English Literary Renaissance.*

I am indebted financially to Vanderbilt University, both to the college and the graduate School, for assistance in meeting clerical and incidental expenses. I am also grateful to the University for the leave time afforded me for this work.

The librarian and fellows of Pembroke College, Cambridge, afforded me access to their collection, and the assistant librarian, Pamela Judd, was unfailingly courteous and helpful. I owe an especial debt at Cambridge to Elisabeth Leedham-Green, archivist at the university library. Without her unselfish and remarkably efficient help, both in Cambridge and in correspondence, the project would have been impossible.

I have enjoyed the good editorial services of Christine Benagh, George Core of *The Sewanee Review,* and my student Clinton Brand. Professor William H. Race of the Vanderbilt classics department spent a great deal of his valuable time assisting me with Greek and Latin translations from Renaissance patristic texts.

Finally, I wish to thank fellow Spenser scholars for direction and encouragement, especially Carol V. Kaske, Thomas P. Roche, A.C. Hamilton, and Thomas Cain.

The book is dedicated to the friend and scholar who suggested this approach to Spenser and who has helped me most.

Mirrors of Celestial Grace:
Patristic Theology in Spenser's Allegory

Introduction

Attempts to read the theological allegory of *The Faerie Queene* with reference to any single set of beliefs have proved frustrating, if not to those who have made the attempts, at least to many of the readers they have sought to persuade. Most of these interpretations are Protestant, and that Spenser was in more than one sense a Protestant poet is scarcely debatable. He was a member of the Church of England and, at least in the 1590 *Faerie Queene*, a champion of that Church; his allegory, as all readers know, borrows heavily at points from anti-Catholic polemic, especially in his use of Revelation, and his historical and ecclesiological typology in Book One, as Frank Kermode and others have demonstrated, is conventionally Protestant. Nevertheless, efforts to find a systematic Protestant theology in the allegory have proved reductive. The most obvious instance, and a cautionary one, is Padelford's endeavor to make Spenser a consistent Calvinist.[1] But even Anthea Hume's much less rigorous definition of Protestantism produces readings which strain (as we shall see) against the apparent sense of the poetry; and John King's otherwise persuasive discussions of Spenser's iconography are biased by the author's determination to make the allegory conform to the official iconoclasm of the Tudor Church.[2] King sometimes seems to argue from what Spenser as an Elizabethan Protestant *must* have believed rather than from the beliefs the poetry appears to present. Furthermore, the Protestant interpreters largely ignore such overtly Catholic elements in the allegory as the symbols in the House of Holinesse. Indeed, ever since Lewis's *Allegory of Love* critics have sought to explain these away; Anthea Hume merely writes them off as 'personifications of a profoundly traditional kind,'[3] not seeming to recognize that their presence necessarily qualifies her Protestant interpretation.

I do not suggest as an alternative a Catholic interpretation (like Nelan's)[4] nor even a systematic effort to reconcile Protestant and Catholic elements but simply a reconsideration of Spenser's theological range. How eclectic, in fact, is *The Faerie Queene*? How many different and even contradictory understandings of Christianity does the poem weave together? Catholic as well as Calvinist teachings certainly seem to be there (Spenser introduces the Catholic symbolism in the House of Holinesse with what appears to be a Calvinist statement of belief in total depravity: 'If any strength we haue, it is to ill'),[5] but do these exhaust the possibilities of the allegory? The purpose of this study is to argue that they do not and to propose another point of theological reference.

Discussions of Spenser's religion have always presupposed that the influences to which he was subject were those exerted by particular Churches or Confessions; interpreters have largely ignored the sorts of theology which Spenser could have read in books. One such sort which cries out for consideration on account of its ubiquity in the sixteenth century is that of the pre-Augustinian and Eastern Church Fathers. No historian of Renaissance ideas would dispute the importance of patristic influence in the period, but very few students of English literature have taken that influence seriously into account[6] – in Spenser's case, virtually no one. There is a letter to the *Times Literary Supplement* in 1951 commenting on a resemblance of a passage in the *Shepheardes Calendar* to Saint Basil's *ad adolescentes*; C.A. Patrides argues that Spenser's 'trinall triplicities' (*FQ* I, xii, 39) is owing to Dionysius the Areopagite rather than to Calvin; and there are passing references to various Fathers in various books and articles.[7] But nowhere, not even in so learned and encyclopaedic a study as Nohrnberg's, do we find a sustained argument for the possibility of patristic influence. I advance such an argument in the pages that follow.

No antecedent improbability attaches to the enterprise, for patristic works were readily available. All the principal Fathers – Ambrose, Athanasius, Basil, Chrysostom, Clement of Alexandria, Cyril of Alexandria, Cyril of Jerusalem, Dionysius the Areopagite, Gregory Nazianzen, Gregory of Nyssa, Irenaeus, Origen, Tertullian, and more – are to be found in sixteenth-century, Western European editions, some in the original Greek, some in Latin translations, some in both, a few in English. These patristic editions were not done in a corner; virtually all of them are major scholarly publications from distinguished houses – Froben in Basel, Stephanus in Geneva, Chaudiere in Paris, Aldus Manutius in Venice.[8] The editors were for the most part the major humanists: Pirckheimer, Billius, Musculus, and of course Erasmus, whose contribution to patristic studies is well documented. And the Fathers appear to have been popular: there were at least twelve editions of Irenaeus between 1526 and 1596;[9] Petrus Nannius' translation of Athanasius (1556) went through four editions before the end of the century;[10] *Opera* of Gregory of Nyssa were published at Cologne in 1551 and at Basel in 1562 and 1571, with separate works appearing throughout the century;[11] there were several editions of Gregory of Nazianzus, the most important being a 'complete' Greek version in 1550 and a translation by Jacobus Billius in 1569, to which Billius added a commentary in 1583;[12] Maximus the Confessor's *Four Centuries of Charity* was published at Hagenau in 1531 and his *Five Centuries of Theology* at Paris in 1560.[13] There were numerous editions of John of Damascus, the most important being an *Opera Omnia* by Jacobus Billius (Paris) in 1577, of which we shall have more to say.[14] Chrysostom was the most popular of the Eastern Fathers and was available to sixteenth-century readers in multiple editions; Erasmus' five-volume *Opera*, published by Froben in 1530, was the most complete and remained standard until the beginning of the seventeenth century.[15] Furthermore, by 1545 all of the Byzantine service books were in print in the West, and by late in the century most of them many times over;[16] in view of the close relationship between Eastern patristic theology and Greek liturgy the availability of these liturgical texts (some of which I shall argue Spenser knew) is of great importance.[17]

Though before 1612 none of the major patristic editions comes from England, there is plentiful evidence for their English circulation.[18] There are citations and quotations of the Fathers and the antique liturgies by English theologians and polemicists from More to Hooker, most notably and frequently in works of Cranmer, Jewel, Whitgift, Grindal, and Foxe. Many of these references are cryptic and do not demonstrate profound knowledge of the text in question, but their

very presence indicates the importance of patristic authority in sixteenth-century religious controversy. That the Reformers should
appeal to that authority is especially interesting in view of their supposed commitment to the principle of *Sola Scriptura*. 'The Fathers,' S.L.
Greenslade explains, 'are not in themselves an absolute standard, but
they are positively important as a guide to the meaning of scripture, as
an indication of a scriptural way of life for the Church; they have *auc-
toritas*, weight, they are to be esteemed.' And esteemed in England
they certainly seem to have been; Greenslade quotes from the Westminster Conference of 1559: '"By the custom of the primitive church
we mean the order most generally used in the church for the space of
five hundred years after Christ; in which times lived the most notable
fathers, as Justin, Irenaeus, Tertullian, Cyprian, Basil, Chrysostom,
Hierome, Ambrose, Augustine, etc."' Greenslade also quotes Jewel's
hyperbole that '"The first five hundred years of the church are more
worth than the whole thousand that followed afterward."'[19] That is a
common sixteenth-century sentiment in England. Cranmer echoes it in
his Preface to the Great Bible (1540), where he quotes extensively from
both Chrysostom and Basil as representatives of the Church's greatest
age,[20] and an anonymous translator of Chrysostom's homilies on Ephesians tells his 'Reader': 'The time, wherin this golden father Chrysostome liued, seemeth to be the golden age, wherein Religion and
Learning, were lincked togither, with true pietie: in the which time ...
not onelie this Author, but also Gregorie Nazianzen, and Basil the
great, liued ...'[21] Such statements bespeak not only knowledge of but
reverence for the Fathers – the sort of reverence that could inspire a
poet to read them and draw upon them for the purposes of his art.

   That would be all the more likely if Spenser encountered them in his
intellectually formative years, which could easily have happened at
Cambridge. Thanks to the University's preserving probate records we
know that 176 scholars who died in residence between 1535 and 1599
owned among them 277 copies of editions of the following Greek
Fathers: 21 of Athanasius; 24 of Gregory Nazianzen; 5 of Gregory of
Nyssa; 32 of Basil; 18 of Cyril of Alexandria; 2 of Cyril of Jerusalem; 9
of Dionysius the Areopagite; 16 of Irenaeus; 25 of John of Damascus;
and a surprising 125 of Chrysostom. (I say surprising in view of there
being only a few more, 129, of Augustine, whom one would expect to
be far more widely read; only 87 of Luther, and only 5 of Thomas Cart-

wright.) Of the pre-Augustinian Latin Fathers, there were 42 copies of editions of Ambrose, 40 of Cyprian, and 24 of Tertullian.[22] These figures suggest that patristic texts and doctrines made a part of the Elizabethan intellectual milieu and that Spenser was educated in an ambiance in which the Fathers could easily have been known to him.

We can be more precise – not just Cambridge in general but Spenser's College, Pembroke, in particular. John Welles, BA, who died in 1569 and is described in the probate inventory as a 'pensioner in Pembroke Hall,' left, besides editions of Augustine and Aquinas, an 'Opera Tertuliani 1 volumine,' an 'Opera basilii magni 1 volumine,' an 'Opera Crisostomi .5. voluminibus,' and a 'Lexicon grecum.'[23] He would not have required the lexicon for the Chrysostom, there being no five-volume Greek *Opera* in 1569. The edition Welles owned may be Erasmus' translation of 1530,[24] of which the Pembroke library also owned a copy (acquired in 1536 and still in the collection).[25] There were almost certainly other editions of the Fathers at Pembroke in the 1560s and 1570s though of the many Renaissance patristic editions now in the collection, only the five-volume Chrysostom can be traced with certainty to a pre-Spenserian date. There are, however, half a dozen others which could as easily have been there then as not;[26] no records of acquisition are available. One group of these which, though post-Spenserian in date of accession, brings us tantalizingly close to Spenser is inscribed *Ex dono Lanceloti Andrews, Episcopi Wintoniensis*, 1589. Spenser and Andrewes were fellow students both at Merchant Taylors School and later at Pembroke. That means they were associated academically (and in a small group of scholars) for at least a decade. They could scarcely have avoided knowing each other, and knowing each other intellectually; there being no biographical evidence of mutual influence does not preclude the possibility and, one would think the probability, thereof. Andrewes became one of England's best patristic scholars, and Spenser could have learned from him, at Cambridge or, for all we know, later.[27]

Pembroke had been associated with the Fathers before Welles, Andrewes, and Spenser arrived there – at least since the time of Edmund Grindal's (Algrind's) presidency and mastership (1549–1562). Patrick Collinson has discovered editions of 'Athanasius, Basil, Ambrose, Gregory of Nazianzus, and many others' among books which Grindal bequeathed to Queen's College, Oxford,[28] and the

Archbishop's *Remains* includes dozens of citations of the Fathers pertinent to questions both of doctrine and of discipline. As Bishop of London, in 1567, Grindal chose as a gift 'worthy to be presented to the Queen's majesty, both for the author's sake, and the rarity' 'thirty Homilies of Chrysostom, upon the eleven first chapters of Genesis.' This is a manuscript ('the Greek copy is not in print to my knowledge'); Grindal is confident of its authenticity, 'for it agreeth with the Latin translation set forth by Œcolampadius, in the 5th tome of Chrysostom's works in Latin'[29] (again the Erasmus edition, which contains translations by several hands). Grindal is writing to William Cecil, Lord Burghley, who was himself a Greek scholar and familiar with the Fathers; in 1553 Burghley presented his second wife, Mildred, with a 1529 Veronese edition of Chrysostom's homilies on the Pauline epistles (the only Greek edition of these homilies available until 1596).[30] (Cecil's first wife was sister of his Greek tutor at Cambridge, John Cheke.) The further one looks into the world in which Spenser moved – at least before his departure for Ireland – the more evidence one finds of interest in the Fathers. At Pembroke itself that study was to all appearances sustained after Grindal's departure by Whitgift, who became Master in 1567 and who was in that position when Spenser matriculated; by Andrewes, who became a fellow of the college in 1576, the year of Spenser's departure, and Master in 1589; and by John Young, who became Master in 1567 upon Grindal's recommendation and whom, as Bishop of Rochester, Spenser served as secretary in 1576-7.[31]

None of that *proves* that Spenser had read the Fathers at Cambridge, but such evidence of patristic interest among his associates (and in the instance of Grindal a man we have reason to believe Spenser revered) demonstrates the possibility. I shall try to show that the poetry demonstrates the probability. Taking patristic theology as a measure for certain episodes either makes sense of allegorical developments which have hitherto proved puzzling or suggests new and more convincing ways of reading other passages which we have interpreted as 'Protestant' or 'Anglican.' At the very least the Fathers' theology provides an effective heuristic tool, helping us to see in Spenser things which, however they got there, seem certainly to be there and which have not been seen before. That they got there because Spenser read the Fathers and the ancient liturgies seems considerably more likely to me than that the

resemblances are mere coincidences; but I trust that the reader whom I
may not convince of influence will profit nevertheless from the fresh
perspectives which the hypothesis of influence makes available. If he
profits enough, he may ultimately become convinced of the hypothesis
itself.

II

A central episode in Book One demonstrates how our knowledge of a
patristic work available to Spenser contributes to a reading of his allegory. In 1581 Binneman and Newberie of London published an anonymous English translation of Saint John Chrysostom's homilies on
Ephesians;[32] in them Chrysostom devotes a great deal of attention to
the Pauline metaphor of Christian armor. Given the popularity of the
conceit in devotional works of all kinds, there would be no compelling
reason to single out Chrysostom as a source for Spenser's 'armour of a
Christian man' were it not for some distinctive similarities between
Chrysostom's and Spenser's use of the motif. Both emphasize the
disastrous spiritual consequences of going unarmed, and in much the
same vocabulary. The prelude to Red Crosse's seduction by Duessa is
his being 'Disarmed all of yron-coted Plate' (I, vii, 2), and Chrysostom
asks the Christian soldier, 'Howe commeth it to passe, that thou liuest
deliciously [as Red Crosse does at this juncture]? How art thou dissolute? how can we get the victorie, when we are unarmed?'[33] To illustrate Spenser's delight in word-play and etymological puns, A.C.
Hamilton cites Una's characterization of Red Crosse as 'dissolute' (I,
vii, 51: 'disarmed, dissolute, dismaid'): 'This term means "debauched,"
"enfeebled," "relaxed," and "careless."' 'Also,' Hamilton adds, 'it implies "dissolved" (OED I), from the Latin *dissolutus*, loose: the Knight
was betrayed when he lay "Pourd out in loosnesse on the grassy
ground."' Furthermore, 'the Knight is "dissolute" in the precise sense
of being dissolved: by drinking from the fountain, his 'cheareful bloud
in faintnesse chill did melt."'[34] And Hamilton glosses Spenser's 'Pourd
out' with the 'Lat. *effusus*'; Red Crosse, 'sexually expended and
exhausted ... is like the water he drank.'[35]

Chrysostom's *dissolute* also has liquid associations; his disarmed
miles Christi is not only dissolute but 'floweth ouer.' And for both *dissolute* and 'Pourd out' Hamilton could have as plausibly cited the Greek

διακεχυμένος (Chrysostom's participle) as the Latin *effusus*. Chrysostom asks the disarmed soldier, 'How art thou *dissolute?*' πῶς διακεχυμένος εἶ? 'He that standeth right, standeth, not dissolutely' οὐ διακεχυμένος 'but such as stand not, can not be straight, *but loose, and dissolute*' ἀλλὰ διαλελυμένοι, καὶ διακεχυμένοι.[36] The participle is of διαχέω, 'to pour forth' or 'disperse,' and ultimately from χέω, to 'pour.' The closest Latin equivalent is *diffusus* (our 'diffuse'), but Hamilton's *effusus*, 'poured out,' is a legitimate synonym. It is therefore possible that Spenser's 'Pourd out in loosnesse' may be less a metaphoric extrapolation from the English *dissolute* than a literal translation of Chrysostom's adjective for those who discard the 'armour of a Christian man.'[37] It is interesting in that regard that Henri Estienne's *Thesaurus Graecae Linguae* (1572), which a sixteenth-century translator of Chrysostom would have been likely to consult, cites the very passage in question as a gloss on διακεχυμένος and offers *effusus* as a synonym – 'to describe those who are brought up softly (or "deliciously").'[38] Still more interesting in view of Spenser's language is that Estienne pairs *effusus* with *solutus* (according to Sir Thomas Elyot's dictionary, 'lewsed or louse'). In other words, Estienne tells us that Chrysostom's διακεχυμένος in the Ephesian homilies means 'poured out and loose,' from which Spenser's 'Pourd out in loosnesse' is an easy step. And as for 'grassy grownd,' Chrysostom's 'disarmed, dissolute' soldier 'hath all his thoughts trailing upon the ground.'[39]

Such resemblances no more constitute proof of influence than does the accessibility of patristic texts. But, given the availability of Chrysostom's homily both in English and in Greek, the congruence of subject matter, and the similarity in vocabulary and word-play, there is some reason to believe that Chrysostom contributed to the symbolism and verbal wit of Book One. What he did not contribute in this particular instance is anything distinctively patristic; his interpretation of the Christian armor manifests none of the devotional or doctrinal characteristics which frequently distinguish the Fathers' exegesis from that of later Catholic and of Protestant interpreters. In that respect this illustration of possible influence is different from those in succeeding chapters where I argue for reinterpretations of Spenser's allegory in light of patristic *peculiarities* – for a reconsideration of familiar figures and episodes in *The Faerie Queene* in view of the possible influence of theologically distinctive works and teachings. In Part One, for instance, I suggest that Spenser's knowing the catechetical homilies of John Chrysostom, Cyril of Jerusalem, Dionysius the Areopagite, and Ambrose, along with the baptismal treatises of Tertullian and Basil, could account for the way he represents baptism, the Harrowing of Hell, the Resurrection, and the 'marriage supper of the Lamb' in cantos eleven and twelve of Book One. In showing how those ancient interpretations of the paschal mysteries differ from later Western treatments I suggest fresh ways of conceiving Spenser's allegory of holiness. Also in Part One, also under the rubric of holiness, I argue that peculiarly Eastern conceptions of the Transfiguration inform Spenser's use of that Gospel narrative in his description of Dame Nature in the Mutabilitie Cantos. Parts Two and Three deal with more strictly ethical issues and seek to show that Spenser's understandings of temperance and of original sin are more nearly Eastern-patristic than Western, whether Catholic or Protestant, in character. The results are fresh interpretations of four passages in Book Two – of Belphoebe's appearance in canto three (and of her place in a legend of temperance), of Guyon's notorious faint, of Ruddymane's unwashable hands, and of Arthur's battle with Maleger. In these analyses, I suggest influence upon the allegory of such ascetical treatises as Basil's *ascetica* and parts of Clement of Alexandria's *Stromateis*. Finally in the Epilogue I broach the possibility that patristic attitudes toward eros (mostly negative) affect Spenser's treatment of love and marriage in Books Three, Four, and Six.

One thing this book does not presume to do is offer a complete reinterpretation of the theological allegory. I deal with only seven issues in *The Faerie Queene*, six of them in Books One and Two (my discussions of Three, Four, and Six are tangential and suggestive in nature). I do not believe that Spenser's theology was any more consistently patristic in character than it was consistently Protestant. The Protestant elements are unmistakable, and I do not see how an unbiased reader of the poem can deny that Catholic elements are as well. How, if at all, Spenser rationalized his interweaving of frequently contradictory and even hostile theologies, I do not speculate, though such speculation might well be the subject of another study. My purpose here is much less ambitious – simply to argue for the presence of *another* ingredient in the mix, one not previously considered and which, when we do consider it, opens our eyes to new meanings in the poem and to new ways of understanding its Christianity. These do not invariably displace the

old ways, but at important points they qualify them. Some of the qual-
ifications are radical, but I leave for the future the sorting out of exact
relationships.

III

If this study is unsystematic in its treatment of *The Faerie Queene*, it is
equally so in its dealings with the Fathers. I can imagine a patristic
scholar being dismayed that I make no consistent effort to distinguish
among schools or periods – between, for instance, the Alexandrians
and the Chalcedonians. My reason for not doing so is that I see no reason to believe that Spenser would have. In a few instances I argue for
the influence of specific works, such as that of John of Damascus's
Homily on the Transfiguration on the Mutabilitie Cantos; but where I
find evidence of persistent patristic motifs, such as deification or the
quest for passionlessness, I detect no fine distinctions. Nor would we
expect Spenser to make them. Cranmer's evocation of Chrysostom and
Basil as teachers of true religion in the Church's golden age does not
discriminate between the two, for Cranmer like most of his contemporaries appealed to the Fathers as a group and as a composite authority.
Patrides remarks upon 'that most characteristic of Renaissance tactics,
the ahistorical and highly eclectic appeal to all "authorities" which
could be invoked to sustain any given outlook,'[40] and nowhere do we
find that tactic better illustrated than in Renaissance patrology. In effect
I have followed that tactic, piling Father upon Father, text upon text, to
illustrate themes and contexts from which I believe Spenser drew,
because if I am correct that he read the Fathers, that was probably the
way he read them. My treatment, therefore, is 'ahistorical and highly
eclectic' and deliberately so. I have, however, been very careful not to
ascribe to Spenser knowledge of any Father or patristic work which
would not have been available to him. One can never be certain that
what appears as part of a Father's corpus in the *Patrologia* or in other
modern editions was known in the sixteenth century. In any given
work, moreover, sentences or sometimes whole passages which appear
in modern editions may be missing in earlier ones, or the converse; and
the Latin translations printed in the sixteenth century may differ considerably from more recent ones, even when the Greek text is constant.
Some Fathers were not edited at all in Spenser's day and may not have

been known to Spenser (I have not investigated manuscript sources). Lest therefore I should contend foolishly for the influence of a writer or a work unavailable in the Renaissance, I have gone directly to six-teenth-century editions, quoting exclusively from them and making certain that when I have argued for possible influence, the possibility of influence was there. Finally, when I have cited (ahistorically and eclectically) a variety of Fathers to illustrate the persistence of a theme or teaching, I have relied most heavily on the ones most frequently edited in the sixteenth century, assuming that the number of editions is an index of a writer's popularity and influence.

As I have already indicated, this book is not strictly a source study, though I hope I shall convince the reader that the Fathers *are* a source for Spenser's allegory. I am also interested – finally more interested – in what the allegory means. Perhaps I can best characterize my position by saying it is slightly 'before' Hamilton. Hamilton set Spenser studies on a new course in 1961 when he sought to liberate them from a 'schizophrenic image of Spenser' in which 'poet and thinker conflict.'[41] Hamilton is referring, of course, to the tradition of scholarship that comes from the *Variorum* which was generally more concerned with the idea than with the image that conveys it. Hamilton will 'focus upon the image itself, rather than seek the idea hidden behind the image,' because he believes what Spenser 'labours to express is an image rather than moral ideas. These may inform and sustain the image, but the image itself is primary.' I would not flatly deny that primacy (the image is the only vehicle we have for meaning), but being just 'before' Hamilton – as it were a little closer to the *Variorum* scholars – I am more concerned than he is with the 'moral [and theological] ideas'; I believe Spenser was more concerned. Another way to state the difference would be to emphasize more strenuously than Hamilton that the ideas 'inform and sustain the image.' In allegory, after all, images are *of* ideas, and that remains so even in allegories like Spenser's where there is seldom a one-for-one equivalence. Hamilton says that the 'meaning which is usually considered to lie behind the image, I find to lie within the image, *being defined by it*.'[42] I question the phrase I have empha-sized; in Spenser's allegory, does not the idea define the image rather than the reverse? Perhaps it works both ways; perhaps the image shapes our apprehension of the idea while at the same time the idea, behind as well as within, shapes the image; but in my judgment the lat-

ter is the more important influence upon the reader. We want to know
what Spenser's images *mean*, and discovering the meaning is a great
part of the pleasure of reading him. When the meaning we grasp seems
inadequate to account for the details of the image, we remain unsatis-
fied, however rich and powerful the image in itself may be. Spenser
scholarship attests to that phenomenon – the number of different interpretations of the Garden of Adonis reflects scholarly dissatisfaction
with the ideas we have thus far found behind the image. There is no
consensus about meaning so we continue to investigate. That does not
mean that we are interested *only* in meaning or that we simply translate image into idea; but we do want to know what the idea is. I agree
with Heninger that 'with Spenser ... it is the moral that finally counts,
not the pictures, or even the tale.'[43] The ensuing arguments for patristic influence attempt to provide some new and more satisfying meanings for some very familiar Spenserian images.

If my approach to image and meaning is a little 'earlier' than Hamilton's, it is at least the three ensuing decades earlier than some recent
readings of Spenser's 'moral ideas.' (I am not concerned here with
deconstructionist and New Historicist interpretations, for which meaning in my and Hamilton's sense is largely irrelevant.) Two studies, concerned as mine is with Spenser's philosophical and theological
antecedents, invite comparison.

Sean Kane quotes Rosemond Tuve to the effect that '"Allegory is a
method of reading in which we are made to think about things we
already know."' I take that to be another way of saying that the idea
informs the image and that we read for the sake of what the image
means. Kane, much more radically than Hamilton, rejects this 'flatten-
ing of the text with history, so that the poem is read as if it were the
uncritical celebration of an ideology [or a theology?].' He praises the
great Spenser scholarship of the 1960s, from Hamilton to Hankins,
which reads allegorically and 'speaks from the harmony of faith and
reason that offers a direct philosophical life-line back to Spenser.' But
'this tradition of scholarship may now be finished; the shift in intellectual climate has led to a more ironic criticism,' with which Kane is
seemingly in sympathy. I could perhaps best characterize the difference between his and my approaches to 'Spenser's moral allegory,' by
saying that I am still speaking, or trying to, 'from the harmony of faith
and reason that offers a ... life-line back to Spenser' and arguing for a

new, at least hitherto unrecognized, note in that harmony – not a different ('more ironic') approach to Spenser's moral ideas but simply some new suggestions about what those ideas are. Kane laments that 'it is always hard ... to avoid [the] tendency to read a text according to the beliefs of its time.'[44] I am not trying to avoid that tendency; rather I am suggesting that we have not previously recognized some of the beliefs of Spenser's time which manifest themselves in his allegory. (Oddly in view of his Preface, Kane's interpretations are remarkably traditional. His Spenser is Augustinian, a believer in a hierarchical and spiritual conception of man and enemy of an encroaching, secular 'polarization' of flesh and spirit which Kane sees as the harbinger of modernity. In a very considerable measure Kane is still reading allegorically with a concern for the moral and spiritual meaning of Spenser's images. One wonders whether Spenser's poetry will finally allow an honest critic, whatever his predisposition, to read otherwise.)

Both Elizabeth Bieman and I are concerned with Spenser's appropriation of his spiritual antecedents, and to the extent that patristic theology is Platonic we are concerned with some of the same antecedents. Her range, however, is much broader than mine and her approach much more subjective. She offers us her 'readings of the traditional materials, and of Spenser ... as mimetic enactments of "personal knowing,"'[45] Mine may be that, but they are not offered as such. My intention is to be as objective as possible in determining exactly what 'the traditional materials' are – what the Fathers, in this instance, teach – and how Spenser's allegory reflects those teachings. 'To define my critical position,' says Professor Bieman, 'I would suggest that this book describes a process of reconstructive, or recreative, hermeneusis.'[46] I should characterize the hermeneutic value of a patristic interpretation of Spenser's allegory not as recreative or reconstructive but as – well, hermeneutic. The 'traditional materials' should help us to understand the meaning that is there, in the allegory, and where it came from rather than encouraging us to enact personal knowings. Like Kane, Professor Bieman acknowledges her debt to the earlier, more traditional Renaissance scholars of the century; but, like Kane also, she rejects what he calls their 'allegorical reasoning' – their assumption 'that any instance of paradigmatic language was carrying as freight the doctrines traditionally associated with such patterns.' Whereas I make precisely that assumption and am arguing that the freight included doctrines not previously recognized by Spenser's readers, she regrets that that older way of reading caused its practitioners 'to miss ironies, equivocation, evidences of skeptical thinking, and much of the humane richness we now find in the texts.'[47] To counter, as I might, that perhaps we find those elements in ourselves rather than in the texts would be to little purpose, since Professor Bieman has already told us that her readings are 'personal knowing[s].' The phrase, 'humane richness,' seems especially personal, for it appears to deny that richness to 'the doctrines traditionally associated' with 'paradigmatic language.' The bias here seems to be the modern identification of the humane with uncertainty about 'traditional materials' – with 'ironies, equivocation, evidences of skeptical thinking.' She speaks of a 'sceptical strain in the Platonic tradition' which 'provides something quite other than the logocentric set-pieces of Platonic myth.' 'Spenser's poetry is, of course, "logocentric,"' but not, it appears, because ideas inform its images. It does not 'open itself' to meaning but 'to a mysterious absence beyond itself.' It is 'deconstructive insofar as it prevents the consciousness of either narrator or reader from closing upon anything resembling a dogmatic centre.' Then she returns to her insistence upon personal knowing: 'When Spenser deconstructs, he does so serving many freedoms, not least the creative freedom we as readers can achieve in reconstructive, recreative, interpretations.'[48] Because I believe Spenser's theological allegory does close upon dogmatic centers, I am much less interested than Professor Bieman is in my 'creative freedom' as a reader and much more in discovering what the dogmas at the centers are.

To illustrate the difference, I examine one of her recreative interpretations and compare it to my dogmatic one. When Arthur takes his leave of Red Crosse in canto nine of Book One he gives him

> a boxe of Diamond sure,
> Embowd with gold and gorgeous ornament,
> Wherein were closd few drops of liquor pure,
> Of wondrous worth, and vertue excellent,
> That any wound could heale incontinent
>
> (I, ix, 19).

For the reader who believes there is a meaning behind as well as within the image, the obvious question to ask about this 'liquor pure' is: what does it signify? A second question follows hard upon: does the diamond box 'embowd with gold and gorgeous ornament' also have a meaning? Does it refer to some kind of vessel or container we are supposed to recognize?

Professor Bieman approaches these images from several directions. She focuses first on the relation between 'the merely ornamental outer shell' (the box) and the 'inner substance' and finds an 'analogy to the Zoharic notion of text as shell and the understanding derived in the course of hermeneusis as the kernel.' That reading seems far enough removed from the literal level of the allegory to qualify as 'reconstructive' or 'recreative'; however interesting or suggestive in its own right, it does not help us a great deal in discovering what the image means. Her next suggestion is an analogy to Belphoebe's 'soueraigne salue, in secret store,' 'that sweet Cordiall, which can restore / A loue-sick hart,' but which Belphoebe denies to the love-sick Timias (III, v, 50). Here Belphoebe is presumably the diamond box and the love which she withholds, the 'liquor pure.' That reading suggests 'that Spenser regards the precious inner substance as one that calls for circulation.'[49] Since Belphoebe's salve is entirely figurative and Arthur's (so far as the literal level of the allegory is concerned) physical, that comparison too seems far removed from the facts of the poem. Furthermore, Arthur does 'circulate' his ointment; the diamond box does not impose the kind of constriction that the comparison with Belphoebe implies. However, the contrast between constriction and circulation is germane to Professor Bieman's understanding of the matter, for even when she comes to something approaching a 'dogmatic' reading of these images, the restrictive character of the box is still a chief concern. The contents of the box 'sound like the clear contents of a baptismal font'; there we have a 'meaning' in my sense of the term (though not the meaning I believe Spenser intended), but what interests Professor Bieman is not meaning as such but that when Spenser presents baptism in canto eleven, he 'abandons the box and turns to a well and a tree.' Why? Because 'nothing crafted by human hand, however splendid, can serve as well to figure forth God's abundant saving grace as the natural symbols of water and tree.' 'No explicit criticism arises in Canto 11 of the heroic splendour of Arthur's earlier gift. Yet when its disappearance is questioned, the field of understanding is widened

and the contrast intensified between wealth and natural loving goodness.'[50]

That contrast sounds anachronistic, more Romantic or modern than
Spenserian. Finding it in *The Faerie Queene* can perhaps be justified as
an exercise of the reader's 'creative freedom,' but that exercise helps us
very little if at all with the images in question. Given their Scriptural
and liturgical provenance (which Professor Bieman fully acknowledges) the Well of Life and the Tree of Life are not likely to have conveyed to Spenser or his contemporaries (or to many of his readers
since) the Romantic vitalism which Professor Bieman senses. We can be
reasonably certain that the Well represents the baptismal font; and the
two traditional meanings of the Tree of Life are the original tree in
Eden forbidden to Adam and Eve after the Fall and the Cross, which
restores the grace forfeited by the Fall; in conventional exegesis, the
tree in Eden is the type, the Cross the antitype. Sometimes Christ himself, as the source of the sacraments, is the Tree of Life. One can be reasonably certain that Spenser took those meanings for granted and
expected his readers to.

Do Arthur's precious liquor and gorgeous box have equally certain
points of reference? Perhaps not *equally* certain, for neither object has
the self-evident scriptural and liturgical authority of the Well and Tree;
but if we consider the two images in their context we can, I believe,
achieve a reasonable assurance about their meanings. By context, I
refer to the pairing of Arthur's gift with Red Crosse's. Since the latter is
the 'Saueours testament,' we naturally assume (and properly, I believe)
that the former is an equally important Christian symbol, an equivalent means of grace and salvation. What, we then ask, is the traditional
complement of Scripture, of the Word? What do we conventionally
pair with the Bible as the other principal instrument of salvation? The
obvious answer is: the sacraments; and Arthur's gift being material
sustains that inference. It is not an especially startling inference, but
interpreters have been hesitant to make it: Hamilton suggests that the
liquor is '"my blood of the Newe testament,"'[51] but he stops short of
identifying it with the eucharist; it reminds Professor Bieman, as we
have seen, of 'the clear contents of a baptismal font,' but as we have
also seen she is less concerned with the identification than with the
artificiality of the box and the naturalness of Well and Tree. Both suggestions, however, merit careful consideration, because if Spenser's

image is in fact sacramental, it is also fluid and must therefore refer to a sacrament whose matter (in the Scholastic sense) is a liquid. The eucharist and baptism are two of three possibilities.

We cannot eliminate either with complete certainty, but neither seems self-evidently right. Why, for instance, should either be housed in a box? The chalice and the font are their obvious receptacles, and since Spenser's religious imagery in Book One is biblical and traditional, there is no reason to suspect an obscure symbolism in this instance. In canto ten he presents the eucharist in a chalice (Fidelia's 'cup of gold, / With wine and water fild'), and the Well of Life is as obvious and conventional a symbol of baptism as the font. Why should we expect an esoteric variation here? Furthermore, a 'few drops' seems a very small quantity for either communion or baptism; we picture a cup full of wine (Fidelia's is 'fild vp to the hight') and a font with enough water to immerse a child (the 1559 Prayer Book requires immersion unless the child be weak or sick). In that respect too the image contradicts our expectations, and to no discernible purpose. In short, there is no inherent reason to identify a few drops in a box with either baptism or communion, and there is nothing else in the allegory to impose a reason.

The third possibility, the third liquid sacrament, is unction, and that that is the meaning within and behind this symbol seems likely in view of another reference to Arthur's 'liquor pure.' In Book Four the Prince anoints the wounded Amoret with 'that pretious liquour ... / Which he in store about him kept alway' (IV, viii, 20). Hamilton is certainly correct in reminding us at this point of the gift to Red Crosse and in discovering a pun on *incontinent* ('any wound could heale incontinent' [I, ix, 19]);[52] Amoret's wounds are ultimately a consequence of her imprisonment by Lust, and Red Crosse has recently been sorely wounded and brought close to death by his incontinence with Duessa. Since sacramental unction is medicinal, the extremity of Red Crosse's condition is also noteworthy. At the end of canto eight, not long before he receives Arthur's gift, 'all his vitall powres [are] / Decayd, and all his flesh shronk vp like withered flowres' (I, viii, 41); and even after his liberation from Orgoglio's dungeon, at the beginning of canto nine, he is still 'that weake captive wight.' Spenser adds, that he is 'now wexed strong' (I, ix, 2), but before the canto ends we discover (as Arthur may foresee) that his recovery is more apparent than real. In view of such feebleness, both past and to come, a therapeutic sacrament seems an entirely appropriate gift for him. (By traditional acceptation, unction heals both sin and sickness, soul and body.) 'A few drops,' moreover, is an appropriate quantity for this sacrament, precisely what we should expect for unction (interestingly, Arthur also anoints Amoret with a 'few drops'); and though there is no compelling reason, liturgical or iconographic, to associate unction with an elaborate box, such a container would be far more appropriate for holy oil than for baptismal water or eucharistic wine. Moreover, Spenser had precedent for his image in the Gospel account of 'a woman having an alabaster box of very precious ointment,' who broke the box and poured the ointment on Christ's head 'as he sat at meat' in the 'house of Simon the leper.' (The story is told with variations in all four Gospels; the box is mentioned in Matthew, Mark, and Luke; John identifies the woman as Mary, the sister of Martha and Lazarus.)[53] Alabaster is not diamond, but in each instance a materially precious box houses a spiritually precious liquid; and Spenser may have altered the material so as to associate the box with another of Arthur's instruments of grace, his diamond shield.

IV

The differences between my and Professor Bieman's approaches to Spenser's allegory should require little further comment. I do not offer mine as a rebuttal of hers but as an instance of what I mean by placing myself a little before Hamilton and thus much before some important recent interpreters of the 'traditional material.' Beginning with the assumption that the meanings *within* Spenser's theological images are defined by meanings *behind* them and that Spenser anticipates our looking behind, I have used Arthur's gift to show how one can tease those meanings out. That we can be more certain about some meanings than others – about Fidelia's cup, for instance, than Arthur's box – goes without saying, and how much conviction any interpretation carries will always be a question for the reader to answer. But disagreement with an argument for a certain meaning does not mean that no meaning is to be found; the skeptic should look elsewhere. Indeed the purpose of this book is to question some theological meanings which have become conventional and to look elsewhere, in this instance to the Church Fathers, for alternatives.

I begin with those two images whose importance for Professor Bieman inheres primarily in their naturalness rather than in their meaning, the Well of Life and the Tree of Life. I shall explore their meaning. What precisely does each signify, and how is each related to the other? I shall try to show that certain teachings which, if not peculiar to the Fathers, are more fully developed by them than by later Christians, and which Spenser's interpreters have not taken into account afford more convincing answers than those conventionally given.

PART ONE

HOLINESS

CHAPTER ONE

The Well and the Balm

I

The conventional interpretation of the Well as an allegory of baptism is almost certainly correct. A spring of water possessing powers to quench the flames of concupiscence and give victory over the Old Serpent is probably the font, and Red Crosse's hands, after his immersion, are 'baptized.' There are problems, however, with Spenser's timing and with some associations attaching to the Well. Rosemond Tuve, the most persuasive dissenter from the traditional reading, argues that baptism ought to come earlier in Red Crosse's career; we 'harm the poem's action when we introduce notions of the new Christian's first renunciation of the devil' seeing that Red Crosse 'has fought him already for one whole anguished day.' Furthermore Christian initiation seems inappropriate for someone who has already been cleansed and renewed in the House of Holinesse; by identifying the Well exclusively with the font we make 'nonsense ... of canto x.' And what, she asks, are we to make of Spenser's military metaphors? The '"secret vertue" (force and size)' which the Well imparts to Red Crosse's hands and 'the strength that had hardened even the brandished steel blade ... are details which fit no scene at a font.' She finds the Well's 'ancient paradisiacal place' and its 'medicinal strength' equally incongruous with baptism.[1] None of these objections has been satisfactorily answered, though there have been several addresses to the problem of timing.[2]

The conventional interpretation of the Balm as holy communion presents even more difficulties – enough to call the convention into question. Almost certainly the presupposition that Spenser's Protestantism dictated his presenting the two sacraments of the Reformed Churches has displaced critical judgment. If we look only to the poetry, there is little to support the traditional reading. That the Tree of Life itself should have eucharistic associations is not surprising, for as a type of the Cross and of Christ its fruit may signify the sacramental elements. Spenser's vermilion apples, bestowing life everlasting on all 'which thereon fed' (I, xi, 46), probably do. But the Balm, though it flows from the Tree, in no way resembles holy communion. Red Crosse does not eat and drink; he is 'besmeard' (I, xi, 50). Surely this liquid must be precisely what Spenser says it is, a 'gratious *ointment*' (I, xi, 48; italics added); and if it is sacramental, as Spenser's pairing it with baptism suggests it is, it must be one of the sacraments which involve anointing. Recognizing that, Hankins and Nohrnberg (two dissenters from the conventional interpretation) suggest extreme unction.[3] That may be a step in the right direction, but the exact meaning is obscured by the nomenclature. Extreme unction, which is usually associated with death, is more correctly 'the Sacrament of the Unction of the Sick' and is for the healing of the infirm as well as for the repose of the dying. Peter Lombard was the first to call it 'extreme,' and the Eastern Church has consistently repudiated the restrictive designation. If Hankins and Nohrnberg use the term to mean a sacrament of healing, it applies well enough, for Red Crosse is certainly in need of that. But its usual acceptation as preparation for the soul's departure from the body is at odds with the poetry; and that seems to be both scholars' meaning. Nohrnberg associates the Balm with the *viaticum*, and Hankins stresses that Red Crosse is in peril of death. That he is, but the Balm, rather than ensuring him a holy death, 'did from death him saue' (I, xi, 48). The scene is not a sickroom but a battlefield, and the unction is clearly for strength to fight and win rather than to succumb gracefully.

We lack, therefore, a full rationale for two of the central images in the allegory of holiness. Despite considerable reason for believing that the Well signifies the font, we have not accounted for all the ramifications of the symbolism, and we have no consistently convincing interpretation of the Balm. Patristic baptismal theology supplies both needs. It affords precedents for those characteristics of the Well which seem to modern readers inconsistent with baptism, and it offers a new and more convincing explanation of the subsequent unction.

II

The most immediately obvious resemblance between the Fathers' baptismal theology and Spenser's allegory – and therefore the most immediately obvious reason for looking to that theology for an interpretation of the allegory – is the centrality to both of paschal themes and symbols. Interpreters of Book One have long recognized that Red Crosse's dragon fight represents the Harrowing of Hell, and its three-day duration the *triduum sanctum*; and that is the context in which the Church Fathers most frequently discuss baptism. They teach with remarkable consistency that immersion initiates the new Christian into Christ's struggle with Satan in the depths of the earth between Good Friday and Easter day and that the Resurrection gives him Christ's victory. Hence the theologically appropriate time for baptism is Holy Saturday, at the Easter vigil, and the ancient mystagogia take the paschal liturgy for their setting; these works are at once paschal homilies and baptismal catecheses. While Christ is beneath the earth, conquering Hades, the catechumen descends with him by going down into the baptismal pool. Coming up out of the water, he rises with Him on the third day, entering with Adam and Eve, whom Christ has freed from age-long bondage, into a restored Eden. Red Crosse appears to act out an allegorical and romance version of these liturgical events.

The mere fact of the parallels argues more strongly for patristic influence than one might think: where else could Spenser have found the paschal-baptismal symbolism he employs? There were, of course, other sources, such as the Holy Saturday liturgy in the Sarum Missal and Manual (though, as a matter of fact, that liturgy itself is probably patristic – Ambrosian – in origin); but the bare rite, without commentary, is not likely to have afforded Spenser the understanding of Easter baptism which (as I shall try to show) canto eleven exhibits. And commentary other than the Fathers' would have been hard to come by in the sixteenth century. The link between Easter and baptism became tenuous in the West after Augustine; that the articles on baptism in the *Summa Theologica* do not so much as mention its original paschal context is symptomatic. Protestants broke the link altogether: Calvin rejected the Holy Saturday liturgy as an 'adventitious medley' and a human addition to 'the institution of Christ'; for Cranmer Easter baptism was a custom 'grown out of use ... [which] cannot for many considerations be well restored again.'[4] That Spenser in effect restored it points to his having deliberately rejected a Protestant rejection and to his having turned for his allegory to ancient doctrines that even the medieval Church had lost sight of.

In those doctrines, and in the rites and ceremonies to which they point, we find precedents for most of the characteristics of the Well of Life that have puzzled critics. Spenser's military metaphors are an instance. These are common in other than patristic treatments of baptism and should not have seemed so strange to Rosemond Tuve as they do; the Prayer Book, for instance, prays for the baptized child grace 'manfully to fight ... against sin, the world, and the devil, and to continue Christ's faithful soldier.'[5] But there can be no doubt that Christian warfare is a more pervasive and persistent theme in the ancient mystagogia than in later, Western baptismal literature and liturgy; and it is the paschal setting – specifically the Harrowing – that makes the difference. Since the catechumen is initiated into Christ's battle with Satan, it comes naturally to the Fathers to talk of arming a soldier. They would find nothing incongruous in the font's serving to harden the Christian's spiritual sword or to strengthen his spiritual hands. They use, in fact, comparable metaphors. In Erasmus' 1530 edition of Chrysostom, Spenser could have read a baptismal homily, *Ad Neophytos*, which, as its title indicates, is addressed to a congregation of catechumens.[6] The text makes clear that Chrysostom was preaching on Easter morning to a group of men and women baptized the night before during the Holy Saturday vigil, and most of the sermon is concerned with combat, either military or athletic (Chrysostom mixes his metaphors). Lent, just past, has been a 'school for training and exercise.' Now, says Chrysostom, 'the arena stands open, the contest is at hand'[7] (*arena* almost certainly alludes to the traditional setting of martyrdoms, for the martyr's 'passion' is for the Fathers still another version of the Harrowing). Then, with a sudden shift of symbols, the Christian wrestler becomes a Christian knight: though the neophyte finds himself in the arena – now the battlefield – he need not fear, for by baptism 'Christ has put on us armor that is more glittering than gold, stronger than any steel.' This symbolism approximates Spenser's: though Red Crosse is furnished with 'the armour of a Christian man' before he goes down into the Well, he only wears it to good effect afterwards; on the first day of battle it proves an impediment rather than an aid. Chrysostom says that this armor does not weigh the warrior down but raises him up – which in the paschal context presumably alludes to the Resurrection and Ascension – 'It gives wings to [his] limbs and lifts them up.' If you wish to 'take flight to heaven, this armor is no hindrance.'[8] When Red Crosse rises from the Well to fight a second day, he 'mounts vnto the skies' and is like a fledgling hawk who 'marueiles at himselfe, still as he flies' (I, xi, 34). A pre-baptismal unction was part of the Holy Saturday rite, and Chrysostom interprets that as a shield or weapon with which the catechumen equips himself before he goes into battle: Christ 'anointed us as we went into the combat, but he fettered the devil; He anointed us with the oil of gladness, but He bound the devil with fetters ... to keep him shackled ... for the combat.'[9]

These same metaphors, of contest and combat, were to be found in other recently printed patristic treatises. In the *Ecclesiastical Hierarchy* (familiar to the Middle Ages and available to a sixteenth-century reader in a variety of editions)[10] Dionysius the Areopagite characterizes the anointing before baptism as the oiling of a wrestler's body for a match: the ceremony calls 'the initiate to the holy contests in which, with Christ as judge, he will take part.' And Christ is not only judge of the match but a fellow athlete: 'He enters into the contests beside [the catechumens], fighting for their freedom and their victory over the forces of death and corruption.' The neophyte 'is enrolled under a good Lord and Leader' and follows 'in the footsteps of the Athlete first in goodness.'[11] Cyril of Jerusalem in his *Mystagogical Catecheses*[12] prefers the military to the athletic metaphor: 'As Christ after baptism and the descent of the Holy Spirit went forth and vanquished the adversary, so likewise, after holy baptism and the mystical chrism [of which more subsequently] ... do ye stand against the power of the enemy and vanquish it.' The ellipsis in this quotation is of especial interest to Spenserians, for it identifies receiving baptism with putting on the 'armour of a Christian man specified by Saint Paul v. Ephes.': 'So likewise after holy baptism and the mystical chrism, *having put on the whole armor of the Holy Spirit*, do ye stand ...'[13] Unction on the breast signifies 'having put on the breastplate of righteousness [Ephesians 6:14] [that the catechumen] may stand against the wiles of the devil.'[14] Red Crosse now stands, which, before, he signally failed to do. (Cyril, moreover, introduces a dragon as the neophyte's adversary: 'Great indeed is the proffered baptism, but a dragon by the road is watching

the passerby ... Thou art going to the Father of Spirits, but thou art
going past that dragon.'

III

These athletic and military metaphors remind us that the Fathers envi-
sioned the baptism of grown men and women, and in this difference
between patristic expectations and ours lies a possible solution to the
problem of Spenser's timing: why baptize Red Crosse at the end rather
than the beginning of his pilgrimage? Should the Christian sacrament
of initiation not introduce rather than serve as culmination of a quest
for holiness? If, with Rosemond Tuve, we assume it should, we must
either reject an interpretation of the Well as baptism (despite strong
evidence for such a reading) or (like Virgil Whitaker) argue, somewhat
against the grain of the narrative, for a thematic rather than chronolog-
ical arrangement of events. If, however, we think of adult baptism, we
place ourselves in an entirely different frame of reference, in which
baptism seems more appropriate as an end than as a beginning. Lent,
as we have seen, was a 'wrestling school,' arduous training for ultimate victory to be won on Holy Saturday in the baptistery; hence baptism was naturally conceived as the fulfillment of long preparation
(often longer than a single Lent – as much as three years in some parts
of the Church). The paschal context contributed to the same conception, for just as Christ's final defeat of Satan consummated rather than
inaugurated His earthly ministry, the catechumen's baptism into
Christ, at the end of his own preparation, was his personal consummation, with eschatological dimensions. Christ's Resurrection introduced
the life of the age to come, and the catechumen entered that life
through baptism. In more nearly practical terms, baptism for adults,
especially those born as pagans, was as much a triumph over an old
life as the beginning of a new one – in that respect less the undertaking
of a quest than its completion.

Sometimes the quest seems to have lasted a lifetime, baptism coming
in old age or, as in Constantine's case, on a deathbed. The Fathers
preach against excessive delay, and their admonitions would have
afforded Spenser a clear picture of ancient attitudes and practices.
'Though always learning have you not yet come to know?' asks Basil.
'A searcher through life, will you be exploring until old age, will you

ever become a Christian?'[16] And Gregory Nazianzus: 'Let us be baptized today, that we suffer not violence tomorrow; and let us not put off
the blessing as if it were an injury, nor wait till we get more wicked that
more may be forgiven us.'[17] We have no evidence of Red Crosse's having deliberately 'put off the blessing,' but he has become 'more wicked'
as he has pursued his quest; exhortations like Basil's and Gregory's
seem applicable to his repeated backslidings. Clearly the pursuit of
holiness begins before the Christian comes to the font; baptism effects a
conclusion. 'Let us then be baptized,' says Gregory, not that we may
begin to fight, but 'that we may win the victory.'[18]

Rosemond Tuve also asked how the Well can signify baptism when
the effects of baptism have already been conveyed to Red Crosse in the
House of Holinesse. After the purging and acquisition of virtue
effected there, an allegory of baptism seems redundant, making 'nonsense ... of canto x.'[19] Not only were catechumens in the early centuries
prepared for baptism throughout Lent, but on the very night, in the
course of the Easter vigil, they were exorcised, shriven, and made a confession of Faith – activities comparable to the disciplines of the House
of Holinesse. All the ancient Easter liturgies seem to have contained
these preparations, and Spenser could have seen an instance in the
Sarum Manual – an 'Ordo for Making Catechumens' (*ordo ad cathecumi-
num faciendum*) immediately preceding baptism on Holy Saturday.[20]
There are no structural or verbal resemblances between this service and
Dame Celia's medieval Catholic hospital (here, if anywhere, the allegory is eclectic), but their purposes seem much the same: to make the
catechumen (Red Crosse) 'invincible and free' and to bestow upon
him the 'constancy of the godlike state' and a 'holy love of truth.'[21]

These quoted phrases come from Dionysius' formulation of the
effects of pre-baptismal cleansing, and he is representative of the
Fathers in conceiving such virtues not, as we should be likely to, as the
fruits of baptism but as its prerequisites. Since baptism is a warfare, the
catechumen must go into the pool well prepared; without such preparation he is likely to suffer defeat. John of Damascus says explicitly that
without the preliminary rites of penance and instruction the effects of
baptism are diminished: though 'remission of sins ... is granted alike to
all through baptism ... the grace of the Spirit is proportional to the faith
[which the catechumen receives through instruction] and previous
purification.'[22] Saint Basil says, 'It is necessary ... to receive instruction

before Baptism,' and instruction is contingent upon removing 'any impediment to learning.' The impediment is of course sin; therefore the catechumen must make his confession, receive absolution, and be exorcised. That is roughly analogous to Spenser's sequence: Red Crosse is put to school by Una and Fidelia, and his sins are washed away. He repents and does penance; plucking out his rotten 'superfluous flesh' with 'pincers firie whot' (I, x, 26) is arguably an allegory of pre-baptismal exorcism. Spenser's account of the 'impediment' also accords with Basil's; the sin in question is not merely wrongdoing but the source of wrongdoing – a radical corruption of the soul and body. 'Outwardly,' says Basil to his flock of catechumens, you 'appear to men just; but inwardly you are full of hypocrisy and iniquity.'[23] When Red Crosse arrives at the House of Holinesse, he is in a similar circumstance; he has been delivered from various instances of wrongdoing by Una and Arthur, but 'Inward corruption, and infected sin, / Not purg'd nor heald, behind remained still' (I, x, 25). Only when this 'stubborn malady' is remedied can Red Crosse make further progress in virtue and only then is he ready for baptism. If we are prepared to interpret the House of Holinesse in this fashion – as a place of preparation and as a 'way to heauenly blesse' (I, x, Arg.) rather than the bliss's source – we may place Dame Celia's establishment in a recognizable liturgical sequence. So far from making nonsense of canto ten, a reading of the Well as the font may make clear sense of it.

IV

The Well's medicinal powers also have patristic precedents. I have discovered one instance (in Tertullian's *De Baptismo*) of an unmistakably literal belief in the font's capacity to effect physical cures;[24] but the belief was obviously not peculiar to Tertullian. Indeed Protestants were sufficiently aware of it to be afraid of it; G.W. Bromiley says the Anglican Reformers deliberately avoided the subject lest it 'give rise to the grossest of superstitions.'[25] The belief probably echoes in the Fathers' use of healing streams and wells as baptismal types; Eastern liturgy treats as such both the cure of the paralytic at the pool of Bethsaida (John 5:1–15) and of the blind man at Siloam (John 9:1–38).[26] In these instances one cannot be certain whether the therapeutic virtue of the type transfers to baptism symbolically, literally, or in both ways. Tertullian takes Bethsaida literally, using it as an argument for his belief in healing miracles wrought by the font; Ambrose employs Siloam as a more general figure of the sacrament, though one cannot be certain that Ambrose speaks *only* symbolically.[27] So when Spenser uses Siloam as a type of the Well of Life and applies its medicinal virtue literally, he is easily within the boundaries of patristic baptismal symbolism (and well outside those of baptismal symbolism in his own time). He also had patristic precedent for treating the Jordan as a healing stream. We should expect it of course to be a type of baptism, but Spenser says the Well of Life excels the Jordan (as the antitype always excels the type) specifically in its capacity to 'recure' the sick. That seems an oddly misplaced emphasis until we discover that the cure of Naaman's leprosy in the Jordan played almost as large a part in patristic typology as Christ's baptism. At least two Fathers, Ambrose and Gregory of Nyssa, cite only Naaman's healing as rationale for that typology.[28] That the Catechism of the Council of Trent is careful to exclude any reference to healing in its citation of Naaman suggests that Renaissance Catholics were no less uneasy than Protestants about belief in baptismal healing. The Tridentine Church interpreted the removal of Naaman's leprosy to signify that 'the remission of all sin, whether original or actual, is ... the proper effect of baptism'[29] – that is what we now call demythologizing. Spenser's emphasis on healing, like so much of his baptismal symbolism, is decidedly archaic by sixteenth-century standards and bespeaks the probability of archaic precedents.

The 'ancient paradisiacal place' enters baptismal symbolism specifically by way of the link with Easter. To place the font figuratively in Eden came naturally to writers who believed that baptism initiated the catechumen into Christ's rising from the dead; for the Resurrection effected a new creation which though superior to was also analogous to the original one. Baptism, therefore, returns man to his Edenic condition. The blessing of the font in the ancient Latin rite employs this symbolism to the full: the water of baptism is the antitype of the primordial water over which, in the beginning, God's spirit moved to bring forth life; now from the font, through the moving of the Holy Spirit, whom the celebrant invokes, will come forth the new life of the baptized.[30] Consequently the liturgy characterizes the font as a spring of water in Eden whence issue the four rivers which 'water all the earth' (*et in quattuor fluminibus totam terram rigare precepit*) and as a well which God caused to 'spring forth from Paradise' (*de paradyso manere*);[31] Spenser's is also a '*springing* well' – was he consciously translating *manere*? – and from it comes, if not four rivers, at least one, a 'siluer flood,' a discrepancy in number which need not trouble us greatly since when Una tells her story to Arthur in canto seven, she names three of the four rivers of Eden. The single stream mentioned in canto eleven is said to be 'Full of great vertues' (I, xi, 29), and in the Latin rite the priest rehearses numerous virtues inhering in the paradisal-baptismal spring.

Patristic commentary also invokes Christ's restoring Adam and Eve to Paradise. The newly baptized catechumen is the old Adam delivered by the new. Israel, says Basil, 'entered the Promised Land through baptism'; 'how will you,' he asks, 'enter Paradise, if you have not been sealed by baptism?'[32] Cyril calls baptism itself 'paradise' and a 'fragrant meadow' and reminds the catechumen that if he can get past the dragon he can enter the 'pleasures of paradise.'[33] Through the grace given him by the Well and the Balm, Red Crosse slays the dragon and enters Eden. Some ancient *baptisteria* were decorated to represent Eden; Spenser may not have known that, but he could have read patristic references to this symbolism. Gregory of Nyssa reminds catechumens waiting to enter the baptistery that they are 'still outside paradise.' They 'share in the exile of Adam, our first father. Now, however, the gate is opened to you again. Step inside then to the place from whence you departed.'[34] Eden is always eastward, and so presumably is Spenser's paradise; we infer as much from Una's being the daughter of the Eastern Emperor and antithetical to the Western Duessa. Cyril employs a similar directional symbolism; before the catechumen enters the baptistery, he looks west and renounces Satan (common ancient practice prior to baptism on Holy Saturday); then, 'turning from west to east,' he enters 'the place of light,' the baptistery. 'There is opened to thee,' says Cyril, 'the Paradise of God, which He planted in the east.'[35]

V

'The Paradise of God' is not, however, opened *to* Red Crosse; rather he opens it. He does not enter Eden merely as the forgiven sinner or recipient of grace but as the victor over Satan on the morning of the third day and soon to be the Heavenly Bridegroom at the marriage supper of the Lamb. In other words, Red Crosse becomes Christ. 'Refreshed by the water from the Well of Life and by the fruit from the Tree of Life, [he] is the second Adam who regains the Paradise that the first Adam lost.'[36] The Knight of Holiness is transformed from '*miles christi*' into 'Christ himself (whose bride Una is the Church).'[37]

Oddly, this development in the allegory has not raised the kinds of questions Rosemond Tuve has asked about inherently less startling effects of the Well and the Tree, and critical reticence on the subject is strange. For the modern reader is much less likely to expect baptism to deify than to arm the initiate for battle or to heal his wounds. Even interpreters like Hamilton and Kermode who have addressed the subject seem oblivious to its implications. When '*miles christi*' becomes 'Christ himself,' we are surely prompted to ask, as Kermode does not, how such a transformation is possible and what it can possibly signify. That no one has probed such matters suggests that no one has taken Spenser's allegory of deification literally – that commentators regard Red Crosse's *theosis* as a figure of speech, as merely a metaphor for his increased holiness, as a way of saying he has become that conventional figure of the imitator of Christ, or 'only a type of Christ' (Kellogg and Steele),[38] a conception closer to 'sanctification' in its common acceptation than to anything so startling as a literal 'becoming Christ.' That Spenser meant to startle is a possibility no one has taken into serious consideration.

Readers fail to recognize and therefore explain away conceptions for which they have no frame of reference. In this instance ignorance of any Christian precedent for a literal *theosis* of the believer has probably hindered our hearing what Spenser is saying. By providing such a frame and by thus helping us to understand an otherwise puzzling element in the poetry, the Fathers – in this case the Eastern Fathers – make still another claim upon our attention. For deification is a distinctive emphasis in Greek patrology and in the history of Christianity very nearly peculiar to it and to its subsequent Byzantine development. Indeed in reference to *theosis* even more pointedly than to Easter baptism we may ask where else than in Greek treatises could Spenser have found the conception. To say nowhere else would perhaps be incautious, but that it is alien to Western, post-Augustinian soteriology is scarcely debatable.[39] When Anselm of Canterbury asked *Why God became man* (*Cur deus homo*), he answered with what Jaroslav Pelikan calls 'the most representative Western formulation of the doctrine of the Atonement' – to render satisfaction, as only the God-man could, to the justice of God.[40] So universal is this conception in Western Christendom, both Catholic and Protestant, that many people, knowing of no other, take it to be simply *the* Christian doctrine of salvation. But when Athanasius asked *Cur deus homo*, he answered without any reference to the Atonement, in a phrase which he borrowed (without acknowledgment) from Irenaeus: '[God] was made man that we might be made God.'[41] We could vary Pelikan's characterization of Anselm's treatise and call Athanasius' 'the most representative Eastern formulation of the doctrine of man's salvation.' By uniting divine to human nature in the Incarnation and by raising mortal flesh from the tomb in the Resurrection, God made human nature divine. Christ overcame death in the flesh, thereby bestowing God's life on flesh. If not the only Greek patristic conception of salvation, this is beyond any question the most pervasive one – sufficiently pervasive that we may regard it as a signature of that ancient theology and a likely earmark of that theology's influence when we encounter it elsewhere.

Athanasius' treatment of *theosis* is of particular interest both because his work would have been readily available to a sixteenth-century reader and because he discusses deification in great detail, using the doctrine as a weapon against Arius. If, as Arius claimed, the Son is not God and not equal in divinity to the Father, man cannot have been made divine by the Incarnation; but making man divine was the very purpose of the Incarnation: men, 'being by nature creatures,' could not become sons of God 'otherwise than by receiving the Spirit of the natural and true Son. Wherefore, that this might be, "The Word became flesh," that He might make man *capable of Godhead*.'[42] Deification, according to Athanasius, secures victory over the dragon, 'for the Word being clothed in the flesh ... every bite of the serpent began to be utterly staunched from out it; and ... death also was abolished.' Being thus liberated from Satan and death and 'being joined to God, no longer do we abide upon earth.'[43] Rather deified man lives, appropriately, in heaven, in the flesh of the risen and ascended Christ: Christ assumed the created and human body 'that having renewed it as its Framer, He might deify it in Himself, and thus might introduce us all into the kingdom of heaven after His likeness.' The Incarnation united 'what is man by nature to Him who is in the nature of the Godhead, [that man's] salvation and deification might be sure.'[44]

Deification or θέωσις manifests itself in a variety of patristic contexts. Chrysostom in his second homily on Saint Matthew, in a discussion of the Nativity, reminds his hearer or reader that God 'suffered Himself to be called also Son of David, that He might make thee Son of God ... For it is far more difficult, judging by human reason, for God to become man, than for a man to be declared a Son of God. When therefore thou art told that the Son of God is Son of David and of Abraham, doubt not any more, that thou too, the son of Adam, shalt be son of God. For not at random, nor in vain did He abase Himself so greatly, only He was minded to exalt us. Thus He was born after the flesh, that thou mightest be born after the Spirit; He was born of a woman that thou mightest cease to be the son of a woman.'[45] In other words, 'God became man that we might become God.' John of Damascus, in his discussion of the two natures of Christ and with the specific purpose of defending Mary's motherhood of God against the Nestorians, explains that 'as soon as [Christ] was brought forth into being,' the nature which he had assumed in the Virgin's womb 'was deified by Him, so that these three things took place simultaneously, the assumption of our nature, the coming into being, and the deification of the assumed nature by the Word.' Mary is therefore properly named 'Mother of God, not only because of the [divine] nature of the Word, but also because of the deification of man's nature' – that is to say that the manhood which she bore had also become God.[46] Irenaeus conceives deification in terms of light: 'The Word was made flesh' to illuminate and, by illuminating, to deify man – so that 'the Father's Light might meet us in the Flesh of our Lord, and might come to us from His glorious Body, and so man might arrive at incorruption, being compassed about with the brightness of the Father.' Here incorruption signifies a divine condition, freedom from death and decay, as subsequent statements make clear: 'For as those who see the light are in the light, and partake of its splendour, so those who see God *are in God*, partaking of His splendour. *And the brightness quickens them.*' God's light becomes the source of life in an altogether literal sense: 'Men therefore will see God so as to live: by the vision *made immortal, and reaching even unto God*' (italics added).[47]

Since the deifying grace of the Incarnation is communicated to man through the font, most patristic baptismal homilies discuss *theosis*. Baptismal regeneration, for many of the Fathers, especially the Greeks, is virtually synonymous with deification. Basil the Great compares man's fallen nature to a 'statue which has been shattered into fragments and in which the glorious image of the king [the *imago dei*] is no longer discernible.' Baptism 'shapes it anew and restores its former splendor.'[48] To renew the Image of God in man is to make man divine. That conception is closely linked to the symbolism of returning to Paradise. Our original, unfallen condition was deified because we possessed the divine Image without stain and in perfect wholeness; to be cleansed of stain and reconstituted by baptism is to return to that condition. Another frequent metaphor is 'putting on Christ' as though he were a garment. The phrase (Galatians 3:27) figures in many patristic discussions of *theosis*: 'For as many of you as have been baptized into Christ have put on Christ' (sung with *alleluias* in the Byzantine Easter liturgy). Chrysostom interprets the statement to mean becoming Christ: 'If Christ is the Son of God, and thou hast put Him on, having the Son on thyself thou art made like Him, having been brought into one kindred and one nature [or 'form'] with him.'[49] In a homily not known in the sixteenth century but which is representative of the exegetical tradition, Chrysostom says that in baptism '"We put off the old garment which was made filthy with the abundance of our sins; we put on the new one which is free from every stain."' That is conventional baptismal symbolism with no distinguishing theological coloring, but what follows is patristic: '"What am I saying? *We put on Christ Himself*"' (italics added).[50]

Chrysostom is not, however, referring to baptism proper; he attaches the symbolism of the garment to the anointing which followed. This is the unction with the holy oil of chrism, commonly called chrismation, to which thus far we have referred only in passing.[51] Chrismation made a very important part – indeed it was the culminating moment – in the Holy Saturday baptismal rite, and all the mystagogia devote homilies to it. When the catechumen ascended from the baptismal pool, he was chrismated before being clothed in white and brought to the altar for his first communion. Not only did this unction complete baptism; it is the part of the sacrament to which the Fathers ascribe deifying virtue; more decisively than the water, it marked the new Christian as Christ. Indeed the very word, *chrism*, signifies deification, for as Tertullian explains, the person anointed 'is called a Christ, from

"Chrism" which is [the Greek for] "anointing": and from this also our
Lord obtained his title' – Christ.[52] Cyril in the *Catecheses* is more
explicit; he quotes Psalm 82 (a standard patristic text for the doctrine of
theosis): 'I haue sayde, ye are Gods, and ye all are the chyldren of the
most hyghest'; 'Thou, a pitiable man,' Cyril says, 'dost receive the
name of God.'[53] 'The name of God,' here, is 'Christ,' bestowed by
chrism: as Christ after His baptism in the Jordan 'was anointed with
the spiritual oil of gladness, which is the Holy Spirit ... so ye also were
anointed with ointment, having been made communicants and partak-
ers of Christ.'[54] Athanasius says that Christ was anointed (by the Holy
Spirit) after baptism not that He might become God, 'for He was so
even before,' but that 'He might provide for us men, not only exalta-
tion and resurrection, but the indwelling and intimacy of the Spirit.'
'The Spirit's descent on Him in Jordan was a descent upon us, because
of His bearing our body ... that we might share His anointing,' His
'Christing.'[55] Both Athanasius and Cyril cite Aaron as an Old Testament type of the chrismated or anointed one – an anticipation at once
of Christ Himself and the Christian who is anointed and thus deified in
Christ. Moses made Aaron high priest by first washing and then chris-
mating him. Aaron, says Cyril, 'was called Christ [or anointed] from
the emblematical chrism'[56] – only emblematical in the Old Testament
because the type had not yet been fulfilled in the Incarnation. Aaron
was *'called* Christ' by anticipation; Christians by unction *become* Christ.
In Saint Ambrose's language, 'You have received the seal unto His likeness, that you may rise again unto His form, may live unto His figure,
who was crucified to sin and liveth unto God.'[57]

VI

Chrismation brings us of course, and properly last, to Red Crosse's
unction in the Balm from the Tree of Life. If the Well signifies baptism,
what could be more likely than that the ensuing unction is that which
the Fathers understood as the indispensible, deifying complement of
baptism? We could, in fact, make a strong case for the Balm as chrism
even without patristic reference, for Spenser could have known of
post-baptismal unction in several ways. Unlike some facets of patristic
teaching and practice, chrismation did not end in the West after
Augustine. It was administered in England in Spenser's lifetime; had

he been born a year later than he was, after Mary's accession, he would presumably have been 'besmeard' as well as baptized (or if for any reason he was baptized after his infancy and before Mary's death, he almost certainly received chrismation). Unction is to be found in the Sarum Easter liturgy and in the only slightly altered *ordo* for Easter baptism in the new Tridentine Missal (officially banned but circulated surreptitiously). Spenser might even have witnessed baptism with chrismation in Ireland. Furthermore, the Reformers who rejected the rite mention it; it was evidently familiar enough to Englishmen that Hooker could allude to it as a matter of common knowledge.[58] Or Spenser could have known Scholastic commentaries on the sacraments, like Aquinas', which reads rather like a sketch (though only that) for the allegory of canto eleven: by immersion in water (baptism proper) man receives 'power to do those things which pertain to his own salvation' (the Well saves Red Crosse from the dragon's fire) whereas the subsequent unction bestows 'power to do those things which pertain to the spiritual combat with the enemies of the Faith' (to slay the dragon) (*ST*, III, 72, 5). The chrism 'strengthen[s] [the believer] in his outward combat' (*ST*, III, 72, 4); Spenser's Balm strengthens Red Crosse to win his battle.[59]

The Catholic rationale is much more persuasive than the Protestant glosses which identify the Balm with the eucharist,[60] but the patristic is more persuasive still. The need for my parenthetic additions to the quotations from Aquinas is indicative; he does not identify 'combat with the enemies of the Faith' with slaying the dragon because (as we have already mentioned) he makes no connection between baptism and the Harrowing. Nor does he have anything to say about chrism's deifying power, which is so major an emphasis in patristic commentary (deification does not form any significant part of medieval or Renaissance Catholicism). Furthermore, Aquinas is clearly thinking of chrismation as part of an initiatory rite – power for spiritual combat implies the beginning of a battle – whereas according to the Fathers, chrismation, by deifying, completes and gives the final victory. Dionysius the Areopagite calls chrismation a 'perfective anointing.'[61]

Spenser's Balm is certainly a consummation rather than an initiation for Red Crosse. Indeed all its effects seem to represent the Fathers' understanding of chrismation very faithfully, especially in respect of its deifying virtue. The transformation from *miles christi* into 'Christ himself' does not take place – or at least is not complete – until Red Crosse has been anointed. Even after rising from the Well, healed and strengthened for battle, he is still in some measure Cyril's 'pitiable man,' who is yet to become Christ and conquer Satan. He has been purged of sin and instructed in true faith in the House of Holinesse (if our interpretation is correct, in pre-baptismal, Holy Saturday rites), and he has received the grace of baptismal immersion but not yet the deifying grace of unction. He can fight better after immersion but not yet well enough to win, for he has not yet been made Christ, and only Christ can conquer (has conquered) Satan. Having been 'besmeard' with chrism, however, he can win and win handily; by means of the oil he becomes the victorious Χριστός.

Carol Kaske has offered an analogous interpretation of the timing of these episodes; but she works within the framework of Reformation theology, and patristic conceptions make her persuasive argument even more persuasive. The battle begins, she says, 'with unregenerate man under law – identified as such by his inconvenient armor, his defeat through unchecked concupiscence, and his subsequent baptism; it progresses through Christian regenerate man, identified by his use and need of both sacraments and his qualified victory over concupiscence; it culminates in Christ the perfect man, showing his swift and final victory over Satan ...'[62] When she refers to 'both sacraments,' she means of course baptism and the eucharist rather than baptism and chrismation. She recognizes – one of the strengths of her analysis – that 'it is the Tree [the Balm] alone and not both reinforcements ... which transforms Red Crosse from a Christian into a Christ figure,'[63] but she does not explain why holy communion should be peculiarly appropriate for that purpose. As the sacrament of the body and blood of Christ the eucharist does in fact deify (the Fathers, as we shall see in a moment, teach that), but deification is not associated with communion so directly (and peculiarly) as with chrismation. For that reason (as well as the others we have advanced) the latter seems a far more likely referent for Spenser's Balm and a valuable addition to Mrs. Kaske's interpretation. As the sacrament which bestows the 'whole armor of God,' chrism affords the Christian his 'swift and final victory over Satan'; as preeminently the sacrament of deification it transforms each Christian into 'Christ the perfect man.'

Spenser may foreshadow that transformation in an image we have already examined; interpreting the Balm as chrism introduces a possible linkage which identification of the Balm as communion obscures. Arthur's 'liquor pure' reminds Elizabeth Bieman of the water of baptism and thus anticipates, though for her inversely, the Well and the Tree. It reminds me of the Balm (both are healing unctions) and anticipates all we have found chrismation may mean.[64] The possible biblical source of the box strengthens the association by providing a paschal context. When the harlot breaks the alabaster box and pours its fragrant contents on Christ's head, He says, 'In that she hath poured this ointment on my body, she did it for my burial' (Matthew 26:12). The statement anticipates the futile attempt by the three Marys on Easter morning to anoint Christ for burial – futile, of course, because he has risen and there is no body to anoint. The traditional identification of one of the three, Mary Magdalene, with the harlot who broke the box strengthens the association between the two episodes and thus the paschal character of the former.[65] Furthermore, Matthew's version of the story is included in the Passion Gospel (in the Book of Common Prayer) for Palm Sunday and Mark's version in the Gospel for Holy Monday. Since anyone familiar with this context, as we may assume Spenser was, would discern in the anointing at Simon's table a prophecy of the mysteries of the *triduum sanctum*, it is entirely possible that Arthur's gift is to be regarded as similarly prophetic – of the allegorical version of the Three Days in canto eleven. If so, the seemingly inconsequential episode of the gift-giving (literally inconsequential – nothing appears to follow from it) takes its place convincingly in the pattern of the allegory. Arthur, in effect, anoints Red Crosse for burial – burial of course in baptism, the burial in and with Christ which with the ensuing chrismation deifies Red Crosse and gives him the victory of the Resurrection. What Arthur gives Red Crosse in canto nine, Red Crosse receives at the foot of the Tree of Life in canto eleven.

VII

We find then in patristic exegesis and ancient liturgical practice analogues for most of the details of the allegory in canto eleven: evidence to sustain our conventional interpretation of the Well of Life as baptism, a coherent explanation of the Balm as the traditional complement of immersion and as a necessary part of a full allegory of baptism, numerous precedents for associating baptism with warfare, a logic for conceiving this sacrament as the consummation rather than as the inauguration of the Christian quest and in that logic an answer to the hitherto unresolved problem of Spenser's timing, a plausible explanation of the relation of the Well and the Balm to the House of Holinesse (as well as to Arthur's diamond box and 'liquor pure'), precedents for ascribing medicinal virtue to the Well and for placing it in Paradise, and, both prior to and uniting all these themes, firm theological and liturgical grounds for Spenser's setting the Well and Balm in an allegory of Christ's Harrowing of Hell and Resurrection. Finally, in the patristic interpretation of holiness as deification effected by baptism and – especially – chrismation, we find a link between the symbolism of canto eleven and the titular virtue of Book One. The Fathers thus help us to understand what Spenser meant by holiness. Bits and pieces of this theological material would have been available to a Renaissance poet from medieval and contemporary sources, but nowhere except in patristic theology and liturgy could he have found them all together and constituting a thematic whole analogous to that of the allegory of canto eleven.

CHAPTER TWO

The True Saint George

I

Patristic influence – especially as we encounter it in Byzantine liturgy – may also explain Spenser's choice of George as hero of Book One. To the modern reader the choice may not seem to require explanation, and in terms of the political allegory it does not; what other legendary figure, except perhaps Arthur, could represent English patriotism so well as the nation's patron, symbol of the Order of the Garter, paradigm of medieval knighthood, and popular subject of Lord Mayors' pageants? But Spenser also uses George as an exemplar of holiness, and the Saint's qualification for that role (his primary one) is less certain. (If it seems certain to us now, that is partly owing, as I shall try to show, to Spenser himself.) Padelford and O'Connor argued confidently in the *Variorum* that George served 'equally the purpose of the spiritual and the political allegory,'[1] but that assertion ignores doubts which have been present since the beginning of Spenser scholarship. William Nelson is closer to the mark in saying that 'No Renaissance humanist could have thought the legendary life of St. George a respectable literary model,'[2] and there is good reason to believe that no Renaissance Christian who took his religion as seriously as Spenser apparently did could have thought the legendary George a respectable model for theological allegory. Nelson may be thinking of Gabriel Harvey's 'Hobgoblin runne away with the Garland from *Apollo*'[3] – a literary objection certainly, but possibly theological as well. Harvey may have been alluding to Calvin's caustic comment that those men dishonor Christ 'who consider his intercession as unavailing without the assistance of George and Hippolytus, and other such phantasms.'[4] *Phantasms* translates Calvin's *larvae*, and a *larva* is a ghost or bogey. Sir Thomas Elyot says a 'goblin,' and Lewis and Short say specifically, 'hobgoblin,' used 'as a term of reproach.' The latter is almost certainly both Calvin's and Harvey's meaning, and whether or not Harvey alludes to Calvin, both reflect George's contemporary reputation among both Reformers and humanists. The new learning had combined with the new religion to call his legend into serious question; it contained too much of the far-fetched to escape the skepticism of the enlightened. 'By the sixteenth century accretions of impossible adventure,' says Nelson, 'and the buffoonery of village St. George plays must have rendered the story ridiculous.'[5]

We might question whether Spenser was either a humanist or Reformer, whether he shared either Harvey's or Calvin's tastes, and argue that, given the medieval flavor of Book One, George's role as hero is not to be wondered at. But skepticism about George was not altogether Protestant and contemporary. As early as the fifth century, Pope Gelasius questioned the authenticity of miracles attributed to the saint, and, in the Renaissance, Catholic theologians as well as Protestant rejected the cult.[6] Erasmus is as outspoken on the subject as Calvin: Folly praises fools who 'in George ... have discovered a new Hercules, just as they have found a new Hippolytus. They all but worship George's horse, most religiously decked out in breastplates and bosses, and from time to time oblige him with some little gift. To swear by his bronze helmet is thought to be an oath fit for a king.'[7] (That both Erasmus and Calvin link George to an Hippolytus is curious – one to the classical demigod, the other to the saint and anti-Pope.) On this subject as well as so many others the Church of England seems to have embraced both Catholic and Protestant views; though George was the nation's patron, the national Church rejected him. He vanished from the calendar in 1549, and though his name was restored in 1552, neither collect, epistle, nor Gospel were appointed for his feast. One suspects that Cranmer also thought him a hobgoblin, and Book One of *The Faerie Queene* presents the anomaly of celebrating as patron of English Christianity a saint discarded by the English Church.

The very seriousness with which Spenser treats George in cantos eleven and twelve adds to the puzzle. By representing him not only as holy in the conventional sense but as 'Christ himself,' Spenser makes a higher claim for his hero than the legend had ever made. 'In medieval poetry and romance' where George is 'par excellence' the knight of

holiness (Padelford and O'Connor), he never attains such an eminence
of virtue as Spenser raises him to. Though he is 'Crystes owen knight'
(Lydgate), and though his martyrdom is associated with Christ's passion, nowhere in the legend does he represent the new Adam, the Harrower, the Heavenly Bridegroom.[8] Spenser seems not only to be flying
in the face of George's contemporary debunkers but even to be going
the George of folk tale and cultus one better. Grace Warren Landrum
says that by the late sixteenth century 'the glow of holiness that once
enveloped' George had disappeared.[9] Spenser evidently intended not
only to re-illumine him but to make him shine more brilliantly, and
with a more serious holiness, than before.

                                  II

Why? Why choose for an exponent of holiness a saint of whom neither
Catholic theologians, Continental Reformers, nor the Church of
England any longer approved and then claim for him a measure of
sanctity which by any contemporary standard would seem exorbitant?
A possible – and on the face of it a plausible – answer is that Spenser
had in mind and expected some of his readers to recognize quite
another George from the one whom Harvey, Calvin, Erasmus, and
Cranmer had repudiated. Such another was in fact available to him in
the same liturgical material from which he seems to have derived the
paschal-baptismal symbolism of canto eleven. When Nelson refers to
the 'legendary life' of Saint George, he means the story of the dragon-
slaying and subsequent martyrdom which Spenser and his contemporaries knew primarily from de Voragine, Lydgate, Mantuan, and Barclay, and whose popularity in the Renaissance is well documented.[10] It
is the George of these versions who had become the subject both of
popular devotion and intellectual scorn and who has occupied the
exclusive attention of Spenser's interpreters. The other George, the
George of patristic liturgy, who was accessible to Spenser in contemporary editions of Byzantine service books, is an authentically holy figure
of whom the hero of medieval legend is a vestige heavily overlaid with
pagan accretions. This 'true *Saint George*' (I, ii, 12) is arguably better
qualified than any other saint in the calendar for the role in which
Spenser casts him, not only by virtue of his holiness but because the lit-

urgies treat him – just as Spenser does – as a type of the victorious Christ, closely identified with the Harrowing and Resurrection. He is the most paschal of saints.

These associations are owing to the date of his feast – 23 April – which in the Eastern calendar usually falls within and fairly near the beginning of the forty days of Easter. Even if it falls earlier, however, it is always celebrated in the paschal season, for the Eastern Church considers George's festival sufficiently important to transfer out of Lent (the only commemoration within Lent is the Annunciation on 25 March). Consequently, in a year in which Easter comes after 23 April, George is honored on Easter Monday. His commemoration is always therefore in conjunction with the Resurrection, as the propers for his feast indicate. These are drawn from three different texts, whose names are probably stranger to us than they would have been to Spenser: each of them was printed several times over in Western Europe in the sixteenth century; the various Greek liturgical books appear in catalogues of private libraries; and scholars like Cranmer and Andrewes make use of them. The prayers and hymns written specifically for Saint George appear in the April *Menaion*, and these, as we shall see, are heavily paschal in emphasis. They are supplemented with others from the Easter liturgy itself, from the *Pentecostarion*, in such a fashion as to attribute to George motifs pertaining properly to Christ; George is virtually christified by liturgical association. If George is commemorated in Easter week or on a Sunday in the paschal season, the *Menaion* text is still further augmented, with propers from the Byzantine Sunday cycle in the *Octoechos*. This latter material is also paschal in character, for the Eastern Church treats each Sunday as a festival of the Resurrection; consequently hymns from the *Octoechos* are appointed for the successive days of Easter week (and of course for the subsequent Sundays), so if George's feast falls in that week or on one of those Sundays, the *Octoechos* hymns are added to his liturgy.[11]

The following matins hymn from the *Menaion* is indicative of the way Easter themes permeate George's commemoration: 'Behold, the spring of grace hath arisen, the Resurrection of Christ shines upon all, and with it now shines forth the all festive and light-bearing day of the martyr George.'[12] There is much more to the same effect. In fact the theme of the feast is announced at vespers on 22 April in hymns which focus on the Resurrection to the exclusion of any direct reference to the saint; whoever wrote the liturgy seems to have taken George's assimilation to the risen Christ for granted and to have assumed that worshippers would do the same: 'Clap your hands all ye people; let us shout to God our Saviour, for lifted up upon the cross, and descending into the tomb, He conquered Hades and raised the dead with Himself ...' Two other vespers hymns repeat the motif: 'Come lovers of martyrs, let us bring lyrical hymns to Christ rising from the tomb'; 'Let us lovers of martyrs, singing together, offer a song of songs to Christ, for He the noble champion hast cast down the tyrant, the foe, having overcome him in combat.'[13]

The obvious reference to the Harrowing in this last passage is one of many; George is characterized throughout his liturgy as a warrior saint, whose struggles are assimilated to Christ's battle with Satan. George is a 'soldier of the great King.' He is also the 'pride of athletes,'[14] an epithet which as we have seen has paschal significance and which associates George with 'the Athlete first in goodness' (Dionysius), in whose strength and indeed in whose person catechumens win the paschal-baptismal contest. Worshippers are bidden to honor George for 'trampling on Satan's power,'[15] and 'as a divine hero' George is praised for having 'turned the ranks of demons.' He accomplished those feats, literally, through his martyrdom, but the Easter setting transfers our attention to the Harrowing: 'Suffering with the Saviour and by death willingly imitating His death, thou dost reign with Him in light.'[16]

Hymns added to the *Menaion* from the *Pentecostarion* (Easter cycle) repeat these motifs, for the principal emphasis in Byzantine paschal liturgy is on the victory in Hades rather than the empty tomb. The Easter *kontakion* (collect), sung at all services during the forty days of Pascha and thus at all services on Saint George's day whenever it occurs, states the theme of the Harrowing clearly: 'O Christ our God, though Thou didst descend into the grave, yet didst Thou overthrow the power of Hades and didst arise as victor.'[17] In a stanza from Saint John of Damascus' paschal canon which is repeated at matins throughout the season and thus forms a part of George's celebration,[18] Christ descends 'into the deepest parts of the earth' and shatters 'the everlasting bars which held fast those who were fettered.'[19] They are, of course, Adam and Eve, the patriarchs and prophets, who await the

coming of Christ – those imprisoned citizens of Eden whom Red
Crosse liberates. Whenever during the paschal season George might be
commemorated, the choir would also sing: 'O King and Lord, Thou
didst sleep in the flesh as a mortal and rise on the third day, having
raised up Adam from corruption and destroyed death.'[20] Spenser's
George sleeps twice as a mortal, but the second time 'in a dreame of
deepe delight' because he is 'Besmeard with pretious Balme,' the deifying chrism, sacrament of his participation in Christ's victory. From that
sleep he 'freshly vp arose' on the third day and raised up Adam, the
'most mighty king of *Eden* faire' (I, xi, 50, 52 & xii, 26).

The *Octoechos* Sunday hymns contain similar passages. If 23 April
fell on Easter Tuesday or on the fourth Sunday after Easter the following *troparia* from the Sunday cycle would be sung at vespers: 'O
mighty one, Thou as God didst break the chains of death. Wherefore
we worship Thy Resurrection from the dead, shouting with joy ...' The
chains symbolize, of course, the age-long bondage of Adam and Eve
and thus constitute an obvious reference to the Harrowing. So too do
the gates which Christ-George breaks: 'Thou hast broken the gates of
Hades, O Lord, and by death Thou hast destroyed the Kingdom of
death.'[21] These gates are customarily 'brazen,' for they derive from
Psalm 107: 'For he hath broken the gates of brasse: and smitten the
barres of yron in sunder' – a verse interpreted by the Fathers as prophetic of the release of Adam and Eve. The metaphor is common in the
Pentecostarion and *Octoechos* and is employed in the same vespers
sequence from which we have been quoting: 'Thou hast shattered the
gates of brass and broken asunder the chains, O Christ our God, and
raised up the fallen race of man.'[22] Appropriately, Spenser has his Saint
George open or, more precisely, effect the opening of a brazen gate.
This time, however, the gate is to Paradise rather than to Hades; once
Una's father becomes certain that the dragon is dead, 'He bad to open
wyde his brazen gate' (I, xii, 3). I know no liturgical precedent for a brazen *Edenic* gate, but Spenser could have found a portal of unspecified
material in a sequence of Easter verses which would have been sung
both at matins and vespers on Saint George's day had the commemoration fallen at any time in Easter week (its most likely date of occur-
rence) or on any of the subsequent Sundays before the Ascension: the
Resurrection has 'opened to us the gates of Paradise.'[23] Spenser's gate
may be designed by virtue of its substance to combine these two litur-

gically opposite symbols so as to meet the demands of the allegorical fiction. In canto eleven we are required to picture Hell as the plain where the dragon fight takes place, and such a setting does not allow for a gate (that that same plain is the usurped land of Eden need not trouble us unduly in an allegory as protean as Spenser's). What better way to save the otherwise unusable liturgical motif of the gates of brass than to combine it with another, equally familiar paschal symbol? Certainly the fusion of the two does no violence to the significance of either: the opening of either signifies the release of Adam and Eve from the dragon's bondage.

On the wall above the gate of Spenser's paradise stands a watchman, who also may have been transferred from his liturgical place in Hades. His presence in canto twelve is usually ascribed to the iconography of Saint George and the dragon in which a walled and towered city is depicted with people looking from the battlements. In those pictures, however, there is not a single watchman but usually a king and queen, corresponding to Una's parents (who in the poem never appear on the wall), and sometimes other citizens. A more likely source than these pictures for Spenser's single figure, whose sole purpose seems to be to watch for the coming liberator, is the John of Damascus paschal canon. The third ode begins, 'Upon the divine watchtower let the God-seeing prophet Habakkuk stand and with us show forth the radiant angel [the angel of the Resurrection], who says with vibrant voice, "Today salvation [hath come] to the world, for Christ hath arisen as almighty."'[24] As an Old Testament prophet of the Incarnation, Habakkuk is one of those in Hades who await the opening of the gate – precisely the role in which Spenser casts his watchman. Indeed Spenser prepares for the motif very carefully, mentioning the same watchman at the beginning of canto eleven, where, like the ancient prophets, he is 'wayting tydings glad to heare' (I, xi, 3). Along with the gates he has probably been moved from Hades to Eden for the purposes of Spenser's narrative.

Furthermore, what he sees and announces may derive from the same passage in the Easter rite in which the gate of Paradise is mentioned. This is a series of short hymns sung as responses to the opening verses of Psalm 68, 'Let God aryse, and let his enemies be scattered: let them also that hate him flee before Him. Like as the smoke vanisheth, so shalt thou dryue them awaye ... But let the rightous be glad.'[25] Red

Crosse scatters his enemies by slaying the dragon, and the righteous citizens of Eden are glad; but the truly tantalizing detail here is the vanishing smoke: the watchman infers Red Crosse's victory from the dragon's 'last deadly smoke' (I, xii, 2) steaming aloft. There we have either a fairly remarkable coincidence of both theme and symbol or evidence of Spenser's drawing details of his allegory from the liturgical texts. The latter possibility is enhanced by the thematic coherence of these images – the opened, brazen gate, the watchman, the vanishing smoke – which combine in *The Faerie Queene* to the same effect, if not in the same symbolic place, as in John of Damascus' hymns.

Other liturgical themes anticipating Spenser's symbolism cluster around these. In the ode of the Easter canon immediately subsequent to that in which the watchman appears, worshippers, presumably responding to Habakkuk's proclamation, are bidden to rise with the women who went to Christ's tomb on Easter morning and 'in the deep dawn' (ὄρθρου βαθέος) see the rising of 'Christ the Sun of Righteousness, who causes life to rise for all.'[26] The point of the metaphor is that Christ's rising 'in the *deep* dawn' precedes, as is fitting, the sun's. After the Well, Spenser's George rises only *with* the sun; but after the unction he rises as Christ does – for being anointed he *is* Christ – before it, when Aurora, not Phoebus, appears (I, xi, 51). The third stanza of the same ode introduces a motif which plays an important part in canto twelve – that of the Heavenly Bridegroom. The worshippers whom John of Damascus dispatches with the women to the tomb are bidden to go with lamps in hand to meet Christ coming forth as a bridegroom.[27] The lamps allude to those of the wise virgins in the parable of the wedding feast, but in a paschal context they no doubt refer as well to the candles given newly baptized catechumens as symbols of the light of the Resurrection. That light is, of course, Christ Himself, and other hymns in Easter (and Saint George) matins link the Savior's role as bridegroom with his being a source of pre-dawn, supernatural light – the mystical 'Sun of Righteousness.' Jerusalem rejoices to 'see Christ the King as a bridegroom come forth from the tomb,' and 'From the tomb as from a bridal chamber, Christ today shone forth.'[28]

His *shining* rather than merely *coming* forth connects the various facets of this symbolism. The allusion is to Psalm 19, in which the sun 'cometh forth as a bridegroom out of his chamber, & reioyseth as a giaunt to run his course'; Spenser uses the second half of the verse when Red Crosse rises the first time, *with* the sun, when '*Titan* rose to runne his daily race' (I, xi, 33). The author of the liturgy has identified the bridal chamber with the tomb and the sun with Christ – not only Christ the Sun of Righteousness whose rising precedes the natural sun's but also Christ the Heavenly Bridegroom who rises victorious to become (as Red Crosse – Saint George – does in canto twelve) the Church's spouse. That Jerusalem in this instance rather than Paradise receives Him may account for Spenser's presenting Eden as a city rather than a garden (a matter of which we shall have more to say); and that possibility is enhanced by yet another hymn from the Damascene canon, 'Shine, shine New Jerusalem, for the glory of the Lord is risen upon thee.'[29]

III

Spenser could have known John of Damascus' paschal canon without having seen a *Pentecostarion*;[30] and there is a greater probability of his having seen a *Pentecostarion* than a less important text such as one of the twelve *Menaions*.[31] One could therefore argue that the paschal motifs in cantos eleven and twelve came to his attention in the context of the Easter baptismal liturgy without reference to Saint George and that putting the two together was his own imaginative conception rather than a debt to the prior liturgical combination. Against that possibility, however, we must set a number of resemblances between the characterizations of George in the *Menaion* and *The Faerie Queene* which are not paschal in character and which cannot, therefore, be attributed to a general knowledge of ancient Easter liturgy.

Like Spenser's George, the George of liturgy is prepared for battle by the three theological virtues: 'opposing desire by *faith*, thrusting off fear with *hope*, thou didst attain heaven by *charity*.'[32] Also the liturgical George, like Spenser's, wears the Christian armor of Ephesians 6: 'Having put on the whole armor of Christ' (except for *Christ*, rather than *God*, a direct quotation in the liturgy of Ephesians 6:11), George shouts 'to the transgressors of the law, "I go for a soldier to Christ my king."'[33] The motif is repeated in another hymn with further direct quotation from Saint Paul: 'Fenced around with the breastplate of faith and with the shield of grace and with the spear of the Cross, O George, thou didst become invincible to the enemies.'[34] This is the only instance I have discovered other than *The Faerie Queene* itself in which George is depicted as wearing the armor of Ephesians 6; there is no precedent for the conceit in de Voragine, Lydgate, Mantuan, or Barclay. Furthermore, George's armor in the *Menaion*, as in canto eleven, is associated with trial by fire. 'Having put on the whole armor of Christ,' George is 'burned for Christ': 'dangers hardened [lit. 'forged'] him who was burned for Christ;'[35] he became a 'whole burnt offering, living and spiritual, and a sacrifice well accepted and most pure;'[36] he was 'set on fire with burning desire for the Master.'[37] Red Crosse's fiery ordeal on the first day of battle may signify, as Carol Kaske has ably argued, a residue of concupiscence in his not yet baptized flesh,[38] but at the same time (and multiple significance in Spenser is never improbable) the torment is a consequence of his contending for holiness. Even if Spenser's George is burned on account of a defect, he is arguably also being 'burned for Christ' on whose account and in whom he fights.

There is also an important verbal (as distinguished from thematic) resemblance between the *Menaion* liturgy and the poem – a repetition in both of *victory* and *victorious*. From the moment Red Crosse learns he is George, the word attaches to him: Contemplation promises that George will be 'the signe of *victoree*' (I, x, 61), 'when thou famous *victorie* hast wonne' (I, x, 60; italics added). Red Crosse fulfills that prophecy when he overthrows the dragon, gaining thereby 'most glorious *victory*' (I, xi, Arg.; italics added); Una's parents come to salute him bringing laurel branches, 'Glad signe of *victoree*' (I, xii, 5; italics added); and the other inhabitants of Eden, rushing 'To see the face of that *victorious* man' (I, xii, 9; italics added) proclaim 'to heauen ... happie *victorie*' (I, xii, 4; italics added). *Victory* is also the liturgical George's identifying characteristic; in fact Spenser's 'signe of *victoree*' translates the saint's epithet, τροπαιοφόρος. In modern English versions this is usually rendered as 'trophy bearer,' but it can also mean 'victory bearer' or simply 'victorious.' If Spenser, however, had read the hymns in which the word appears and attended carefully to the Greek, he might well have derived a translation closer to his designation of Red Crosse. For τρόπαιον is not so accurately rendered by 'trophy' or 'victory' as by *insignia* or *sign* of victory: the George of liturgy is quite literally the bearer of the 'signe of victoree.'[39]

Τροπαιοφόρος occurs not only in the heading of the liturgy for

23 April – feast of 'the holy great martyr George, bearer of the sign of victory' – but also in several hymns, two of which recall other facets of Red Crosse's character. In the *Apolutikion* of the commemoration, the hymn which states the theme of the day and is repeated several times, George is a 'liberator of captives,' 'champion of kings' (Red Crosse liberates the citizens of Eden and champions their king), and 'bearer of the sign of victory.'[40] In one of the vespers hymns George is a 'brilliant star,' 'son of the day' (both phrases recall Red Crosse's identification with light and his rising at dawn) and 'bearer of the sign of victory.'[41] Other hymns repeat the motif, using instead the word νίκη; George, having 'finished his course and [kept] the faith, receives ... the crown of *victory* (νίκης),' and he reigns with the risen Christ, 'distinguished by the crown of *victory* (νίκης).'[42]

IV

How much of this material could Spenser have found in the 'legendary life'? Not, in fact, a great deal, and parallels which earlier critics have cited are considerably less persuasive than the ones we have been examining. When, for instance, Padelford and O'Connor argue that 'the mere mention of the bright steel armor of St. George [in Lydgate's version] was seemingly enough of a hint for the later poet to identify it with that armor of the Christian which he assigns to the Red Crosse Knight,'[43] we are reminded that the liturgy offers more than a hint, bestowing on George that very Pauline metaphor. When Patrick Grant says that George's breaking idols and driving fiends into Hell (in the part of the legend dealing with his martyrdom) is 'a kind of harrowing,'[44] we cannot but remember that the George of liturgy is explicitly identified with Christ the Harrower; Grant's gloss seems far-fetched by comparison. And although Grant and others have been at pains to show that the legend presents a pre-eminently holy George and thus a persuasive original for a patron of holiness, there is nowhere any suggestion of the deification or literal identification with Christ which is so prominent an element in the Saint George liturgy and so explicit a theme in cantos eleven and twelve.

That is not to deny that Spenser drew upon the legend – he obviously did – but he subjects it to a radical reconstruction, and we can find liturgical precedents for most of his changes. The walled city to which we have alluded is an instance. Though this citadel appears both in the legend and the iconography, it is nowhere save in *The Faerie Queene* identified as Eden and its king and queen as Adam and Eve. In the legend it is named Silena, a city in Libya, and until George preaches the Gospel there it is a pagan place. Nothing about its traditional representation suggests the recovered Eden of canto twelve. Silena does seem to have undergone a theological development prior to *The Faerie Queene* but one quite distinct from what we find there. Kellogg and Steele, following Panofsky, argue convincingly that in Carpaccio's famous version Silena represents Augustine's City of Man, and though Kellogg and Steele do not say so directly, they imply that Spenser intended the same meaning.[45] They are almost certainly correct in their reading of the fresco, but they are mistaken I believe in implying that Spenser embraced the Augustinian interpretation. The question they never raise is how the City of Man can also be the recovered Eden, which we know Spenser's city to be. Perhaps Augustine's metaphor could be regarded as an historical extension of a fallen Eden (though Augustine himself does not make that connection), but that will not square with Spenser's emphasis. His paradise is not lost but regained, and his theme in cantos eleven and twelve is obviously not the first Adam's fall but the second Adam's victory. The City of Man has really no place in such an allegory, for Saint George (as Christ) has restored the City of God.

That, as we have seen, is the city which appears in the paschal liturgy – New Jerusalem (which Spenser's Saint George, we must not forget, has been promised) shining with the light of the Resurrection, and Jerusalem rejoicing to receive Christ as bridegroom. New Jerusalem is admittedly not identical with the restored Eden; but the two are typologically consonant, and one suspects that Spenser was deliberately fusing them. Though Eden is conventionally represented as walled and gated, it is never conceived as a city with king, queen, lords, and commons. Such a representation must be owing in part to the presence of the walled city in the legend and the paintings, but Spenser leaves little doubt that he also intends a reference to Jerusalem. As Hamilton has pointed out, there are two allusions in canto twelve to Christ's entry on Palm Sunday: when Red Crosse enters Eden its citizens throw 'laurell boughes' at his feet (I, xii, 6) 'And with their garments strowes the paued street' (I, xii, 13).[46] In liturgical typology, the Palm Sunday triumph signifies precisely what Spenser's allegory suggests, Christ's entry in glory into *New* Jerusalem and the eschatological nuptials of Christ and His Church: 'See ... how he weds the new Sion [who is] chaste ... As in a marriage uncorrupt and pure the pure and sinless children come together rejoicing.'[47] To complete his pattern Spenser could have found in the same liturgy references to the Harrowing; like Red Crosse, Christ not only enters Jerusalem to wed His Church but to release Adam from the dragon. 'Out of the mouth of guileless babes and sucklings Thou didst perfect the praise of thy servants; Thou hast destroyed the adversary ... and avenged the ancient fall of Adam.'[48] Worshippers are admonished to bear 'spiritual' palms and with the children of Jerusalem cry to Christ with a loud voice: 'Blessed art Thou, O Saviour, who cometh into the world to save Adam from the ancient curse.'[49] The celebration which ensues upon Una's parents' release responds in spirit and in some details to that admonition. Silena of the legend appears to have been subsumed in the Eden-New Jerusalem of antique liturgy – a theological development quite different from that which Spenser would have been likely to derive from Carpaccio's allegorization.

Within Silena, after George slays the dragon, there springs up a magic well, whose waters possess power to heal those poisoned by the dragon and even to restore the wasted land. There is no well within the walls of Spenser's city, but the Well of Life with its healing virtue may owe something to Silena's fountain.[50] As a symbol of baptism, however, Spenser's Well is much more convincingly glossed with reference to the paschal liturgy. Since the George of legend converts and baptizes the pagan populace, Silena's well may have some relation to the font (its presence may be a garbled survival from George's liturgical origins), but in no version of the story is it identified as such. Conversely, since baptism is an integral part of Easter liturgy, since it signifies in that context participation in the Harrowing, and since the liturgy for Saint George identifies him consistently with the paschal Christ, we may reasonably surmise that the *Triodion*, *Pentecostarion*, and *Menaion* (and of course the patristic baptismal homilies which we have examined) were Spenser's primary sources. Furthermore, if we are correct in identifying the Balm as post-baptismal chrism, the addition of that detail (there is no precedent for it in the legend) points to a deliberate renovation of the well of Silena in light of liturgical sources.

Other pieces of the story appear to have been subjected to the same kind of transfiguration. There can be no question that Una and her lamb derive in part from Alcyone and her sheep and from the many representations of that pair in contemporary iconography and pageantry. Except, however, for the barest visual details – the pairing of lady and lamb – Spenser's allegory seems to owe nothing to the legend. Una is not chosen to be a sacrificial victim, her mother and father as Adam and Eve bear no thematic resemblance whatever to Alcyone's pagan parents, and so far from being like Alcyone in need of conversion and baptism, Una is an explicit symbol of Holy Church. Another difference, which may be more significant than it seems on first consideration, is that while the George of legend refuses the offer of Alcyone's hand, Red Crosse accepts Una's joyfully. His doing so makes it possible for Spenser to introduce into the allegory of canto twelve the betrothal ceremony which completes Book One and which obviously symbolizes the eschatological nuptials of Christ and His Church. These, as we have just seen, are a part of the liturgical significance of the entry into Jerusalem on Palm Sunday, and, as we shall see in the next chapter, are integral to the typology of the descent into Hell and the Resurrection. Without this marriage, Saint George's assimilation to the paschal Christ would be incomplete; Spenser's modifying the legend to allow the marriage is, therefore, still another reason to believe that he took the liturgical rather than the legendary George for his principal model. The relations between Alcyone and the George of legend at Silena are so remote from such paschal and eschatological considerations as to constitute only the faintest pretext for Spenser's representation.

Finally there is the dragon fight itself and its transformation into the Harrowing. If we have come to think of Christ's defeat of Satan on Holy Saturday as a part of the Saint George myth (and the relative silence of commentators on the subject suggests we have), Spenser himself is most likely the mythmaker.[51] Had we been reading *The Faerie Queene* in the 1590s, we should probably have found this a surprising development. Saint George is so nearly ubiquitous in the Renaissance that one can never be certain of having seen all the pertinent references, but of the analogues usually cited none seems a likely source. The *Variorum* editors and more recently Nohrnberg and Grant have called attention to a number of instances in which George plays

Christ to the dragon's Satan.[52] Most of these, however, are too brief or
obscure to carry much conviction, and several of them cannot possibly
be sources because they were published after Book One of *The Faerie
Queene*. The latter are cited by commentators as evidence of a continuing tradition of interpretation from which Spenser drew somewhat
earlier, but they could just as easily be evidence of his influence on
later writers. That seems especially likely in the case of Raleigh's *History*, and Drayton in the *Poly-olbion* mentions Spenser. According to
Grant, Tristram White's *The Martyrdome of St. George of the Cross* 'begins
by comparing Christ, the "crowned Conquerour of Hell" ... to St.
George, our "owne true Knight,"' and that of course is what Spenser
does;[53] but since White's book was not published until 1614 it well
may have been written with *The Faerie Queene* in mind. The analogue
closest in date but still post-Spenserian is a patriotic poem by Richard
Vennar, *Saint George for England*:

> Saint George the Dragon, Jesus Sathan kill'd
>   Saint George the Princesse and the Lambe preserv'd:
> Jesus his bitter combat hath fulfill'd,
>   And by the Divel's death his Church reserv'd.[54]

That was published in 1601; it may be indicative of a popular allegorization of Saint George which Spenser knew, or it may be owing to
Spenser.

Another problem with these citations is that the struggle between
Christ and Satan as they represent it is not necessarily the Harrowing –
it may or may not be. In Vennar's poem, for instance, Jesus' 'bitter
combat' could be the temptation in the wilderness or the passion of the
Cross. The same ambiguity attends a reference which by virtue of date
and accessibility could be legitimately regarded as a source – the entry
for *Georgius Cappadox* in Charles Estienne's *Dictionarum, Historicum,
Geographicum, Poeticum*. After a brief summary of the dragon fight,
Estienne tells us that 'some theologians' think George's name is a fiction under which Christ is presented, 'liberating the Church from the
tyranny of Satan.' That allegorization may have been inspired as a
response to attacks like Calvin's and Erasmus', and it certainly anticipates Spenser's. We cannot, however, be certain that Estienne intends
the Harrowing; 'liberating the Church from the tyranny of Satan' could

apply to almost anything Christ did. Furthermore, when we compare a reference so brief and general as this to the full development of the same motif in liturgical texts available to a sixteenth-century reader, the latter seem more likely sources.

The full-scale versions of the Saint George legend, those of Lydgate, Mantuan, Barclay, and de Voragine, afford even less convincing precedent for Spenser's interpretation. Of course all dragons in Christian literature are potentially Satanic, but George's less than most; he is not a true dragon but a water beast and patently pagan in character. Spenser would surely have recognized him as a not very well assimilated version of Perseus' adversary and so, he must have realized, would most of his readers. Furthermore, in the legendary account of the fight and of George's victory there is nothing to suggest Spenser's paschal allegory. There is no hint that the battle takes place at Easter or has any association with the Resurrection. Neither is there any precedent in the legend for the struggle's lasting three days. Though baptism, as we have seen, figures in the legend, it is not connected there with the Harrowing and Resurrection as it clearly is in *The Faerie Queene*. Furthermore, in the legend George administers rather than receives the sacrament; the font is not the source of strength for his victory. Indeed all the paschal and related sacramental symbolism which surrounds the dragon fight in the poem seems to be owing to Spenser and, in view of the improbability of contemporary sources, constitutes a strong case for George's antique liturgical character.

Grant and other critics believe that the Easter motif in Spenser's presentation derives from the second half of the medieval legend, of which we have had nothing to say – the account of George's martyrdom. A version of this narrative appears in the *Menaion*, in matins for 23 April,[55] and so would have been available to Spenser in immediate conjunction with the liturgical motifs we have been describing (needless to say there is no dragon in the liturgy). There is almost nothing, however, in this bit of hagiography which offers itself as a convincing precedent for the allegory of Book One. Grant makes a great deal of the fact that George's sufferings are compared with Christ's, but that emphasis is not particularly strong, nor is George in that respect unique among martyrs. If Spenser was acquainted with the conventions of hagiography, he would have found little or nothing in the account of George's passion to mark it as more distinctively paschal than the sufferings of many other saints. Furthermore the legend makes little connection between even those faint (and routine) paschal references and the dragon fight, upon which Spenser concentrates all his paschal symbolism. Finally – and perhaps the most important difference – the legend is concerned almost exclusively with George in relation to the Passion, *The Faerie Queene* with George in relation to the Harrowing and Resurrection. Grant remarks that in Mantuan's version George upon leaving Silena 'makes a pilgrimage to Mount Calvary, visiting the very scene of Christ's passion'; 'in choosing to interpolate this journey to the site of the crucifixion Mantuan seeks to underline the motif [that is, the Passion] which he thought the two sections of the story had in common.'[56] That may well have been Mantuan's intent, but it helps very little to understand Spenser's allegory. Cantos eleven and twelve make no reference whatever to Calvary; for all their paschal implications, the Cross is invisible. Like the liturgy, *The Faerie Queene* hurries us beyond Good Friday to Holy Saturday and Easter day. Recognizing that but not, apparently, understanding its implications, Nohrnberg remarks that 'the tone of the dragon fight will not strike many readers as doing anything like justice to the Crucifixion – it certainly is not the *St. Matthew Passion*.'[57] I believe Spenser would answer, it was not meant to be; it was not meant to 'do justice' to the George of legend and his association (however tentative) with the Passion but to the George of liturgy, a type of the Harrower, the resurrected Lord, and (as we shall now see in greater detail) the Heavenly Bridegroom.

CHAPTER THREE

Una's Betrothal

I

Interpreting the hero of Book One and the events of cantos eleven and twelve with reference to a paschal, liturgical context raises a question about another important part of that context – the eucharist. Does Spenser's legend of holiness include any reference to holy communion? If not, there would be cause for surprise, for one can scarcely imagine an account of Christian sanctification – patristic, Catholic, or Protestant – which found no place for the sacrament which above all others unites the believer to Christ. Though the Balm is almost certainly not holy communion, those generations of critics who have conceived it to be were proceeding on a sound assumption: that one cannot have Christian holiness without the eucharist. Patristic commentary would support that conviction fully, for it treats the eucharist as the supreme sacrament and the consummation of all the rest, including baptism and chrismation. Dionysius calls the Mass the 'mystery of mysteries' both because 'what is common to the other hierarchical mysteries is pre-eminently attributed to this one beyond all the rest' and because the perfections bestowed by the others derive 'from the supremely divine and perfecting gifts of this sacrament.'[1] That means that though chrismation, for instance, may be primarily instrumental in a catechumen's deification, the unction both derives its virtue from the eucharist and is completed by it. In view of such teaching our argument that Spenser was interpreting holiness in patristic terms, as *theosis*, would be undercut if he included no allegory of communion.

Furthermore, the sacramental sequence on the paschal night, which seems to be represented in cantos eleven and the beginning of twelve,

ended in the eucharist; the catechumen's communion completed his
initiation, and all the catecheses end with homilies on what came to be
called in the West, the 'first Mass of Easter.' From the baptistery the catechumen, immersed and anointed, was led to the altar where for the
first time he witnessed the full celebration of the eucharist and
received Christ's body and blood. 'Having put aside,' says Ambrose,
'the defilements of ancient error [in pre-baptismal purgation], renewed
[by baptism and chrismation] in the youth of an eagle' (as Red Crosse
is), the neophytes 'hasten to approach that heavenly banquet.'[2] Jean
Danielou describes very accurately 'the great unity which the whole
process of initiation is ... seen to possess: from Baptism to Communion,
this is all a participation in Christ dead and risen again. There is no
other mystery than the Paschal mystery, this is the mystery which is
the unique object of the whole sacramental life.'[3] That Spenser, if in fact
he knew of that mystery as his allegory suggests he did, should have
represented only part of the whole, omitting its culminating episode, is
improbable.

There is no reason to believe he did that; we need only reconsider
how Book One ends. The eucharist was the catechumen's reward for
his victory over Satan in baptism and chrismation; Red Crosse's
reward for slaying the dragon and liberating Eden is his betrothal to
Una. Does the betrothal rite in the second half of canto twelve represent the eucharist? Habitual identification of the Balm as holy communion has blinded us to the possibility, for a second representation of
the same sacrament would be redundant and unlikely. Conversely, if
the Balm is chrism, what would be more likely than that there should
follow an allegory of the sacrament which always followed unction at
the Easter vigil and which completed the catechumen's deification?
Eucharistic imagery in canto twelve has not gone unnoticed: Upton
recognized an allusion to the 'marriage supper of the Lamb' (Revelation 19:6–7) – the Messianic banquet or eschatological wedding feast –
which both in the New Testament and in patristic commentary serves
as a type of the Mass. Most commentators acknowledge this reference,
but no one has suggested that Spenser intended a precise representation of the paschal eucharist, that the events of canto twelve follow in
direct liturgical sequence from the Well and Balm and dragon fight, or
that the betrothal completes an extended allegory of holiness conceived as *theosis*.

II

Spenser's nuptial symbolism has proved a distraction because it has traditionally been interpreted in pagan terms. When the same symbolism is placed in a Christian – and specifically paschal – frame of reference, it proves a key to the wedding's meaning. Upton, despite his recognizing an allusion to the Messianic banquet, is responsible for the conventional pagan reading; to explain the 'housling fire' and holy water at the beginning of the celebration, he pointed to 'the marriages of Antiquity, which were solemnized "sacramento ignis et aquae."' Most commentators have followed that lead, but Upton himself had doubts: in pagan ceremony the 'holy water was not sprinkled on the fire ... but water was sprinkled on the bride. I wonder whether Spenser did not rather write, "And holy water sprinckled on the bride"'[4] (an altogether amusing suggestion in view of Una's sage and serious demeanor). A simpler explanation is that Spenser never intended reference to pagan or in fact to any marriage customs but that he was using marriage in a traditional Christian way as a metaphor for the Mass. *Housling*, after all, is a synonym for *eucharistic*, and, as Josephine Waters Bennett wrote fifty years ago, 'the lighting of a "housling fire" ... which is sprinkled with holy water and from which an ever burning lamp is lighted, and, finally, the sprinkling of the posts with wine, symbolic of the blood of the Passover – all these rites were, I believe, intended to suggest the symbolism of Christian consecration rather than a pagan wedding.'[5]

Professor Bennett's comment adumbrates an adequate interpretation of the betrothal. Perhaps she would have gone further had she been reading Spenser against the backdrop of patristic commentary, in which the paschal eucharist is frequently represented as a wedding feast. Marriage symbolism runs through the whole of Cyril's *Catecheses*. In his very first homily, the *Procatechesis*, he admonishes his flock to prepare for holy communion as for a marriage: 'If the day of [thy] nuptials lay before thee, wouldest thou not relinquish other things and be anxious about preparation for the celebration? If then thou art about to consecrate, or espouse [thy] soul to a celestial spouse [in the catechumen's first communion], wilt thou not disregard corporeal things in order to receive spiritual?'[6] Since these remarks precede Cyril's homilies on baptism and chrismation, we may reasonably conclude that he regards those sacraments as part of the preparation he is urging upon his flock – just as the Well and Balm serve as Red Crosse's preparation for his betrothal. Nor does Cyril abandon the nuptial symbolism when he comes to the eucharist itself; rather he begins the first of his two eucharistic homilies with a reference to the marriage in Cana of Galilee: we should not wonder at the wine's being transformed into Christ's blood since Christ once turned water into wine. He performed that astounding miracle when invited to 'a bodily marriage'; for the heavenly marriage of the eucharist, 'Shall He not much rather be confessed to have given the enjoyment of His body and blood to the sons of the bridal chamber?'[7] Those sons are, of course, the newly baptized and anointed neophytes who have been enlisted in Christ's ranks and given 'betrothal lamps.'[8]

Patristic commentary frequently characterizes the eucharist in nuptial symbolism drawn from Canticles (a 'Canticum Canticorum translated,' is among Spenser's lost works).[9] Ambrose says to his flock, 'You have come to the altar; the Lord Jesus calls you ... and He says: "Let him kiss me with the kiss of his mouth."' The kiss is the touch of the lips on the host or chalice; it is also, of course, the kiss bestowed by the bride, the Church in the persons of the initiates, on Christ the Bridegroom. Why, asks Ambrose, should Christ invite the kiss? Because 'He sees that you are clean [through baptism and chrismation] of all sin, because transgressions have been wiped away. Thus He judges you worthy of the heavenly sacraments, and thus invites you to the heavenly banquet. "Let Him kiss me with the kiss of His mouth."'[10] Theodoret of Cyrrhus commenting on the same typology says, 'But lest anyone be perturbed by the term kiss, let him consider how in the mystical time [of engagement], receiving the body of the bridegroom, we embrace and kiss [it], and we place [it] with eyes of the heart, and in soul and thought we fashion as it were certain embraces and nuptial unions.' Theodoret makes this symbolism even more explicit in another passage: 'Therefore, eating the members of the bridegroom and drinking His blood, we arrive at his nuptial union.'[11]

Patristic catecheses also afford a precedent for some of the apparently pagan elements which have distracted commentators. Like the fire and water, the sprinkled posts have been ascribed to pre-Christian nuptial celebration. Professor Bennett is almost certainly correct that these constitute an allusion to the Passover and thus signify a 'Christian consecration'; but they may suggest bacchic revelry as well. The fusion of the two motifs in a single symbol seems indecorous and perhaps sacrilegious until we hear Saint Gregory of Nyssa say that for those 'who understand the mystical sense of the Gospels no discrepancy will appear between' the invitation in Canticles, '"Eat, my friends, and drink, and be inebriated, my brothers"' and Christ's institution of the sacrament of His body and blood; for in both instances the exhortation is to eat and drink. To the possible objection that the command in Canticles to be inebriated exceeds the Gospels, Gregory responds that anyone who considers the matter accurately will 'discover this [command] to be consonant with the Gospel language.' Gregory's explanation is that Christ's flesh and blood effects the true inebriation of which the Old Testament's physical drunkenness is the type: 'for what here [in Canticles] is commanded ... in words there [in the Gospels] effects the thing itself.'[12] The Church, says Ambrose, invites us to the sacraments, saying, '"Eat, my neighbors, and drink and be inebriated, my brethren"' because what we eat and drink is Christ; the Holy Spirit explains that elsewhere [Psalm 34] by saying, '"Taste and see that the Lord is sweet."' In another place Ambrose links divine inebriation to the nuptial kiss: '"Let Christ impress a kiss upon me." Why? "For thy breasts are better than wine," that is ... your sacraments are better than wine, than that wine which ... [has in it] worldly pleasure.' As often as you drink this better, eucharistic wine, adds Ambrose, 'You are inebriated in spirit.' 'He who is inebriated with wine totters and sways; he who is inebriated with the Holy Spirit is rooted in Christ ... glorious is ebriety which effects sobriety of mind.'[13] Spenser's wine is probably intended to combine these motifs and to constitute a paradox like the Fathers' sober or sacred drunkenness. (The even more explicit fusion of the holy and the bacchic in the *Epithalamion* may derive from the same tradition of exegesis.)

III

Here then in the same homilies in which Spenser could have learned about paschal baptism and chrismation he could also have found a symbolic rationale for presenting the Easter eucharist as a wedding ceremony and one, attended as is his, by apparently pagan revelry. And there is even more persuasive evidence that he intended the Easter Mass – a striking resemblance between the details of his allegory and the Easter liturgy in the Latin rite. If he drew his conception of Saint George and other paschal symbolism from Byzantine service books, he seems to have relied for the imagery of the betrothal on the Sarum Missal and Manual (or possibly on the new Tridentine liturgical texts). Like Una's betrothal, the Latin Easter liturgy began with fire and holy water. Rubrics instruct the priest to bless and kindle the 'new fire' of Easter – the *novus ignis: sacerdos ... ignem benedicat & accendatur ibidem.*[14] A reader of *The Faerie Queene* who had discerned allusions to paschal rites in canto eleven and who remembered how Easter had been celebrated in the 'old religion' (as many of Spenser's contemporaries must have) would almost certainly have recognized the fire as a signal – to let him know that the betrothal thus begun was an allegory of the sacramental activities of Holy Saturday night. The accompanying water, puzzling to Upton, would have made the signal even clearer, for if pagan Romans sprinkled the bride, Christians, as Una's father does, asperged the paschal fire; immediately after the priest kindles and blesses it he sprinkles it with holy water (*hic aspergatur aqua benedicta super ignem*).[15] Spenser all but translates the rubric: 'And holy water thereon sprinckled wide' (I, xii, 37).

Immediately thereafter Spenser's groom lights a torch – a 'bushy Teade' (I, xii, 37) – and as soon as the priest has sprinkled the fire a deacon – an attendant like the groom – lights the paschal candle, the principal liturgical symbol of Easter: *hic accendatur cereus de novo igne.*[16] 'From the new fire' – Spenser's groom evidently does the same: 'At which the bushy Teade a groome did light.' 'At which' seems on first reading a temporal reference, like 'whereupon,' but *which* could just as easily be pronominal with *fire* for its antecedent. That is obviously the way Professor Bennett understood the line – 'A "housling fire" ... *from which* an ever burning lamp is lighted.' The paschal candle is also 'ever burning'; the phrase does not occur in the liturgy proper, but a Missal rubric stipulates that the candle 'shall burn continuously' (*et ardebit cereus paschale continue*)[17] – literally during all the services of Easter week and at all Masses until Ascension day, but symbolically until the Second Coming. When the deacon blesses the candle, he sings, 'May the morning star [Christ] find it burning, that morning star, I say, that knows no setting' (*flammas eius lucifer matutinus inueniat. Ille inquam lucifer qui nescit occasum*). We are not told how long Spenser's teade is to burn – only that it 'should not be quenched day nor night' – but possibly until Red Crosse returns for the marriage; and that, of course, is an allegory of Christ's return. In the interim of spiritual combat the teade burns 'for feare of euill fates,' and the deacon prays that the paschal candle by 'continuing to shine' (*indificiens perseveret*) – reminiscent of Spenser's 'burnen euer bright' (I, xii, 37) – will scatter the demons, 'all the shades of this night' (*ad noctis huius caliginem destruendam*).[18]

Such parallels suggest that Spenser was writing his account of Una's betrothal with an eye to the details of the Latin Easter liturgy, but do they necessarily indicate that he had the eucharist in mind? The rites of new fire, holy water, and paschal candle are generally paschal, not peculiarly eucharistic; they introduce the entire Easter sequence and thus apply as immediately to baptism and chrismation as to the Mass. Spenser's using them as symbols in his betrothal ceremony does not in itself therefore identify that ceremony with any one paschal sacrament at the expense of the rest. May he not merely be recapitulating at the end of his allegory – this time in Western liturgical symbolism – the Easter motifs which he has already developed? He may in fact be doing that but probably not *merely* that. The first hint that he is moving beyond the allegory of the Harrowing, baptism, and chrismation is his designation of the fire as *housling*. Since the *novus ignis* is no more exclusively eucharistic than it is baptismal or generally paschal, Spenser's making it so points a direction for his reader. He is saying in effect, we are still operating in the context of paschal liturgy but now with specific reference to the Mass. Another, and even clearer, indication of his intention is that after following the sequence of events in the Latin rite very carefully through what might be called its introduction, he then breaks off and goes to something else. In Missal and Manual, after the lighting and blessing of the paschal candle comes a reading of prophecies of the Resurrection and then a procession to the baptistery, followed by baptism and chrismation. There is no hint of any of those events in the allegory of canto twelve (they have been dealt with, after all, in eleven). Instead, as soon as the groom has lighted the teade, 'Then gan they sprinckle all the posts with wine' (I, xii, 38). If Professor Bennett is correct that the wine, at least in its primary significance, is the blood of the Passover, it must also be – by ancient typological association – the wine (and blood) of the eucharist. And that Spenser intended his reader to identify it as such is all the more likely in view of the rehearsal of that typology in the blessing of the paschal candle: 'For this is the paschal feast in which the true Lamb is slain, with whose blood the door posts of the faithful are consecrated.'[19] The blood of 'the true Lamb' can scarcely signify anything other than the consecrated wine of the eucharist.

In short, Spenser's introduction of the sprinkled posts immediately after the lighting of the teade is probably a telescoping of liturgical events, a collapsing of the end of the paschal rites, the Mass, into their beginning – fire, water, candle – omitting the middle – baptism and chrismation – which canto eleven had represented. Spenser's specific reference is probably to the Mass offertory in which the bread and wine prepared for consecration are placed on the altar. That would be liturgically appropriate, for in the Latin Easter rite most of the preliminary ceremonies of the eucharist are omitted; the offertory is the first event of importance after chrismation and so, with the displacement of baptismal rites, would be the first event to be represented after the lighting of the candle. Furthermore Spenser's sprinkling of posts is accompanied by incense – 'They all perfumde with frankincense diuine' (I, xii, 38) – and so is the offertory. Immediately after the priest places the host and chalice on the altar, he censes them and, in turn, the altar, the sanctuary, and the congregation; like the officiants at Una's betrothal, he 'all perfum[es].'

A reference to the offertory seems all the more likely in view of what follows – the angelic voices of stanza thirty-nine. As soon as the priest has completed the censing of the church, the choir or congregation sings the *Sanctus*, the thrice-holy hymn to the Trinity which signifies (and in mystical interpretations of the eucharist participates in) the song of the angelic hosts heard by Isaiah. The prefaces to the *Sanctus* in all ancient liturgies, Eastern and Western, stipulate that these are angel voices, and most name the angelic orders. A vestige of that practice survived in the Book of Common Prayer: 'Therefore with angels and archangels, and with all the company of heaven ...' Spenser gives us, however, not just those two angelic orders but all nine – 'trinall triplicities' – and he could easily have taken the hint from the liturgical prefaces. In the Sarum version God the Father is praised 'through Christ our Lord, through whom *Angels* praise the majesty, *Dominations* adore, *Powers* tremble, the heavens, the *Virtues* of the heavens, and the blessed *Seraphim* together with exultation extol Thee ... And therefore with

Angels and *Archangels*, with *Thrones* and *Dominations*, and with all the hosts of heaven, we sing to Thee without ceasing the hymn of glory' (italics added).[20] There we have seven of the nine orders – sufficient pretext for including all nine, whose names and ranks Spenser would of course have known from non-liturgical sources.[21] Finally Spenser's 'heauenly noise' mingles with human song and is heard locally, 'through all the Pallace' (I, xii, 39). The Sarum preface envisions just such a union of earthly and heavenly voices bidding that 'our voices be joined' to those of the angels (*et nostras voces ut admitti iubeas deprecamur*).[22]

Red Crosse's confession also hints at the Mass offertory. Preparations for the betrothal are interrupted in stanza twenty-four by the arrival of Archimago, who must be dispatched before the solemnities can continue. The function of this episode is to allow Red Crosse to clear his conscience (he seems to have forgotten all too easily about certain encounters with Duessa). In terms of the betrothal allegory, this is the forbidding of banns (Una's father says so), but it also makes clear symbolic sense in the context of the eucharist: as preparation for a proper offering and reception of the sacramental elements one must confess his sins and be shriven. Red Crosse does in fact make confession in stanzas thirty-one and thirty-two, and Una in her role as Holy Church pleads for his forgiveness – in effect absolves him – in stanza thirty-three. Then the rite continues. There is no order of confession and absolution in any of the ancient Mass liturgies (Cranmer's in the Prayer Book may have contributed to Spenser's allegory),[23] but the Fathers insist on the need for repentance in conjunction with the offering of the bread and wine. Cyril's discussion of the matter is of particular interest in the present context, for it ties eucharistic confession to nuptial symbolism, specifically to the kiss (in the Mass, the kiss of peace at the offertory) – 'a sign of the mingling of souls [as Una's and Red Crosse's are soon to be mingled] and the exorcising of all memory of wrongs [as Red Crosse's are exorcised by his confession].' The kiss, says Cyril, 'solicits ... entire forgiveness,' but only if communicants (the new catechumens) confess their sins. To make his point Cyril quotes Christ's familiar admonition in Saint Matthew (5:23): 'If thou bring thy gift to the altar, and remembrest that thy brother hath aught against thee, leave there thy gift upon the altar, and go thy way; first be reconciled to thy brother, and then come and offer thy gift.'[24] What Christ there commands, Una's father requires Red Crosse to perform: 'Let nought be hid from me,' he says, 'that ought to be exprest' (I, xii, 29). Until Red Crosse tells the whole story of his liaison with Duessa, his gift (presumably his suit to Una) remains unacceptable. He in effect goes his way and is reconciled to his brother. The action fulfills very neatly Cyril's prescription for the prospective communicant's proper participation in the eucharist.

IV

If such parallels persuade us to interpret the betrothal as an emblem of the paschal eucharist, we must then consider a thematic question: do Una's and Red Crosse's nuptials complete Spenser's legend of holiness in the way the Fathers say holy communion completes the catechumen's *theosis*? Red Crosse's confession, and indeed his secondary role throughout the ceremony, suggest that just the opposite might be true. We speak of him as the Heavenly Bridegroom, and in the broad signification of the allegory he must be conceived as such; but after he enters Eden as the victorious Harrower, he no longer seems Christlike. His significance is diminished; he plays the role of a penitent; and we are left asking how, if we have been correct in our interpretation of canto eleven, that can be. If by baptism and chrismation he has been transformed into Christ Himself, how, at the ensuing eucharist where we should expect him to be manifest as the Church's divine spouse, can he be a sinner in need of forgiveness? If he is the Heavenly Bridegroom, is it not improper and thematically contradictory that his bride, the Church (Una), should plead for him and in effect absolve him? Should he not be absolving her? Do these apparent inconsistencies tell against a eucharistic interpretation of the betrothal and even perhaps against a patristic interpretation of the whole of cantos eleven and twelve?

Not necessarily. There is plentiful precedent in the mystagogies for such inconsistency. When Cyril urges repentance and confession as preparation for a first communion, we must not forget that he is preaching to the very same catechumens whose deification has been his theme when he preached (two homilies earlier) on chrismation. He evidently discerned no contradiction between these two emphases. And Cyril is characteristic in this regard; patristic commentary shows little if any concern for logical (or psychological) consistency in its treatment of the theme of deification; the matter, after all, is mystical. When a catechumen is baptized and chrismated, he is made divine; that, as I have tried to show, is to be understood literally – just as I believe Spenser meant us to understand Red Crosse's assimilation to Christ the Harrower as literal rather than merely symbolic or hyperbolic. Holiness – deification – is for the Fathers and the ancient liturgies true in fact, not merely in metaphor. But, except for perfected saints, it is true in the mystical and liturgical rather than in the practical and ethical facets of the Christian life. In the latter the catechumen is still moribund, still concupiscent, and though he has just been exorcised, baptized, and chrismated, he is still in need of repentance and confession before making his communion. To enter upon the full significance of the patristic understanding of the Christian life (as I am implying Spenser's allegory does) we must think of ourselves in both these contexts at once, no matter how violently they jar against each other. Any effort to rationalize the paradox cheats the mystery. Another way to state the matter is to vary a familiar Scholastic distinction and say that the Chrisian lives both in the present age (*in via*) and in the age to come (*in patria*). For the Fathers (as we shall see more fully later) the *eschaton* has already arrived with the Harrowing and the Resurrection; but it is also still to come when Christ returns. In the interim (the six remaining years of Red Crosse's service to Gloriana – the six ages of this present dispensation) each Christian is illogically but no less truly both a miserable sinner awaiting the Second Coming with the redemption of the body and a 'partaker of the divine nature,' participating already through baptism, chrismation, and the eucharist in the life of God. By allowing Red Crosse to manifest both these equally Christian though contradictory conditions in immediate succession Spenser is arguably more faithful to the theology of deification than if he had presented his hero and exemplar of holiness more consistently.

The inconsistency also works to Spenser's thematic advantage, allowing him to broaden the significance of his allegory by extending deification beyond the Knight of Holiness. Since Red Crosse can be at once the Heavenly Bridegroom and a penitent Christian, other figures can plausibly change roles as well. Una's father is an instance; he is both the old Adam redeemed by the new – the part he plays consistently, by reputation, throughout Book One and in person at the beginning of canto twelve – and also himself the new Adam, Christ in His role of the great high priest officiating at the heavenly altar and requiring Red Crosse, who a few stanzas earlier was his redeemer, to confess his sins. And that we should witness the Christification of the old Adam is obviously important, for his release from the bondage of the dragon signifies the redemption of the entire human race. But that we should witness a comparable transformation in Una – her unveiling and her assumption of spiritual authority as Red Crosse's intercessor – is even more important. For if her father's redemption by Red Crosse's victory signifies the return of mankind to its original paradisal and deified condition, hers – for she is the Church – places that redemption in its proper ecclesiastical context. That in the second half of the canto, and indeed in the culminating action of Book One, she should emerge as Spenser's principal exponent of holiness is therefore appropriate. She now becomes more important thematically than Red Crosse because as the Church she subsumes him, the individual Christian.

A question, however, confronts us: does Spenser give any indication that Una participates in the paschal sacraments represented in canto eleven? Does she *become* holy as a consequence of baptism and chrismation? Allegorical, and indeed theological, consistency seems to demand that she should. If Spenser is to be faithful to the Fathers' conception of holiness, he must show that the corporate deification of the Church no less than the individual deification of the Christian soul derives from sacramental participation in Christ's descent into Hell and third-day Resurrection. Our first impression is that Spenser does no such thing; as truth Una does not seem to change in the last cantos but to be consistently holy from the beginning to the end of Book One. Her unveiling seems merely a revelation of what she has been. In fact, however, Spenser gives us a good reason for believing her to have been deified by baptism and chrism – a reason which a reader unfamiliar with patristic commentary would be unlikely to recognize.

I refer to the white robe in which she appears for her betrothal: 'And on her now a garment she did weare, / All lilly white, withoutten spot, or pride' (I, xii, 22). We should expect white, of course, for a maiden's nuptials, and perhaps because the change of raiment seems so natural under the circumstances critics have paid the matter slight attention. Thomas Cain says the revesting 'points to the church putting on the vestments of Easter' after laying aside 'the Lenten accouterments of "her wearie journey,"'[25] and that statement, so far as I know, is the only

suggestion that the new vestments have paschal and liturgical significance. By 'vestments of Easter' Cain presumably means priestly vestments – white after Lenten purple – and if so he is close to the mark but
not quite on it. There is another type of white Easter vestment to which
patristic commentary makes copious reference, which is intimately
associated with baptism, chrismation, and the paschal eucharist, and
which, on Una, suggests her participation in those sacraments.

When the newly baptized catechumen came up naked from the pool
(having laid aside his former garments as symbolic of his old, unillu-
minated life), he was first chrismated and then clad for the eucharist in
a robe which Dionysius characterizes as being 'in the form of light.'[26]
Una also lays aside a 'mourneful stole,' and her white vestment,
though not literally luminous, is directly associated with light – 'The
blazing brightnesse of her beauties beame, / And glorious light of her
sunshyny face' (I, xii, 23) had been hidden by her 'sad wimple.' The
Fathers allegorize this new white vestment as a wedding garment,
referring to the parable of the wedding guest who lacking proper raiment was cast out of the feast (Matthew 22:11–14). Their exegesis identifies the wedding as the eucharist and a proper garment as baptism
and, more precisely, chrism. In the Latin liturgy the new Christian is
said to be 'clothed in' (*induatur*) chrism; when he is anointed, he puts
on Christ as a 'white, holy, immaculate vestment.'[27] The Latin rite
obviously understands this chrismal robe as the wedding garment of
the parable, for immediately after the unction the priest hands the catechumen a lamp, admonishing him to preserve the purity of his baptism, so that 'when the Lord shall come to the wedding thou mayest be
able to run with him, one with the saints in the celestial bridal chamber' (*una cum sanctis in aula celesti*).[28] (*Una* here teases with possibilities.) On one level of meaning the bridal chamber is heaven – the
symbolism is eschatalogical. But since the *eschaton* is already present in
the paschal mysteries, the chamber is also the sanctuary of the Church
and the wedding the immediately ensuing eucharist (the bestowal of
the white vestment and the lamp serve in the Latin rite as a transition
from the baptistery to the altar).

Cyril pulls all the symbolic threads together – chrismation, the white
robe, the eucharist, and marriage – affording a convincing precedent
for the linking of these themes in relation to Una. In the *Procatechesis* he
interprets the parable of the wedding guest and his improper vest-

ment: the bridegroom (Christ) 'saw a certain stranger, not having a wedding garment, and he said to him, "Friend, how didst thou enter here? In what a condition! With what a conscience! Be gone!"' The whiteness of the robe is, again, the whiteness of light: 'Bind his hand [says the bridegroom] which did not know how to fit him in a shining garment, and cast him into outer darkness. He is indeed unworthy to bear the wedding lamps.'[29] (Archimago's being bound and cast out of the betrothal into a 'dungeon deepe' [I, xii, 36] may echo this familiar motif.) That by the 'shining garment' Cyril intends *both* baptismal vestments and chrism seems likely from his allegorization of Ecclesiastes. Solomon says, 'Come eat thy bread with joy ... and drink thy wine with a good heart ... and pour oil upon thy head ... and let thy garments be always white.' The ellipses contain mystical interpretations: the bread and wine are to be understood 'spiritually,' which is to say, sacramentally, and the oil likewise – it is 'the mystical chrism.' Cyril does not say in so many words that the white garments are the chrismal vesture, but he seems to intend that when he speaks of them as spiritual and as replacing former vestments which were not white: 'The Lord approved of thy works now thou hast put off the old garments and put on white spiritual ones.'[30] We should not forget that he is preaching to catechumens who have just done that when they came up from the font and were chrismated. ('The shining garment' serves as another link between Saint George and paschal liturgy. In one of the matins hymns from the April *Menaion* the faithful, 'wearing bright robes' – or possibly, 'bearing light,' λαμπροφοροῦντες [the significance in either case being chrismal] – are to celebrate the dual significance of the feast, 'the Resurrection of Christ' and 'the martyr George.'[31] In any year when George's commemoration fell in Easter week, newly baptized and anointed catechumens in their white robes, carrying lamps, would be among the communicants.)

V

A reader acquainted with this pattern of patristic and antique liturgical symbolism (and who was persuaded that Spenser alludes to the paschal rites of baptism and chrismation in canto eleven) would probably conclude that when Una appears in white for the marriage feast of the eucharist, she steps into the catechumen's role. But her bright vestment and luminous face may have a broader significance as well, and one which is also patristic in character. The Fathers place heavy emphasis on the visible manifestations of holiness, especially on the radiant countenance, which like the aureole in iconography signifies deification. (There is no reason to believe Spenser could have seen or had any knowledge of Eastern icons, but the faint possibility is tantalizing in view of the iconographer's intention to depict the deified and illuminated countenance.) No reader of *The Faerie Queene* will need to be reminded that Una's is only the first of several shining faces in the poem: Belphoebe's is a 'glorious mirrhour of celestiall grace' (II, iii, 25), and Britomart 'the maker selfe' resembles 'in her feature' (IV, vi, 17). The deified lady is not, of course, a Spenserian peculiarity; that the lady as 'an agent of heaven, the vessel of celestial values,' and as the 'means ... for the heavenward ascent,'[32] comes down to Spenser from Dante and Petrarch and owes much to Italian Neoplatonism is a critical truism. But that Spenser's treatment of the *donna angelicata* may be influenced by the sacramental context established at the end of Book One is possible as well. The descriptions of Belphoebe and Britomart, for instance, are theologically exact: Belphoebe's being a mirror of grace reminds us of Saint Paul's 'beholding as in a glass the glory of the Lord,' and the most convincing way to account for Britomart's resembling her Maker is to say with Basil that baptism has shaped anew in her and restored to 'its former splendor' 'the glorious image of the king.' That conception, the theology of the *imago dei*, directs us in turn to the far other end of the poem where we encounter, in the Mutabilitie Cantos, still another veiled (and subsequently unveiled) figure, radiant in vestment and countenance and, like Una at her nuptials, epiphanic.

CHAPTER FOUR

Dame Nature's Light

I

'Some doe say' that Dame Nature's face is veiled 'to hide the terror of
her vncouth hew ... that eye of wight could not indure to view.'

> But others tell that it so beautious was,
> And round about such beames of splendor threw,
> That it the Sunne a thousand times did pass,
> Ne could be seene, but like an image in a glass.
>
> (VII, vii, 6)

The second seems to be Spenser's opinion – 'that well may seemen
true.'

Hamilton glosses 'Ne could be seene, but like an image in a glass'
(and surely correctly) with a reference to 2 Corinthians 3:18 (and we
recall Belphoebe): 'But we all, with open face beholding as in a glass
the glory of the Lord.' According to traditional exegesis the glass is
Christ--specifically the face of Christ – who (which) manifests the glory
of the Lord. This is a variation on the theology of the divine Image;
Christ is the mirror of the glory of God by virtue of being Himself the
Image, 'the express image' (Hebrews 1:3) of the Father, in whom, made
flesh, the Father's glory is revealed. Since there was one occasion when
the glory of the infleshed Image was clearly manifest – at the Transfiguration on Mount Tabor – it is scarcely surprising that some of the
Greek Fathers should employ Saint Paul's mirror metaphor as a gloss
on that event and interpret the next clause in verse eighteen as prophetic of the Transfiguration's deifying effect on the beholders: they

'are changed into the same image, from glory to glory.' Irenaeus is almost certainly alluding to the Transfiguration and to that change when he says, 'those who see God are in God ... and the brightness quickens them.'[1] Dionysius the Areopagite (as we shall see) develops the same idea, and John of Damascus takes it entirely for granted that 2 Corinthians 3:18, refers to the Transfiguration. He quotes the verse without comment, obviously assuming that its reference to Tabor is self-evident.[2]

Was it also self-evident to Spenser? The transition from stanza six to stanza seven suggests as much, for he proceeds directly from 'Ne could be seene, but like an image in a glass' to the well known simile in which he compares the effect of Nature's radiance upon himself to that of the transfigured Christ's upon His apostles. It 'well may seemen true' to Spenser that Dame Nature is too bright and beautiful to behold because when he saw her for himself on Arlo Hill,

> Her garment was so bright and wondrous sheene,
> That my fraile wit cannot deuize to what
> It to compare, nor finde like stuffe to that,
> As those three sacred *Saints*, though else most wise,
> Yet on mount *Thabor* quite their wits forgat,
> When they their glorious Lord in strange disguise
> Transfigur'd sawe; his garments so did daze their eyes.
>
> (VII, vii, 7)

The mere fact of Spenser's making a connection between these two scriptures (all apart from his purposes in doing so) points to Greek patristic influence; for except in the writings of the Eastern Fathers I have found no instance of the Transfiguration as a gloss on the Pauline mirror, or the reverse. That is quite possibly because neither the Vulgate nor the sixteenth-century English Bibles make the verbal linkage clear. Saint Paul's verb for 'changed into the same image, from glory to glory' is μεταμορφούμεθα; Matthew and Mark use the same verb to describe the alteration of Christ's face on Thabor; 'He was *transfigured* (μετεμορφώθη) before them' (Matthew 17:2) – hence the Eastern name for the feast, the Metamorphosis. An accurate translation of 2 Corinthians 3:18 would be '*transfigured* into the same image ...' For whatever reason, the Vulgate gives us *transformamur* and the English translations either *transformed* (Wycliff and Rheims) or *changed* (the rest). All, on the other hand, use *transfigured* (*transfiguratus est*) for Christ's transformation on Tabor. Hence all obscure a verbal resemblance which Greek exegesis exploits. Spenser's familiarity with that exegesis seems a likely explanation for his exploiting it himself.

The same familiarity could explain his using the Transfiguration in the first place; the feast (6 August) had comparatively little importance in the West (and less, it appears, in England than elsewhere). It was not observed universally until 1457, and there was no legislation to that effect in England until 1487.[3] That means its English life was short, for though the commemoration appeared in most of the printed Sarum missals from the end of the fifteenth century, Cranmer excluded it from the Prayer Book in 1549. Therefore Spenser would have had no liturgical experience of the Transfiguration, and he would only have heard the gospel accounts read in Church twice a year and then only as parts of entire chapters appointed routinely for Morning or Evening Prayer.[4] We can say with some certainty that the Transfiguration made no large part of English theology and devotion after the Reformation, and even if Spenser had turned to the Catholic propers for the feast in either the Sarum or the new Tridentine missal, he would have found altogether perfunctory liturgical material – little to engage the theological imagination and nothing to suggest the use of the Transfiguration in a symbolic or typological context. Given the relative poverty of this Western material and the great richness of the Eastern, Spenser's debt to the latter seems probable.

The Transfiguration exerted the influence it did in the East because it came to signify the belief in deification which (as we have seen) is so distinctive a characteristic of the Greek Fathers' soteriology. Its principal significance was not, as for the West, the revelation of Christ's divinity (that was secondary) but the *theosis* of his humanity; what he showed to Peter, James, and John was nature made divine by the restoration of the Image in which it was created. Christ on the mountain, says John of Damascus, revealed 'the human substance restored to [lit. having assumed] the archetypal beauty of the image.' 'Those three sacred *Saints*' on Tabor 'quite their wits forgat' because they beheld 'the impress of the archetype, our Savior.'[5] Here the pertinence of Saint Paul's mirror metaphor becomes clear: the three disciples discovered

that by taking flesh Christ had made flesh a mirror in which to behold
– physically, visibly – the glory of the Lord.

Physically, visibly require emphasis in view of the subsequent development of these patristic teachings. In the fourteenth century Gregory
Palamas, an athonite monk, building on those teachings, taught, and
synods of the Eastern Church pronounced as orthodox, that 'the light
on Tabor' was uncreated and a manifestation of divine energies in deified human flesh – a divine light visible to mortal eyes. That that
teaching, a specification of the doctrine of *theosis*, should be rejected by
the medieval Catholic Church is scarcely surprising in view of the
West's well-developed conception of nature as metaphysically autono-
mous – as an order of existence which though entirely dependent on
God for its origin and sustenance has its own created being as distinct
from divine being and which can thus be conceived apart from God.
Nature requires grace for its completion, but grace does not abolish
nature; nature has its own ends and its own, 'natural' goodness. The
theology of the restored image and of deification begins with radically
different ontological assumptions. When Gregory Palamas taught that
the divine energies shone in the human flesh of Christ, he did not
think of that human flesh as having a 'natural' existence apart from
those energies. He thought rather, as all the Eastern Fathers seem to, of
grace not as added to nature but as constitutive of nature: 'The Eastern
tradition,' says Vladimir Lossky, 'knows nothing of "pure nature" to
which grace is added as a supernatural gift. For it, there is no natural
or "normal" state, since grace is implied in the act of creation itself.'
And he adds, 'There is no "natural beatitude" for the creation, which
can have no other end than deification.'[6] That means that restoration
of the divine Image and the resulting *theosis* and illumination of the
creature is in fact the restoration of the creature's very being. Christ on
Tabor reveals what nature is; small wonder then should she resemble
Him.

That resemblance, I suggest, is the point of Spenser's simile, his way
of telling anyone acquainted with the Eastern patristic understanding
of the Transfiguration how nature in the Mutabilitie Cantos is to be
understood: not as most of his readers would presumably be disposed
to understand it – as the antithesis of grace (and whether or not Woodhouse was right about *The Faerie Queene* there is no denying the uni-
versality of that antithesis in Western Christendom), as sublunary and

enslaved to change and decay (that is Mutabilitie's significance), as the subject and source of a theology distinct from revealed theology (that Scholastic distinction presupposes nature's autonomy), as 'great creating nature,' the principle of procreation and vicar of God (but distinctly not God) – not in fact according to any of the understandings of nature current in medieval and Renaissance poetry and theology (or any suggested by Spenser's critics in their various glosses)[7] but as the creature restored in Christ to its original divinity, become a 'mirrhour of celestiall grace,' 'the maker selfe resembling in her feature.' Because the Transfiguration had become an Eastern signature of that conception, Spenser could use it as his own signature. Like Easter baptism and the related liturgical symbols at the end of Book One, the Transfiguration provides a key for unlocking the allegory; it sheds light on a dark conceit, explaining in what sense Dame Nature is divine (as all agree she in some sense is) and why when she rather than God appears in response to Mutabilitie's demand to be judged by 'the highest him ... Father of Gods and men,' everyone from Spenser to the irascible Titaness herself takes the substitution entirely for granted.[8]

Interpreting Dame Nature in this way affords access to many of the mysteries of the Cantos – as I shall try to show – but a preliminary question remains to be asked: how likely is it that Spenser and at least some of his readers would have been conversant with the theological issues I have been sketching? No certain answer is possible, but the argument entails no antecedent impossibilities. Spenser and his contemporaries may not have read Palamas, who was not in print in the sixteenth century, but they could have known *of* him and of his controversial doctrines. They could also have known, and easily have read, the works that Palamas knew and drew upon – various discussions of the Transfiguration by the Eastern Fathers as well as the Eastern liturgies for the feast. These were in print and apparently widely circulated. Moreover, the single most important of the exegetical treatises would have been one of the most accessible; John of Damascus' Homily on the Transfiguration (from which I have been quoting) was published for the first time in the West (and for the first time anywhere in print) in Jacobus Billius' edition of the Damascene's *Opera* in 1577, thus at a time when Spenser's reading it could have contributed to the theology of *The Faerie Queene*.[9] The edition was of sufficient importance in patristic scholarship to attract notice, and within it the Transfiguration homily calls attention to itself in two ways – in being one of only three works for which Billius includes the original Greek in parallel columns with his Latin translation and in being singled out in the table of contents as available in print for the first time: *nunc primum in lucem exeunt*. The importance of the homily, especially for someone previously unacquainted with the Fathers' understanding of the Transfiguration, lies in its comprehensiveness. Here, as in most of his writings, John of Damascus sums up a tradition; coming at the end of the patristic period (b c675–d c749), he draws together and gives what has proven to be lasting form to motifs developed less systematically – sometimes only adumbrated – by his predecessors. In the case of the Transfiguration he offers a compendium of liturgical emphases (he composed part of the Eastern liturgy for 6 August) and of earlier teaching. What Spenser and his readers could have found scattered through the entire patristic corpus, they could have found in this homily as in a digest; and there is little in Palamas that John of Damascus does not anticipate. Indeed one is tempted to argue that all the details of Spenser's allegory of the Transfiguration could have had a Damascene origin.

Finally there is the fascinating possibility, which Hankins introduces, of a debt to John Scotus Erigena, who was fully conversant with and obviously sympathetic to the Greek understanding of nature's deification – to what later came to be regarded as the Palamite position. As a gloss on Dame Nature it is tempting to quote such statements as, 'When through sin [nature] renounced the honour of the divine image ... [it] deservedly lost its being and therefore is said not to be; but when, restored by the grace of the only-begotten Son of God, it is brought back to the former condition of its substance in which it was made after the image of God, it begins to be' or that the 'Divine Nature' is 'the essence of all things' and that 'everything which is said to exist exists not in itself but by participation in the Nature [God's] which truly exists.'[10] As Hankins acknowledges, however, Erigena was not in print in the sixteenth century, and for that reason I have not appealed to him as a possible source – as for the same reason I have not appealed to Palamas. Spenser and his contemporaries could have known either or both (certainly both were known despite lack of editions); but I base the following arguments (the rule of this study) on books Spenser and his readers could have *read*. In these we find precedents for most of what Spenser tells us about Dame Nature.

II

One such precedent is for deifying a personification not only of human but of universal nature. We learn that Dame Nature may be leonine as well as human, male as well as female, and she presides over an assembly of the gods and 'all other creatures, / What-euer life or motion doe retaine' (VII, vii, 4). She appears to be a composite personification of the whole created order, and to allow such a symbol to *be* the 'highest him' or to be assimilated to the transfigured Christ seems very odd to Western ears – odder, I believe, than the deification of human nature alone. No wonder critics have turned to Bruno and other esoteric writers as possible sources, for Spenser here seems to be very far from a recognizable Christian orthodoxy.

He will not, however, seem far at all if we take patristic Christianity as our point of reference, for by its lights *theosis* extends from the individual man (Christ) to mankind (the nature the Logos assumed) and ultimately to the entire creation. Jaroslav Pelikan sets out the terms of this doctrine very clearly: 'The original creation in the image of God ... had been brought about through the Logos; that creation would now achieve not only restoration but consummation and perfection through the same Logos: his incarnation would achieve our deification. *And the whole cosmos would have its proper share in that consummation'* (italics added). Pelikan paraphrases Basil in the *Hexaemeron*, that because Christ, the Logos, created the cosmos, He is not only its beginning but its end, 'the *Goal of the cosmos.*' That means that the whole creation as well as the individual Christian has been (or will be) deified: 'As the Savior of the cosmos, the Logos had not snatched humanity out of the goodness of the created order, but had transformed the created order into a fit setting for a transformed humanity.' And Pelikan quotes Gregory of Nyssa's expectation of '"the restitution of all things [*apokatastasis ton panton*]"' and of the transformation of '"the transient and the earthly [into] the incorruptible and the eternal"'[11] – an expectation reminiscent of the end of canto seven when the deified Dame Nature anticipates all things 'turning to themselues ... againe' and the staying of all things on the pillars of eternity.

Spenser could have found cosmic deification in many of the Eastern liturgical texts published in the sixteenth century. In the Epiphany, for instance, 'the creation [not just individual Christians] finds itself free,' and 'all the earthly nature' is bidden to 'dress itself in white / For now it is lifted up from its fall from heaven.'[12] Since Epiphany is another traditional time for baptism, the probable reference here is to the white baptismal or chrismal vestment. Just as the individual catechumen 'puts on Christ,' so does 'the whole earthly nature.' The liturgy seems in fact to say that the entire creation has been baptized – 'watered with mystical streams' – and like the individual neophyte, illuminated by baptism and carrying a lamp to signify divine radiance, so 'the whole creation shines with light from above.' 'Things from above keep festival with things below, and things below converse with things above'; 'earth and sea share in the joy of the cosmos, and the cosmos is filled with joy.'[13] In both matins and vespers for Holy Saturday, the day of Christ's descent into Hell and victory over the dragon, we encounter the same emphasis. 'In order to fill *all* things with Thy glory, Thou hast descended into the nethermost parts of the earth'; 'for Thou dost bring *all* things into being and dost make [*all* things] new' (here the original and the new creations are virtually fused). Christ became Adam for the re-creating of Eve, falling 'supernaturally into a sleep which gives life to nature and, as the Almighty One, didst raise up life out of sleep and corruption.'[14] In the Holy Saturday baptismal service the appointed scripture readings begin with the account of the original creation in the first chapter of Genesis and end with the 'Hymn of the Three Children,' which celebrates the joy of the new creation in unmistakably cosmic terms: 'sun and moon,' 'stars of heaven,' 'mountains and hills,' and indeed *all* the works of the Lord,' miraculously delivered from the curse of death as the three children have been, with them 'praise the Lord, bless Him, and exalt Him unto the ages of ages.'[15]

This liturgical emphasis is continuous with what we find in patristic homilies and treatises. Athanasius is as explicit about cosmic as about individual *theosis*, and his formulations are of especial interest because he is so widely recognized as a spokesman for the latter emphasis. The Incarnation, which effected the deification of the individual who is baptized into Christ, also reconstituted the cosmos and made what had before been natural, divine. Or to state the matter another way, Christ made an entire new creation – not just new, divine men and women, but new heavens and new earth – which is united directly to the Creator in a way the old was not. God was 'not far from [the world] before [the Incarnation] since nothing in creation is left empty of Him';[16] but after the Incarnation the life of the creation became itself a divine life rather than a created one. God became man not only to make man God but 'that He might work in man and [through man] show Himself everywhere, *leaving nothing empty and destitute of His divinity and knowledge.*'[17] From the body of Christ divine energies flood the creation, effecting cosmic *theosis*. God the Father 'brought it to pass that in His Word not only "all things consist" [by virtue of His activity as Creator and sustainer of being], but the creation itself ... "shall be delivered ... from the bondage of corruption into the glorious liberty of the children of God."' The Pauline phrase, 'children of God,' signifies deified men and women, for as Athanasius has already said, the deification of the cosmos is wrought through man. Thus the rest of creation waits for its deliverance upon 'the manifestation of the sons of God.' In his second discourse against the Arians Athanasius is even more explicit about the cosmic dimension of *theosis*: 'of this creation thus delivered, the Lord will be First-born, *both of it* [*istius*] and of all those who are made children.'[18] The phrase I have emphasized singles out the cosmos and distinguishes it from man. It reminds us that the Lord will be the first-born [in the Resurrection] of the non-human as well as the human creation, that 'all things,' not just men and women, will be made divine in His risen flesh.

Cosmic deification (illumination) also informs liturgical and patristic interpretations of the Transfiguration. 'The sun, which illuminates the earth, sets again, but Christ, shining like lightning with glory on the mountain, illuminates the universe.'[19] Here, besides the obvious contrast between the sun's temporal and Christ's eternal light, there is also a distinction between the earth (γῆ) and the universe (κόσμος). Christ's light is much further reaching than the sun's; the force of the metaphor is that the radiance of his face and clothing reached out visibly to the boundaries of the cosmos, and since his light deifies, made everything divine. John of Damascus is very explicit about the cosmic consequence of the Transfiguration: God 'wrought *pancosmic* salvation in His only begotten Son,' and John explains how by referring to the familiar conception of man as a microcosm, 'bearing in himself the conjunction of all substance, both visible and invisible.' By joining Himself to that conjunction, Christ imparted His divinity to all substance. 'Truly the Lord and Creator and Ruler of all things was pleased to become in His only-begotten and consubstantial Son the connection of Godhead and manhood and *through this of all created things*, so that God might be all in all.'[20] Thus John adds that the light on Tabor 'wins the victory over *all of nature*. This is the Life which has conquered the cosmos.'[21] The comparison of Dame Nature's light to the transfigured Christ's suggests that she is that 'all of nature' over which Christ's radiance won the victory, the cosmos conquered by Christ's divine life.

III

Spenser's hyperbolic description of that radiance recalls a common patristic hyperbole. In all three Gospel accounts of the Transfiguration, Christ's face is said to have shone as the sun – hence the liturgical conceit in which Christ on the mountain, the 'sun of righteousness,' is compared with the sun in heaven. In introducing the Transfiguration simile, however, Spenser says that Dame Nature's face was brighter than the sun – 'it the Sunne a thousand times did pass' (vii, vii, 6). There is more than one precedent for that amplification: in Transfiguration vespers, for instance, the apostles fall to the earth because they cannot bear the light of Christ's face which 'shone more than the sun,'[22] and Chrysostom qualifies 'as the sun,' with 'or rather more than the sun.'[23] John of Damascus goes into much greater detail, making a considerable issue of that excess of light, feigning discontent with Matthew's comparison: 'What are you saying, O Evangelist?' John asks. 'Why do you compare things essentially incomparable? Why have you placed side by side and put together things which cannot by their nature be put together?' How did the 'light unbearable and unapproachable' shine only 'as the sun which is beheld by all?' Such rhetoric calls attention to the apparent thinness of Matthew's figure and thereby invites an hyperbole such as Spenser's in response. Moreover, Matthew's imagined reply to John's challenge suggests a relation to the transfigured Christ comparable to that in which Spenser stands to Nature. Spenser says his wit is too frail to describe the radiance of Nature's clothing, much less of her face. Matthew says he writes for 'those bound by the flesh' and thus, we infer, frail of wit. Christ's face shone *as* the sun, 'not that he was not more brilliant than the sun, but only so much could the beholders see.'[24] Because Nature's face 'the Sunne a thousand times did pass' (vii, vii, 6), Spenser, bound by the flesh, cannot see. Dame Nature's veil serves the same purpose as Matthew's simile.

IV

Veils anticipate their removals, and such removals are usually eschatological – as is the whole emphasis at the end of canto seven after Nature, rather suddenly and surprisingly, appears 'with open face.' Patristic exegesis also anticipates this development in the allegory. As Jaroslav Pelikan explains the matter, '"deification" was teleological in content, part of the "goal [*telos*]" of human life,' and 'Christ as Second Adam had manifested this teleology, above all in the Transfiguration, where he gave humanity a glimpse of its own eventual destiny ...'[25] The Transfiguration accounts are themselves eschatological or teleological. In each version (Matthew 17:1–8; Mark 9:2–8; Luke 9:28–36) the ascent of Tabor ensues directly upon Christ's saying to his disciples, 'There be some standing here, which shall not taste of death, till they see the Son of man coming in his kingdom' (Matthew 16:28).[26] Those referred to are evidently Peter, James, and John, whom Christ takes with him into the mountain; the sight of the Son's coming in glory is clearly *both* the Transfiguration itself and the second advent. Certainly that is the way most of the Fathers interpret Christ's statement. Chrysostom's commentary is representative of the tradition – when Christ comes again, in His kingdom, we shall not only behold Him in 'far greater brightness' (than on Tabor), but we ourselves, our deification complete, shall shine with His divine light. '*Then shall the righteous shine forth as the sun* or rather more than the sun' just as in anticipation of the final epiphany of *theosis*, Christ '*did shine as the sun.*'[27] Spenser could have found the same interpretation in other patristic treatises. When Irenaeus says, 'The Word was made flesh' so that man might 'arrive at incorruption, being compassed about with the brightness of the Father,'[28] his reference is simultaneously to the deification effected on Tabor and to its fulfillment in the age to come. As Vladimir Lossky, following the Fathers, interprets the passage, 'The prophetic vision [on Tabor] was already a participation in the final state ... in the "Kingdom of God coming in power."'[29] Dionysius makes the same connections between deification, Transfiguration, and the eschaton, and his brief exposition became a *locus classicus* in subsequent patristic exegesis. The

Transfiguration reveals the glory to come when we shall become '[in]corruptible and immortal and ... fulfilled with [Christ's] visible Theophany in holy contemplations, the which shall shine about us with radiant beams of glory (even as once of old it shone around the Disciples at the Divine Transfiguration).'[30] That such an interpretation is a commonplace in patristic exegesis is indicated by Saint Basil's passing reference to it in a homily on the forty-fifth Psalm: 'Peter and the Sons of Thunder saw [Christ's] beauty on the mountain, surpassing in splendor the brilliance of the sun, and they were considered worthy to perceive with their eyes [lit., to receive into their eyes – ὀφθαλμοῖς λαβεῖν] the beginning of His glorious coming.'[31]

Dame Nature's apocalypse in stanza fifty-seven suggests that her radiance is Spenser's version of that beginning. We are now told that 'all creatures' are 'looking in her face' (VII, vii, 57), whereas formerly that face has been covered because it was too bright to behold. Some metaphysical change has obviously occurred or is occurring in 'all creatures,' enabling them to see the divine light without mediation, and our clue to what that change may be is its coordination with Nature's judgment against Mutabilitie. Mutabilitie signifies, of course, change and mortality, and she has claimed to rule 'all creatures.' That they can now look Dame Nature in the face is probably Spenser's way of saying they have been delivered from that claim. Being no longer mutable is in effect to have become immortal, and to have become immortal is to have been deified; they can therefore behold a divine countenance. They fulfill Dionysius' expectation that in the Second Coming we shall be 'incorruptible and immortal and ... fulfilled with [Christ's] visible Theophany' which of old 'shone around the Disciples at the Divine Transfiguration.'[32] With the defeat of Mutabilitie, which is to say, 'the last enemy' (1 Corinthians 15:26), creatures have been 'transfigured into the same image from glory to glory' and no longer require the protection of a veil or the mediation of 'an image in a glass.' Nature herself now speaks of a time (which of course could not be temporal) when 'all shall changed bee' and 'none no more change shall see' (VII, vii, 59); and her subsequent disappearance appears to fulfill that prophecy. For though deified she is still Nature, and when the cosmos (which she also is) reaches its *telos*, the life of the age to come begins – 'the stedfast rest of all things firmely stayd / Vpon the pillours of Eternity' (VII, viii, 2).

V

Spenser's reserving that stedfast rest (or at least his expectation of it) for canto eight is also in accord with patristic eschatology. In the hexaemeral tradition six signifies the day or age of this present life, for God made the world in six days; seven is the day of God's rest and creation's completion or fullness – the Sabbath. Eight represents the day beyond the world and beyond time or change, the day of the Resurrection and the coming of the Kingdom, of the new and deified creation.[33] Saint Augustine's formulation is representative of this numerology as it developed both among the Greek and Latin Fathers: 'We are now in the sixth epoch ... After this present age God will rest, as it were, on the seventh day, and he will cause us, who are the seventh day, to find our rest in him ... the seventh will be our Sabbath, whose end will not be an evening, but the Lord's day, an eighth day, as it were, which is to last for ever, a day consecrated by the resurrection of Christ, foreshadowing the eternal rest not only of the spirit but of the body also.'[34] Not surprisingly this same typology informs the Holy Saturday baptismal service in the *Triodion*. Holy Saturday 'is the blessed Sabbath,' which Moses 'mystically prefigured' when he wrote, '"And God blessed the Sabbath day."' Moses commanded that the Sabbath be a day of rest, and on this Holy Sabbath 'the only begotten Son of God rested [in the tomb] from all his works [the suffering of the Passion on the sixth day].' Christ fulfilled the Law, obeyed Moses's command, 'through the dispensation of death.' But that was not all He did. Having 'kept the Sabbath in the flesh' through death in the flesh, 'through the Resurrection, returning once again to what He was, He has bestowed upon us eternal life.'[35] The seventh day at one and the same time signifies the rest (completion) of earthly things and anticipates the coming of heavenly things; as Augustine says, its 'end will not be an evening, but the Lord's day, an eighth day.'

The pertinence of this symbolism to the numbering of the Mutabilitie Cantos is obvious (and encourages one to believe the numbering is Spenser's rather than an editor's). Canto six, the day of the present fallen life, divides itself between two versions of the Fall, Mutabilitie's and Faunus's. Canto seven, by demonstrating that Mutabilitie's claims are vain and thus as it were restoring the cosmos to order and harmony – graphically (and ironically) illustrated by Mutabilitie's own pageant

– presents creation in its completed state, its day of rest. Canto eight concerns itself with the eschaton, and Spenser's anticipation of steadfastness indicates, as Saint Augustine and the Holy Saturday liturgy do, that however blessed in itself, the seventh is still only the prelude to perfect and everlasting blessedness in the eighth. Canto seven, by assuring us of the providential character and ultimate goodness of change, triumphs over death *by death*, just as Christ did in the tomb. Canto eight looks forward to the changeless and the deathless – in Alastair Fowler's formulation to 'that eighth day when the sevenfold cosmos will be made new and eternal.'[36]

Fowler is not the only critic to notice this numbering and discern some of its implications, but neither he nor the rest has recognized its probable relationship to Spenser's use of the Transfiguration. That is no doubt because the usual Western versions of hexaemeral numerology – Fowler relies on Hugh of Saint Victor and du Bartas – make no reference to the events on Tabor. For the Greek Fathers, however, there is a very close connection, based on a discrepancy in the Gospel accounts. Matthew and Mark say the ascent of Tabor occurred six days after Christ's prophecy of the Second Coming while Luke says after eight days. John of Damascus follows Chrysostom and others in assuming the discrepancy to be intentional and in taking it as an occasion for allegorical and mystical interpretation. Matthew and Mark speak of six days because in six 'God by a word effected the constitution of all visible things'; Luke says eight days because eight 'bears the figure of the age to come; for the present life is concluded in seven ages. But in the eighth the life of the age to come is named.' Then, as Dionysius had said (and John of Damascus quotes the familiar passage), Christ 'will be seen by his perfect servants' whereas now He is seen by imperfect ones, 'by his apostles on Mount Thabor.'[37] Those perfect servants are the deified men and women whom the apostles and 'all creatures' will become in the eighth day, when they have reached the goal to which the Transfiguration points.

Since the Transfiguration looks forward to the eighth day, it presumably occurred on either the sixth or the seventh. John of Damascus does not raise the question, nor do the other Fathers who employ the numerology, probably because the hexaemeral tradition does not make such precise distinctions. The sixth and seventh days tend to blur into each other when either or both is set in contrast to the eighth, and (as we see in Augustine's formulation) the Sabbath and the eighth day become virtually one in contrast to the sixth. But John may imply the seventh when he says the present life 'is concluded in seven ages,' for the deification and illumination of nature on Tabor, although predicting the age to come, is also the perfection or conclusion of the present dispensation. That, in any event, appears to be Spenser's understanding of the numerology; for placing the Transfiguration simile in the seventh stanza of the seventh canto of the seventh Book must surely identify it with the Sabbath and thus be a way of saying that Dame Nature's illumination – as an allegory of Christ's – both 'conquers the cosmos,' bringing all beings 'to themselues at length againe,' working 'their owne perfection' and simultaneously looks beyond the cosmos to the last and eighth day, when 'all shall changed bee' and 'none no more change shall see' (VII, vii, 58–9). Moreover, by comparing himself with Christ's 'imperfect servants' on Tabor (and indeed emphasizing his and their imperfection), Spenser identifies himself as one of those who looks forward to the 'things of the eighth.' In the seventh he beholds a vision which both reveals the *theosis* of creation and prophecies the completion of that *theosis*, the 'Sabaoths sight.' (Among other things, this reading of the end of the poem justifies Spenser's *Sabaoth* as opposed to Upton's emendation: not only does the sight for which Spenser longs belong to the eighth day – and canto – rather than the seventh; Christ's Second Coming presupposes the presence of His hosts.)

VI

The Fathers' using the same hexaemeral numerology to interpret both Easter and the Transfiguration establishes a closer relation between the two feasts than someone ignorant of ancient exegesis would be likely to discern. The possibility of Spenser's having discerned it brings us full circle, to the continuity from Una at the poem's beginning (through Belphoebe and Britomart) to Dame Nature at its end.

The liturgy for 6 August calls the Transfiguration a 'foretype' of the Resurrection:[38] in His 'love for man' Christ was willing 'before the Cross' to 'show the radiance of the Resurrection.'[39] That is a frequent motif and by itself could account for Spenser's discerning a resemblance between the illumination which results from paschal baptism –

Una's, if I have interpreted her face and white vestment correctly – and the light on Tabor. But we need not rely on such speculation; patristic exegesis focuses on that very resemblance. Ambrose explains that the newly baptized at the paschal liturgy put on white 'because the garments of Christ were white as snow, when in the Gospel He showed the glory of His Resurrection.'[40] 'When in the Gospel' is unmistakably at the Transfiguration, for 'white as snow' is Saint Mark's simile (9:3). Anyone recognizing the quotation would see immediately, as Ambrose surely intended they should, that the deification symbolized by the white baptismal vestment was to be understood as represented also by the illuminated garments of Christ transfigured. Gregory of Nyssa relies on the same typology; when the catechumen puts on baptismal and chrismal white, he puts on 'the tunic of the Lord, without seam, equal to the sun ... such as He revealed on the Mount of the Transfiguration.'[41] When we recall that not only Christ's transfigured clothing but His face 'shone as the sun' and that when Una appears in baptismal white her face is 'sunshyny,' we have reason to believe that Spenser is drawing on patristic typology to unify his allegory – that Nature illuminated and in a garment 'bright and wondrous sheene' (VII, vii, 7) reveals the cosmic and eschatological consequences of paschal baptism and chrismation. On that reading, Book Seven completes the allegory of holiness begun in Book One and interprets not only Una's radiance but Belphoebe's and Britomart's (and of course Gloriana's, which we never see but hear of). That at crucial moments in *The Faerie Queene* these luminous ladies look backward to Una and forward to Dame Nature suggests that deification effected by baptism and chrismation, manifested in the Transfiguration, and to be perfected in the final unveiling, informs all the poem's virtues.

If Spenser in fact intended us to understand his motif of illuminated faces and shining garments in that way, we must reconsider the conventional attribution of Una's radiance to the 'woman clothed with the sun' (Revelation 12:1) and, indeed, the entire debate about Marian influence upon Spenser's ascriptions of divinity to his various representatives of Elizabeth. Against Robin Wells's demonstration of close typological resemblances John King argues the persuasive historical point that owing to 'the Elizabethan eradication' of Marian devotion, 'Mariological images' are not likely to have survived in *The Faerie Queene* in so 'undiluted' a form as Wells believes.[42] Even to those of us

who think the poem (and the poet) less consistently Protestant than
King does, the likelihood of Spenser's embracing Marian symbolism
uncritically seems small. What neither King nor Wells considers is the
possibility which the baptismal symbolism of Book One and the Transfiguration simile of Seven introduce: that the divinity of all Spenser's
royal virgins derives from a belief in deification which of course
includes Mary's but is by no means limited to hers. (The paschal and
Transfiguration homilies and liturgies say in fact almost nothing about
her.) That this belief is thoroughly Christocentric – the Incarnation
being its basis and the Resurrection and Transfiguration its principal
manifestations – would presumably make it more appealing to a member and defender of Elizabeth's Church than a symbolism derived
exclusively from Mary. To the extent that the poem does echo Marian
devotion (and Wells is persuasive on this matter), Spenser may simply
be influenced by the popular (and well-documented) adaptation of
that devotion to Elizabeth. Another possibility, however, is that he is
deliberately using Marian themes without committing himself to their
Catholic interpretation – that he is adapting this traditional material to
the theology of deification which the Fathers provide. He may in fact
be doing with Marian devotion what I have argued he does with Saint
George – transposing a symbolism which he is likely to have regarded
as semi-pagan and discredited into a theological context which justifies
his use of it for allegorical purposes.

                                    VII

Dame Nature may be a similarly transposed figure. That possibility
affords a possible answer to a question which my reading of Book
Seven cannot ultimately ignore: if the Fathers' theology of the Transfiguration affords more convincing glosses for the Mutabilitie Cantos
than the conventional ones drawn from Western and medieval sources,
why does Spenser himself, in the poem itself (vii, vii, 9), send us to two
Western and medieval sources – to *Foules parley* and *Plaint of kindes*?

A possible – I think probable – answer is, to show us how much his
Nature differs from her antecedents in the *natura* tradition. No one, so
far as I know, has suggested such a thing; we have dutifully glossed
her with references to Alane, Dan Geffrey, and other medieval exponents of *natura*, working sometimes against the grain of the poetry to

demonstrate similarities. But Dame Nature does differ radically: she reinterprets her antecedents, who are much less distinctly and explicitly Christian than she. Medieval *natura* is a divinity – at least an allegorical divinity – and God's vicar in creation, but her provenance and ethos are more nearly pagan than Christian.[43] Chartrian thought exalts her, and Josephine Waters Bennett's appeal to the Florentine Neoplatonic Logos to explain Spenser's Transfiguration symbolism carries a measure of conviction;[44] but that Spenser gives us a much fuller – indeed a much simpler and more direct – Christianization should be obvious to anyone who has compared the various texts. The very difference in idiom is telling: the gods of Chartrian and Florentine philosophy to which *natura* is in a measure assimilated, though versions of Christian deity, are nonetheless the gods of the philosophers. The God with whose light Spenser compares Dame Nature's – the 'glorious Lord ... Transfigur'd' beheld in awe by 'three sacred *Saints*' – is unmistakably the God of our Fathers.

That Spenser wanted us to register these differences rather than gloss them over with learned comparisons like Professor Bennett's seems probable from his timing; he refers us to Chaucer and Alan only after (and directly after) he has introduced the Transfiguration. Consequently when we go off to read *Foules parley* and *Plaint of kindes*, we can scarcely miss the theological difference which the Light on Tabor makes. Moreover, Spenser refers us to the medieval poems specifically for an account of Dame Nature's 'vestiments' on the very heels of telling us that on Arlo Hill they shone with an intensity comparable to Christ's. The comparison shows us clearly what Spenser has added to the topos. Chaucer defers to Alan (as Spenser reminds us), and Alan's Nature's garments, though luminous, are not white like Christ's but multicolored; the colors moreover, being kaleidoscopic and constantly shifting, identify their wearer more nearly with Mutabilitie than with the 'highest him.' Furthermore, their being embroidered with fish, flesh, and foul associate Alan's Nature primarily with the physical creation rather than the intellectual or divine (which given her role in the poem as apologist for procreativity is entirely fitting). In other words, Alan's Nature's 'vestiments' simply signify her being nature; those of Spenser's Nature signify her being 'an image of God himself.' The difference is distinct, and if we take the poetry seriously, we must assume that Spenser meant us to recognize it.

Our doing so should entail our recognizing as well that Spenser is probably transposing *natura* from one context to another and thereby reconstituting her, giving her a more specifically Christian identity than she had had before – that he wants us to recall her antecedents and see how she differs from them for the same reason he wants us to recall the legendary George slaying the dragon while we watch the true Saint George harrowing Hell and opening Paradise. In each instance Spenser transforms a semi-mythical, semi-pagan figure for the purposes of Christian allegory, informing it with what he must have conceived to be a sounder and more consistent theology than pertained to the original. And if the transmutation of George's dragon fight into the Harrowing and his victory into the Resurrection was meant to surprise, so, surely, was the transfiguration of *natura*. The latter surprises, moreover, to greater purpose, for while a dragon-slaying is intellectually neutral and susceptible of a variety of allegorizations, the Nature of *Foules parley* and *Plaint of kindes* has a distinct philosophical content. To impose a new content on her – perhaps quite literally to baptize her and to put Christ on her, the raiment white as light – qualifies for praise as a genuinely original act of historical and theological – and of course, poetic – imagination.

PART TWO

TEMPERANCE

CHAPTER FIVE

Temperance

I

Transfiguring Nature's countenance and clothing her in baptismal white is primarily – but not exclusively – the work of grace. Thus far I have argued for Spenser's indebtedness to the sacramental, mystical, and eschatological dimensions of patristic theology, but there is another equally important element in the Fathers' understanding of holiness, the ascetical; and the ascetical is for them so intimately bound to the mystical (deification requires mortification) that acquaintance with the one would scarcely be possible without acquaintance with the other. We should not therefore be surprised if an allegory of holiness informed by patristic conceptions should have as its corollary an allegory of *ascesis* – a legend of temperance to complement a legend of holiness. The possibility of such a theological link between Books One and Two, of Spenser's conceiving temperance less as a distinct virtue than as a facet of holiness, calls for a reconsideration of Book Two and of its pertinence to One.

There is a long debate, still unresolved, as to what Spenser meant by temperance: is the virtue of Book Two really temperance or is it continence? Is Spenser's conception classical (pagan) or Christian? Does Guyon serve as a negative or positive example of temperance (however we conceive temperance)? Does his famous faint illustrate his personal weakness or the weakness of the titular virtue of his legend or both (or neither)? No one asks a corollary question: What attitude does Spenser take toward the passions? Since the subject of temperance, however we conceive it, is the passions and their government, determining what view a writer takes of those basic impulses of flesh and spirit should enable us to understand in turn how he conceives their control.

What view should we expect Spenser to take? Probably one which descends from the Greeks, which medieval Christianity embraced, and to which Augustine gave classical articulation: that the passions are 'bad, if the love is bad, and good if the love is good.'[1] Aquinas expands this: if we consider the passions 'in themselves, to wit, as movements of the irrational appetite ... there is no moral good or evil in them ... If, however, they be considered as subject to the command of the reason and will, then moral good and evil are in them.' When the passions are 'commanded by the reason, they are proper to man' (*ST*, I–II, 24, 1).[2] In other words, the passions as such are neutral; whether they are virtuous or vicious depends not on themselves but on how well they are governed. Hence both Augustine and Aquinas reject what they identify as a Stoic doctrine: that the passions are by their nature and in themselves '*diseases or disturbances of the soul*';[3] 'for passions are not called *diseases* or *disturbances* of the soul, save when they are not controlled by reason,' and 'Cicero [representing the Stoic position] was wrong in disapproving of the Peripatetic theory [Aristotle's] of a mean in the passions, when he says that *every evil, though moderate, should be shunned*' (*ST*, I–II, 24, 2).[4] Aristotle's doctrine of moderation, Christianized by Aquinas, assumes of course the direction of passions to their right end by reason; Cicero, as Aquinas interprets him, assumes instead that the passions are in themselves corrupting.

The Fathers (again primarily the Greek Fathers) make Cicero's assumption (though not for Cicero's reasons). Once more the issue at stake for them is the theology of the *imago dei*; and here we see precisely why the ascetical and mystical elements in patristic thought are inseparable: the deifying Image (Christ), the source of nature's divinity, was initially obscured and corrupted by the passions. If the creature is to return to its original sanctity, if the Image is to be restored and shine in transfigured flesh, the obscuring and corrupting passions must be eradicated. Saint Basil the Great's 'Ascetical Discourse,' one of the most influential patristic texts (and available to a sixteenth-century reader in both Greek and Latin and in multiple editions) develops this conception in detail: 'Man was made after the image and likeness of God; but sin marred the beauty of the image by dragging the soul down to passionate desires ... when man lost his likeness to God, he lost his participation in the true life ... [and] it is impossible for him to enjoy the blessedness of the divine life.'⁵ Consequently Basil admonishes his flock to mortify the passions in order to restore the image of God: 'Let us return, then, to the grace [which was ours] in the beginning and from which we have alienated ourselves by sin, and let us again adorn ourselves with the beauty of God's image, *being made like to our Creator through the quieting of our passions*' (italics added). Since man lost deification by becoming passible, let him regain it by becoming again impassible; that is the motive of Christian *ascesis* as the Fathers taught it. 'He who, to the best of his ability, copies within himself the tranquility of the divine nature attains to a likeness with the very soul of God; and, being made like to God ... he also achieves in full a semblance to the divine life and abides continually in unending blessedness.'⁶ To be dispassionate, as to be immortal, is to be like God, which all Christians are called to be. Therefore to put the passions to death rather than merely to govern or temper them is essential to salvation.

Between this position and the Augustinian-Thomist one lies the same difference we have already discerned between Eastern-patristic and Western views of nature. Aquinas's adaptation of Aristotelian ethics in reference to the government of passion reflects his belief in the existence and essential goodness of a natural order as distinct from a divine one; Basil's teaching clearly does not. 'Whatever,' says Thomas, 'is contrary to the natural order is vicious. Now nature has introduced pleasure into the operations that are necessary for man's life. Wherefore the natural order requires that man should make use of these pleasures, in so far as they are necessary for man's well-being, as regards the preservation either of the individual or of the species.' Again the crucial distinction between pleasures which are vicious and those which are virtuous lies in the government of reason, for to be rational is also natural. Therefore it is sometimes virtuous (which is to say, reasonable) to abstain altogether from pleasure as Daniel did, but 'not through any horror of pleasure as though it were evil in itself, but for some praiseworthy end, in order, namely, to adapt himself to the heights of contemplation by abstaining from pleasures of the body.' Contemplation, however, is a special calling; as a rule, nature demands that man 'sustain his body in order that he may use his reason ... [and] the body is sustained by means of operations that afford pleasure:

wherefore the good of reason cannot be in a man if he abstain from all pleasures' (*ST*, ii–ii, 142, 1).[7] Thomistic temperance takes nature and the reasonable use of natural pleasures into full account: 'Temperance takes the need of this life, as the rule of the pleasurable objects of which it makes use, and uses them only for as much as the need of this life requires' (*ST*, ii–ii, 141, 6).[8] Therefore 'temperance ... denotes a kind of moderation' and is 'chiefly concerned with those passions that tend towards sensible goods' (*ST*, ii–ii, 141, 3).[9]

An accurate way to characterize the difference between this conception and Basil's is to say that the latter, rather than envisioning contemplation as a special and supernatural vocation reserved for such seers as Daniel, understands it as *the* activity for which man was created – to recover in the soul 'the tranquility of the divine nature.' Therefore to be passionless is to be natural, just as to be deified in Christ is to be natural, for the two conditions are synonymous. Instead of being moderate in reference to 'those passions that tend towards sensible goods,' we should seek altogether to overcome them; since by doing that 'we regain the image of God [*theosis*] ... let us devote ourselves to this pursuit in preference to all others.' 'All that springs from the passions mars in some way the purity of the soul and is an impediment in attaining to the divine life.'[10] In view of such statements Basil would scarcely allow, with Aquinas, that 'perfection of moral virtue does not wholly take away the passions, but regulates them' (*ST*, i, 95, 2).[11] He would be more likely to say that the very presence of the passions is a signature of man's loss of perfection.

II

When Nohrnberg says that 'the change from Book i to Book ii corresponds to a ... shift ... from the martyr's passion, to ... the spiritual and interior martyrdom of ascesis and Lenten self-denial: St. George is followed by St. Anthony,'[12] he comes very close to saying that Spenser is representing the relationship between *theosis* and mortification which Saint Basil is developing. Nohrnberg does not pursue the point, but he might have done so by reminding us that Anthony was a symbol for the Fathers of complete victory over passion – a man who by total rejection of pleasures had recovered divine tranquility. Nohrnberg might also have quoted from Athanasius' *Life of Anthony*, which became for Athanasius' successors a kind of textbook on asceticism (and which was also readily available in several sixteenth-century editions):[13] Anthony's soul was pure, for 'never in excessive merriment was it loosened in laughter, nor ever in recollection of sin did its border contract in sorrow, nor was it exalted by high praise.'[14] Anthony by the 'interior martyrdom of ascesis' had achieved not moderation but impassibility. In passages quoted from Anthony's homilies, Athanasius makes clear that the passions are not natural to man, not inherently innocent impulses of the sensitive soul requiring the government of reason for their proper use, but disturbances or diseases which pervert the soul from its truly natural (which is to say, 'divine') condition: the soul is upright 'when its primal integrity is unstained by any blemish of faults; if it should change its nature [its original impassibility], then it is said to be perverse. If its [original] creation [in the divine image] is preserved, it is virtuous. God has commended our soul to us; let us preserve the trust as we have received it ... Let Him recognize His creature, which He made: let Him find His work as He created it.'[15] Since He made it passionless, He will not recognize it if it is obscured by a veil of passions.

Most of the Fathers echo these admonitions. Maximus the Confessor explains that the Christian must practice *ascesis*, not in order to lead a moderate life under the control of reason but because his 'heavenly abode is a dispassionate state of virtue.' Reaching that abode requires 'complete rejection of impassioned thoughts in the soul' – attaining a state of being in which 'there are ... no impassioned thoughts to incite [the soul] to action.' Then 'the soul, ravished by longing, is totally rapt in ecstasy above the realm of created beings.'[16] Chrysostom interprets the chief theological virtue, charity, as being identical with practice of a mortifying, and deifying, asceticism. When Saint Paul says that charity 'is not easily provoked,' Chrysostom understands him to mean that the charitable man is beyond perturbation of passion: Paul did not say, '"though provoked, she overcomes," but, *is not even provoked.*' 'Seest thou how by degrees charity makes her nursling an angel [angels, of course, are impassible]? For when he is void of anger, and pure from envy, and free from every tyrannical passion, consider that *even from the nature of man* he is delivered from henceforth, and hath arrived in a port, at the very serenity of the angels.'[17] To be delivered even from the nature of man is a conception radically different from one which regards the passions when properly governed as constitutive of that nature; and to identify this conception with charity is flatly to contradict the doctrine that our passions are good when our loves are good. What love could be better than charity?

The Fathers' preference of virginity to marriage elucidates this relation between impassibility and *theosis*. Marriage, according to Gregory of Nyssa, is a state contrary to man's original, Edenic condition: the 'reasoning and intelligent creature, man, at once the work and the likeness of the Divine and Imperishable Mind [Gr. & Lat., *nature*] ... did not in the course of his first production have united to the very essence of his nature the liability to passion and to death.'[18] Had man, therefore, remained in Paradise, he would no more have 'needed the assistance of marriage' and carnal union for the begetting of children than do the angels, who though they have no bodies nor passions nevertheless exist in 'countless myriads.' God gave man sexual organs and desire, the 'animal and irrational mode by which they now succeed one another,' only as a remedy for man's 'declension from the angelic life, in order that the multitude of human souls might not be cut short by its fall from that mode by which the angels were increased and multiplied.'[19] Since man's *theosis* entails a recovery of angelic impassibility, it necessarily entails also a virgin state. Virginity is, therefore, a symbol as well as a means of man's return to divine tranquility and recovery of the image of God – 'an actual representation,' says Gregory, 'of the blessedness in the world to come ... For our Lord has announced that the life after our resurrection shall be as that of the angels.'[20] Chrysostom's emphasis is the same. On the one hand he defends marriage against those who prohibit it for heretical reasons, and in his commentary on Ephesians he is eloquent in praise of married love – a 'certaine loue that lieth lurking in our nature, and priuilie ioineth togither these bodies,' from whence comes 'verie great good, both unto (priuate) houses, and (whole) cities.' But from this same love 'are ingendred great euils,' from which virginity delivers the soul.[21] Virginity is therefore more excellent than marriage, and the very act of refraining from marriage is an ascetic discipline with its reward. Virginity is to marriage as heaven is to earth or as angels are to men, for angels 'neither marry nor are given in marriage' and therefore need not 'endure the tumult of passions.' As one is able 'to see the heaven at high noon clear of any interference of clouds, even so the nature of angels remains, perforce, transparent and radiant, without any interference of passion.'[22] Chrysostom agrees with Gregory that Adam and Eve before the Fall were as the angels and that had man remained in Paradise there would have been 'no question of marriage'; they lived there 'as in heaven.' 'Desire of carnal union and conception and pangs of childbirth and birth and every form of corruption were absent from their souls.'[23]

Since Israel's departure from Egypt is a type of man's deliverance from 'every form of corruption' and his return to Paradise, we are not surprised that Gregory of Nyssa (in his *Life of Moses*) interprets many of the events of the Exodus with reference to the quelling of passions. The slaughter of the Egyptian firstborn is the destruction of the sources of passion – specifically wrath and lust. Because all other passions spring from these (as Book Two indicates Spenser knew), they may be regarded as the first-born sons of the Egyptian evils.[24] Those evils signify man's mortality and enslavement to desires of the flesh, from which baptism (crossing the Red Sea) releases him. The serpents which attack the Israelites in the wilderness are 'unruly desires,' which Christ, the brazen serpent, puts to death. Here Gregory connects mortification directly with *theosis*, identifying the ascetic struggle with the reception of deifying grace in the Incarnation. The brazen serpent's therapeutic power is the effect of the impassible Christ's becoming passible man: 'Mankind ... is freed from sin through him who put on the form of sin and became like us who had changed into the form of a serpent'; 'the person who looks to Him who was lifted up upon the Cross puts away passion.'[25]

Antique liturgies also attribute achievement of dispassion to Christ's Passion's having been passionless. Just as Christ is represented as submitting to death in order to destroy death, He is also frequently depicted as submitting to a passionless Passion to release man from passion. Two *troparia* from one of the Byzantine matins canons state these motifs, the one after the other, suggesting their identity by contiguity and rhetorical parallels:

Thou didst remain without participation in passions, O Word of God, having conversed with the passions in the flesh; but Thou dost loose mankind from the passions, our Saviour ... for Thou only art impassible and almighty.

Having accepted the corruption of death, Thou hast preserved Thy body without taste of corruption: and Thy life-creating and divine soul, O Master, hast not been left in Hell; but, having arisen as from sleep, Thou hast awaked us with Thee.[26]

The union of the passible with Christ destroys passibility just as the union of corruption (death) with Christ destroys corruptibility; and the second passage identifies this victory explicitly with the Resurrection, which is to say with the Harrowing and man's consequent deification.

These motifs are subject to various liturgical interpretations, but Christ's antithesis to Adam is consistently presented not only as an opposition of divine life to death but also of divine impassibility to passion. 'Our flesh, not being incorruptible before the Passion, having been assumed by the Maker has been rendered impervious to corruption after the Passion and the Resurrection, and [this] renews mortal men.'[27] Here death is the evil which *theosis* is to remedy; in the following passage, passibility: 'By thy sufferings, O lover of men, Thou hast given dispassion to all men, having put to death the passions of my flesh by Thy Cross.'[28] Sometimes the ascetic fuses directly with the sacramental:[29] Christ 'causes to gush forth from the Passion incorruption and freedom from passion ... and lets fall an immortal fountain from the holy side and everlasting life from the tomb.'[30] That symbolism virtually identifies impassibility with baptism and both with the Passion.

That sounds as though dispassion is wholly a gift rather than the fruit of asceticism, but that would oversimplify. The Fathers say it is both at once, and here we encounter a paradox: man must mortify the passions so as to achieve divine impassibility; yet that divine impassibility is not something he achieves but something Christ communicates to him in the sacraments. 'Having put to death the burning impulses and commotions of the passions *through temperance*, the martyrs of Christ *received the grace* ... to work wonders.'[31] They are deified – become workers of miracles – by grace received but, concurrently, by control exercised. Athanasius interprets Anthony's asceticism in the same paradoxical way: after describing an early contest with a spirit of fornication, Athanasius remarks, 'This, moreover, was Anthony's first victory over the Devil; nay, I should rather say that the strength in Anthony was the Saviour's.' 'Indeed, the Lord aided his servant, He who taking flesh for our sakes, gave to [Anthony's] body victory over the Devil.'[32] The deification of Anthony's flesh through Christ's taking flesh, gives Anthony Christ's victory; but Anthony's rigorous temperance drove out the spirit of fornication.

A statement by Maximus the Confessor involves the same apparent contradiction: because of the Incarnation, man can no longer 'plead the weakness of the flesh [its enslavement to the passions] as an excuse when he sins,' for deified flesh is no longer weak and passionate. 'The union of our humanity with the divine Logos ... has renewed the whole of nature.' That renewal, however, demands rigorous asceticism; what Christ has done for man, man must also do for himself. Precisely because Christ has 'renewed the whole of nature,' the Christian must combat and conquer the 'desires or impulses of the passions which are contrary to nature.'[33] The achievement of divine impassibility is wholly by grace (by deification in baptism) and wholly by human ascetic labor, there being no difference between the two since God became man and made man God. This divine-human activity is what later Byzantine theologians called *synergy* – the union of divine with (deified) human energies in the work of salvation.[34] George in Christ slays the dragon; Christ in George slays the dragon. Anthony in Christ slays the passions; Christ in Anthony slays the passions. Man works out his *own* salvation (as Saint Paul admonishes him to do), Christ working in man; Christ works out man's salvation, man being in Christ. The human operation is divine and the divine operation human. Grace and works, like grace and nature, become synonymous in the risen (and transfigured) flesh of Christ.

III

If Spenser's attitude toward the passions in Book Two is patristic, any one or all of the passages I have quoted could have been his source. More likely, however, than any of them is a book which I have not yet mentioned, the *Stromateis* (or *Miscellanies*) of Clement of Alexandria. Clement's is the earliest full explication of the patristic ascetic ideal, and its influence on the works of later Fathers can scarcely be exaggerated. The *Stromateis* stand behind Athanasius' interpretation of Anthony and behind Basil's *ascetica*. Clement defines in detail conceptions which later Fathers, like Basil, Maximus, and Chrysostom, take for granted. The *Stromateis* were available to sixteenth-century readers both in Greek and Latin,[35] and even if Spenser had read nothing else on the subject, he could have found in them a full picture of asceticism as the divinely communicated (yet humanly wrought) means of *theosis*.

The key to Clement's teaching is his definition of the 'gnostic.' This is the man who, like Anthony, has quelled all the passions, who has endured temptations to wrath and lust and overcome them. The gnostic does not achieve 'perfection of moral virtue' by regulating the passions; he achieves deification through impassibility. His soul becomes 'an image divine ... very like God,' and he beholds God in the mirror of that passionless soul. Christ 'is the only-begotten by nature, the image of the glory of the King of all and almighty Father, *imprinting on the gnostic the perfect reflection according to His* [own] *image*' (italics added). By destroying the passions the gnostic becomes Christ; 'there is now,' therefore, 'a third divine image which is conformed in so far as possible to the Second Cause, to the true Life through whom we live the true life.'[36] The First Cause is the Father or 'King of all,' the Second, Christ, the Father's image, and the third, the impassible, deified man on whom that image is stamped. 'This,' says Clement, 'is the good man indeed, who is outside the passions ... *having gone beyond the whole life of passion*' (italics added).[37]

To be entirely outside the passions and beyond their life produces what Clement and many Fathers after him call *apathy* (ἀπάθεια). This is in fact the word which Basil uses to characterize the divine nature and which I translated as 'tranquility.' The reason for doing so is obvious – the pejorative connotation of *apathy* in contemporary English. Ἀπάθεια does not have that connotation; for Clement the word simply means to be without passion – a divine defect. The gnostic's apathy is the 'perfecting of the believer through charity unto the perfect man, unto the measure of manhood; moving forward, [the gnostic] arrives at the divine likeness, being made like to God, having become truly equal to an angel.'[38] The Christian who has attained to this condition no longer needs to struggle against the impulses of the flesh; rather he is 'already as if fleshless and has come to a holiness above this earth.'[39] 'Such an one is perfected [having grown into] God out of manhood.'[40]

Like Basil and like the composers of the liturgies from which I have quoted, Clement links the achievement of apathy to the paschal mysteries. This is most easily seen in his attack on Marcionite heretics, who deny the good of creation and of sexual procreation. They quote Christ's admonition to Philip, 'Let the dead bury their dead, but do thou follow me' (Matt. 8:22; Luke 9:60), which they interpret to mean that the living, because they are in the flesh and have been generated sexually, are in effect as dead as the literally dead. Clement responds by asking what distinguishes Philip from the rest: since 'he bears the common form of flesh,' is he not as much a dead man as those he is told to leave behind? 'How,' according to Marcionite reasoning, can Philip 'having a body of flesh not be a corpse?' Clement's answer is that Philip's body of flesh has been deified, made deathless by the death of passion which Christ worked in him; Philip 'rose from the tomb when the Lord killed his passions, and he will live in Christ.'[41] Here Clement takes for granted the paschal context of *theosis*, but unlike Cyril of Jerusalem, Dionysius the Areopagite, and other authors of *mystagogia* he emphasizes the ascetic dimension of that context: Philip 'will live in Christ,' because Christ made him impassible. Philip rose from the tomb of passibility and mortality (the two are synonymous) into which Adam sank, when Christ through the Resurrection made man divine. The cause of death is not the flesh or sexual generation as such but the passions which since the Fall have corrupted the flesh and poisoned the sources of life. The way to life, therefore, is not rejection of the flesh but its renewal, which is to say its becoming impassible in the impassible, resurrected flesh of Christ. That is the flesh which shines with the uncreated light.

That argument, like others we have quoted, seems to place all its emphasis on grace, but in other contexts Clement indicates he is aware of the paradox that one must labor for what he is given. Metaphors of athletic contests and military combat (reminding us of those in the *mystagogia*) are frequent in the *Stromateis* and say clearly that though it is Christ on the cross who kills man's passions, man in his own person must battle against them. The reward of victory is divine apathy, but divine apathy is also the gift which makes victory possible; the paradox is always close to the surface of Clement's prose. 'There is one alone who is free from passions from the first,' and that is Christ. 'Whoever strive to be conformed to the image *given* by Him, *struggle with violence* to become free from passions by ascesis.'[42] My emphases make the apparent contradiction clear; man struggles violently and trains himself ascetically so as to receive what he has been given. The gnostic is always the worker and the fighter; apathy entails activity. His soul is 'an earthly image of divine power,'[43] a description suggesting stasis and completed deification, but at the same time 'the gnostic is creating and making himself.'[44] Man being deified by Christ, by *ascesis* deifies himself.

IV

That Spenser presents such a conception of the passions and their discipline I shall argue from the allegory; but prior to that there is lexical evidence. I refer to one of the old debates about Book Two: did Spenser mean Guyon's virtue to be Aristotle's σωφροσύνη or his ἐγκράτεια? The former means balance, rational control, right judgment, prudence, discretion in conduct, seemliness, sanity, and sobriety. Σωφροσύνη is the character and conduct of the σώφρων, the man of sound mind. Ἐγκράτεια signifies the mastery of passion by force. Force, κράτος, is, in fact, its root; and the man who is characterized by ἐγκράτεια is not so much remarkable for balance or discretion as for a capacity to do effective battle against the passions. Σωφροσύνη is the virtue which Cicero translated as *temperantia* (also as *moderatio* and *modestia*)[45] and which, to the extent that later Latin writers considered the Greek at all, is the point of reference for temperance as a cardinal virtue. The translation is in some measure an interpretation; since to temper is to mix or moderate, *temperance* places a heavier (or at least a more exclusive) emphasis than σωφροσύνη does on balance or moderation. Ἐγκράτεια has conventionally been rendered as *continentia* or *continence* and has traditionally been considered as inferior to σωφροσύνη. Aristotle preferred temperance to continence, for though 'both the continent man and the temperate man are such as to do nothing contrary to the rule for the sake of the bodily pleasures ... the former has and the latter has not bad appetites.' The man possessing σωφροσύνη does not 'feel pleasure contrary to the rule' while the man possessing ἐγκράτεια 'is such as to feel pleasure but not to be led by it.'[46] Aristotle does not in fact regard ἐγκράτεια as a virtue in its own right. Aquinas says it can be properly called a virtue only when it is identified as virginity; this he calls 'perfect continence' (*ST*, II-II, 155, 1), a Christian variation upon the classical conception.[47] But *continence* in its usual, Aristotelian acceptation, as the 'opposition [of reason] to the passions ... does not attain to the perfect nature of a moral virtue ...' 'Temperance is far greater than continence' because 'the good of reason flourishes more in the temperate man than in the continent man' (*ST*, II-II, 155, 1, 4).[48]

Given that history of interpretation and translation, one would expect Spenser's temperance to be unequivocally σωφροσύνη, but the matter has been much debated. The *Variorum* editors, Padelford most prominently, argued that when Spenser said *temperance* he really meant *continence*, not σωφροσύνη but ἐγκράτεια; Guyon, rather than being innately balanced and moderate, experiences desires and must combat them forcefully. Padelford also points to Spenser's choosing as a name for his personification of *in*temperance a transliteration of Aristotle's word for incontinence – ἀκρασία. If Spenser had intended Guyon to be the σώφρων, he would have named the villainess Acolasia (ἀκολασία), which Aristotle opposes to σωφροσύνη.[49] Berger's and Hamilton's interpretations of the name do not altogether answer Padelford: that *Acrasia* unites intemperance (ἄκρατος, untempered, unmixed – the antonym of εὔκρατος) with incontinence (ἀκρατής, uncontrolled). Hamilton finds the same fusion (or confusion) in the medieval Latin *acrasia*; and both Berger and Hamilton could have found support for such etymologizing in Estienne's 1572 lexicon, which argues that ἀκρασία is properly the privative of εὐκρασία and has been 'usurped' for ἀκράτεια, 'Id est, Incontinentia.'[50] But Estienne's explanation is historically eccentric; from classical times to the Renaissance (and to the present) the normally accepted translation of ἀκρασία is *incontinence* rather than *intemperance*. That that is true for 'Aristotle and the rest' Estienne's own citations make clear; and sixteenth-century readers of *The Faerie Queene* who recognized the Greek source of *Acrasia* would almost certainly have taken that meaning for granted. Furthermore, Spenser makes Acrates, from ἀκρατής, the adjectival form of ἀκρασία, the father of Pyrochles and Cymochles. If he had wished to indicate that wrath and lust were owing primarily to intemperance rather than to incontinence, he would surely have allowed Acrat_o_s (or perhaps Akolastos) to sire Guyon's adversaries.

'Why, then, [should] Spenser entitle a book based on the Aristotelian continence [and incontinence], "The Legend of Temperaunce"?' That was Viola Hulbert's question more than half a century ago. Her answer: that since 'even a novice at philosophy' could have understood Aristotle's distinctions, Spenser, contrary to his own claim, must not have been relying on the *Ethics* for his conception. Professor Hulbert believed he drew his idea instead from Christian interpreters of temperance (and of Aristotle), from the 'Christian Fathers' to the sixteenth century.[51] That is tantalizing, but the balance of her argument disappoints because of its imprecision. She fails to discriminate among different Christian traditions (which, as we have seen, teach different conceptions of the passions), and her choice of evidence is arbitrary. She allows Ambrose alone to represent the Fathers, making no reference to the Greek tradition; and among Latin writers she quotes more frequently from Macrobius, Isidore, Alcuin, Hugh of St Victor, and Alanus than from Augustine and Aquinas. Furthermore, she seems to lose sight of her target; though she is ostensibly demonstrating a precedent for Spenser's conceiving temperance as ἐγκράτεια, most of her quotations emphasize those very qualities normally associated with temperance as σωφροσύνη – rational control, balance, moderation.

The essay, in short, is muddled, but I cite it because it need not have been. That Spenser could have been heir to distinctively Christian conceptions of temperance and continence is a possibility worth exploring more carefully than Professor Hulbert (or anyone since) has explored it; and such an exploration returns us to patristic ascesis.

That ἐγκράτεια would have been more congenial to the Fathers than σωφροσύνη is easy to imagine in view of their insistence upon complete mortification of passion and denial of all pleasure. Such teaching does not bespeak balance or moderation, and the recurrent metaphors of martyrdom and military conquest suggest forceful overthrow rather than rational government of desire. One could argue that ἀπάθεια, the defining purpose or final cause of patristic asceticism, has more in common with σωφροσύνη than with ἐγκράτεια, and Clement, as we shall see, makes that connection. But Clement also links ἀπάθεια to ἐγκράτεια, and the Fathers in general seem untroubled by the apparent contradiction between images of warfare and praise of impassibility; Clement's gnostic, whose very definition is ἀπάθεια, is the 'true wrestler.' Castiglione says that temperance (σωφροσύνη) is 'like the Captaine that without resistance overcommeth and raigneth ...' Nothing could be further in its flavor from the Fathers' militant apathy. The latter is more nearly conveyed by Castiglione's 'Continencie ... compared to a Captaine that fighteth manly, and though his enimies bee strong and well appointed, yet giveth he them the overthrow ...'[52]

'Chastisement of the body,' says Basil, 'and bringing it under subjection are achieved by no other means as successfully as by the practice of ἐγκράτεια.'[53] Since Basil was fully conversant with Aristotle, one can scarcely regard that statement as other than a tacit rejection of σωφροσύνη in favor of the more militant virtue. And Basil's usage is consistent; he invariably attributes mortification to ἐγκράτεια. Ἐγκράτεια 'destroys sin, quells the passions, and mortifies the body, *even as to its natural affections and desires*'[54] (italics added). That is to ascribe to the virtue the characteristic of patristic ascesis which is least amenable to the idea of temperance-as-moderation. It is also, obviously, to associate ἐγκράτεια directly with ἀπάθεια, the complete transcendence of desire. For Basil, in other words, ἐγκράτεια rather than σωφροσύνη is the virtue which effects deifying mortification and achieves divine tranquility. Not surprisingly, therefore, (and of obvious interest for an interpretation of Book Two) Basil identifies the antonym of ἐγκράτεια as the sin in Eden which deprived Adam and his progeny of *theosis*: 'The first disobedience befell men as a consequence of ἀκρασία.' That Mordant (probably the old Adam) should be Acrasia's victim and that her Bower should signify a fallen Eden accord perfectly with Basil's vocabulary. Ἐγκράτεια, conversely, is man's principal means of redemption and a defining characteristic of the saints, who have recovered the divinity which Adam lost. Through ἐγκράτεια the Three Holy Children in the Babylonian furnace overcame the power of fire; John Baptist's 'whole plan of life was based on the practice of ἐγκράτεια'; and Christ Himself (tempted in the wilderness) 'inaugurated His public manifestation with practice of this virtue.'[55] In other words, ἐγκράτεια and ἀκρασία define for Basil the poles of Christian experience just as they appear to define the psychomachia of Book Two.

That is not to imply that all the Fathers are as consistent in their vocabulary as Basil. Σωφροσύνη was unquestionably a patristic virtue, and some of the Fathers, among them Athanasius, clearly prefer it to ἐγκράτεια.[56] But their doing so does not necessarily set them at odds with Basil, for patristic σωφροσύνη seems in many instances synonymous with ἐγκράτεια. Though the latter (ἐγκρατεύομαι) appears only once in Athanasius' *Life of Anthony*, σωφροσύνη serves to describe the saint's altogether encratic struggles against passion.[57] Clearly Athanasius does not mean to depict Anthony as the Aristotelian σώφρων but as the Clementine gnostic, who fights against desire. If one were to read Basil's ascetic treatises side by side with the *Life of Anthony*, he would likely conclude that Athanasius meant by temperance precisely what Basil meant by continence. Though Clement uses both words, the content of the virtue signified is more nearly encratic than temperate.[58] Sometimes he appears to treat the two as synonyms, as when he says that 'all the epistles of the Apostle teach σωφροσύνη and ἐγκράτεια';[59] if he intends any distinction, he does not spell it out, and one suspects rhetorical doubling. In other passages he makes distinctions, but these are frequently contradictory and thus cancel each other out. In one instance he says that ἐγκράτεια is prior to and a condition of σωφροσύνη: ἐγκράτεια teaches man to 'exercise σωφροσύνη.'[60] If that means we can attain the character of the σώφρων only by first winning our matches as wrestlers, Clement would seem to be approaching Aristotle's demotion of ἐγκράτεια to an ancillary status; but that is not the consistent emphasis of the *Stromateis*. Elsewhere Clement turns the relation on its head and says that without σωφροσύνη it is impossible to be ἐγκρατής;[61] that makes σωφροσύνη the means and ἐγκράτεια both the end and the more important virtue. Clement says the gnostic is both σώφρων and ἀπαθής, and Helen North regards this identification of σωφροσύνη with *theosis* as an important contribution to patristic vocabulary.[62] But Clement makes the same identification with ἐγκράτεια, suggesting that he conceived both virtues as instrumental to deification. Since God is impassible (ἀπαθής), He cannot be said to be continent (ἐγκρατής); but man requires that virtue in order to approach 'by disposition to the divine nature.'[63] There we seem to have Basil's understanding of ἐγκράτεια as the virtue which more efficiently than all others 'mortifies the body even as to its natural affections and desires,' the virtue which redeems man from the Fall by making him divine. In another passage Clement presupposes that meaning of ἐγκράτεια in what appears to be an explicit reversal of Aristotle's distinction. 'Human continence,' according to 'the philosophers of the Greeks,' consists in fighting against desire and not being subject to it. But 'according to us [Christian philosophers],' ἐγκρατεύομαι means, simply, 'not to desire' – 'not that someone tempted by desire should be stedfast [Aristotle's ἐγκράτεια] but that he should be ἐγκρατής even in respect of desire [itself] [Aristotle's σωφροσύνη].'[64] Clement adds that any other conception of ἐγκράτεια is not by the

grace of God. That is not only to reverse the terminology of the *Ethics*
but to make *theosis* specifically encratic.

Helen North's *Sophrosyne* confirms our inference from Basil, Athanasius, and Clement: that the wide range of meaning attaching to Aristotelian σωφροσύνη, including continence, had in patristic usage narrowed down almost exclusively to continence. Professor North reveals her classical bias by calling this development a 'distortion,'[65] and she praises Clement for 'scrupulous moderation in dealing with a subject that for many Christian moralists presented an irresistible temptation to excess.' She cites as illustration a passage in the third of the *Stromateis* in which Clement sounds altogether Aristotelian, using σωφροσύνη to signify the mean between extravagance and niggardliness.[66] To do that, of course, is to emphasize balance and moderation at the expense of any direct reference to discipline of passion. But Professor North is frank to admit that the instance is exceptional – that for Clement (as for most of the Fathers) 'the word normally indicates control of the appetites' and only 'occasionally ... extends to other meanings, equally traditional in classical literature – sobriety, sanity, moderation.'[67] And she cites one instance in which Clement not only assimilates σωφροσύνη to ἐγκράτεια but by virtue of doing so opposes σωφροσύνη to ἀκρασία.[68] That reads rather like a recipe for the nomenclature of Book Two.

If the Fathers are not entirely consistent in their preference of ἐγκράτεια to σωφροσύνη, the Byzantine liturgical texts are. The *Triodion* provides an instance. In the twenty-one pages (Athens 1987) devoted to the week of preparation prior to the first week of Lent, ἐγκράτεια (or a verbal or adjectival form of the word) appears thirty times, σωφροσύνη only twice. Furthermore, in one of those two instances, σωφροσύνη would seem to mean ἐγκράτεια, as it so frequently does in patristic texts: worshippers are bidden to acquire by fasting 'the temperance (σωφροσύνη) of Joseph,'[69] who was, of course, remarkable for doing battle with sexual temptation in the Egyptian court. This heavy imbalance is characteristic of all the Lenten liturgies, suggesting that their authors (some of them Church Fathers) thought of the mortification of passion in preparation for the Passion (and as a means of participating in it) to be pre-eminently the work of ἐγκράτεια. In several instances Lent is characterized as 'the time [or 'season'] of ἐγκράτεια.' The following vespers hymn from Tuesday of the second

week of Lent is illustrative of the way these liturgies link ascetic labor
with the paschal mysteries, in a pattern which seems to be evident in
the relation between Books One and Two of *The Faerie Queene*:

> When Thou wast crucified in the flesh, O Lord,
> Thou hast crucified our old man with Thyself;
> when Thy side was pierced by a spear, Thou hast
> pierced the man-destroying serpent. Nail with
> Thy fear my flesh, and with desire for Thee
> wound my soul, so that beholding Thy Passion in
> continence (ἐγκρατῶς) I shall complete the set
> time of the Fast ...[70]

By the logic of that symbolism, slaying the dragon and practicing
ἐγκράτεια (being Red Crosse and being Guyon) are simply two facets
of the same spiritual activity, carried on conjointly by God and man.

V

What we find then in the Fathers' ascetical treatises and in ancient liturgies – what Spenser could have found in contemporary editions of
those works – is a conception of the passions not as natural impulses to
be governed by the reason but as diseases of the soul and legacies of
the Fall to be extirpated by an ascetical mortification whose purpose is
the restoration of the divine image in man; a paradoxical identification
of that work of mortification with participation in the passionless Passion of Christ and thus with the deifying paschal sacraments which
Spenser appears to be presenting in Book One as the means of holiness;
and a vocabulary of the virtues which appropriates Aristotle's
ἐγκράτεια to describe this sacramental ascesis and which (in salient
instances) redefines his σωφροσύνη for precisely the same purpose. In
other words patristic *ascetica* afford a precedent for conceiving temperance as a means for achieving impassibility and *theosis* and as the
antithesis of and remedy for an incontinence which in the beginning
deprived Adam and his progeny of those gifts. These are conceptions
radically different from those which have hitherto informed scholarly
readings of Book Two; it remains to show that they make clearer sense
of the Legend of Temperaunce than the classical and Western Christian
understanding of the virtues to which critics usually appeal.

CHAPTER SIX

Temperance and Belphoebe

I

That these patristic conceptions have not been introduced into discussions of Book Two is surprising in view of the erudition expended on Spenser's temperance. Even the critics (most of them recent) who deny that Guyon's virtue is Aristotelian and who prefer a Christian to a classical interpretation have not taken patristic asceticism into account. Carol Kaske believes Spenser's allegory reflects 'some inadequacy of classical temperance,' but she spells out no clear alternative; nor does Lauren Silberman, who goes so far as to maintain that Spenser's is 'a coherent poetic strategy of discrediting Classical Temperance as a moral standard ...'[1] The usual appeal is, rather vaguely, to 'Christian humanism,' which is in effect to Augustinian and Thomistic conceptions. Hamilton is characteristic, applying to Spenser Milton's thoroughly Augustinian question: '"Wherefore did [God] create the passions within us, pleasures round us, but that these *rightly tempered* are the very ingredients of virtue?"'[2] (italics added). Peter Stambler reads 'the whole of Book II' as an allegory of 'the supplantation of the Aristotelian or "classical" ethical model ... by a radical Christian standard,'[3] but he does not distinguish among the different Christian standards which Spenser could have known; and save for one quotation from Ambrose (which he takes second hand from Viola Hulbert) he ignores entirely the most radical Christian standard of all.

Save for the ultimately unsatisfactory address to the matter by the *Variorum* scholars, Spenser's attitude toward the relation of temperance to continence has likewise received scant attention. No one has pointed out, for instance, that two important passages, one at the beginning, one at the end of Book Two, seem to exclude σωφροσύνη and *temperantia* and point instead to ἐγκράτεια. The first is the abortive union of Bacchus with the Nymph in canto one; since the mixing of wine and water is an ancient and universal symbol of temperance conceived as moderation or good mixture, Spenser's attributing to their mixture a disastrous consequence in an episode designated as the 'whole subject' of his Book suggests that we are to look elsewhere for the meaning of Guyon's virtue. Mordant's death alone should discourage our agreeing with Berger and Hamilton that Acrasia's name means 'bad mixture' as well as incontinence, for the traditional symbol of 'good mixture,' rather than breaking her spell, puts it into effect. The implication of the allegory would seem to be that balance and moderation in the government of the passions contributes to the evil of sensuality rather than remedying it.

The second passage comes very close to making that implication explicit; I refer to the altogether well mixed atmosphere of the Bower of Bliss. Probably because *loci amoeni* invariably have moderate climates no one seems to have noticed how odd it is for Spenser's chief locus of intemperance to be so temperate. Neither 'scorching heat, nor cold *intemperate*' afflicts the Bower's inhabitants, but 'milde aire with season *moderate* / Gently *attempred*' (II, xii, 51; italics added) breathes upon them. That Spenser intended a specific reference to εὐκρασία is suggested by the description's almost certain source – an account of the climate of the Elysian Fields in the pseudo-Platonic *Axiochus*. In the 1592 version attributed to Spenser the passage reads: 'For the Inhabitants thereof are neither touched with force of cold, nor payned with excesse of heate, but the moderate Aire breatheth on them mildly and calmely, being, lightned with the gentle Sunnebeames.'[4] Resemblance to the climate of the Bower is unmistakable (and, as I have argued elsewhere, supports the traditional ascription of the 1592 *Axiochus* to Spenser).[5] Of principal interest in the present context is the word-play in Greek on εὔκρατος and ἀνακρινάμενος. The root of both words is κεράννυμι, 'to mix,' or 'to temper,' and what the sentence says literally is that 'well-mixed (or temperate) air is poured, well-mixed (or tempered) with the gentle rays of the sun': εὔκρατος ἀὴρ χεῖται, ἁπαλαῖς ἡλίου ἀκτῖσιν ἀνακρινάμενος. The doubling in the original of *mix* (or *temper*) places an obviously heavy emphasis on moderation, which Spenser conveys with an analogous duplication – 'season *moderate* /

Gently *attempred'* ('*milde* air' and '*disposed so well*' reinforce the emphasis). Since *Axiochus* was popular in the late sixteenth century, Spenser may have expected his readers to recognize an allusion to the Greek as well as to the English version. And even if those readers did not know *Axiochus*, they might nevertheless have recognized the sentence in question from Estienne's use of it as a citation for εὐκρασία. By placing Acrasia in a climate so conspicuously characterized by 'good mixture,' Spenser would seem to be rejecting 'bad mixture' as the meaning of her name and moderation as the meaning of temperance. That is in effect to exclude definitive characteristics of σωφροσύνη (and of the 'Christian humanist' idea of temperance) from the virtue of Book Two and, surprisingly, to associate them with its vice. Things *moderate, gently attempred, milde, well disposed,* or *well mixed* appear to belong to Acrasia rather than to the knight of temperance. Guyon is the encratic[6] (and perhaps patristic) opposite of all such when he ravages the temperate Bower.

II

There are, of course, passages in Book Two which appear to identify temperance as moderation or σωφροσύνη, but most of these are subject to subsequent qualification. When Guyon is tempted by Phaedria, we are evidently supposed to approve of his 'fairely tempring fond desire.' But Spenser adds 'subdewd,' leaving us in doubt whether *desire* is the object of the participle or of the verb (II, vi, 26). If the latter, the effect of tempering must be encratic. Other passages which on first reading seem to approve of temperance-as-moderation upon further consideration raise doubts. That Guyon should give Amavia 'goodly counsell ... *tempred* with sweet voice (II, i, 44; italics added) seems appropriate for a knight of temperance, and temperance here is obviously 'good mixture.' It is just as obviously, however, ineffective; Amavia dies in unmitigated grief. In the interim, moreover, she narrates the story of Bacchus and the Nymph, casting serious doubt on Guyon's effort to restore her by what the mixing of wine and water symbolize. The Palmer's commentary on the situation, though a *locus classicus* for those who believe Spenser's virtue classical, seems in context as feckless as Guyon's tempering counsel with sweet voice. To the latter's

'Behold the image of mortalitie' the Palmer responds with temperance as a 'golden squire' which 'can measure out a meane' between 'pleasures whot desire' and 'hartlesse griefe' (II, i, 57–8). Spenser gives no indication that such a mean exists; and there is certainly no reason to believe that either the intensity of Amavia's grief or of Mordant's erotic pleasure should, or could, merely have been moderated. Furthermore Guyon's characterization of mortality militates against the Palmer's Aristotelian formula: nature 'cloth'd with fleshly tyre' is 'feeble,' and 'raging passion with fierce tyrannie / Robs reason of her due regalitie' (II, i, 57). The spiritual circumstance he describes is very like Donne's depiction of his soul in 'Batter My Heart, Three-Personed God': when reason is captive to usurping passion, it cannot exercise its wonted function of control. In Donne's instance a violent God – in Spenser's, arguably, an ascetical temperance – must come to reason's rescue. Acrasia's potion working secretly in Mordant's flesh is a convincing metaphor of an enslavement such as Donne describes – the good that one would he cannot do. And the finality of Amavia's response to grief suggests the impossibility of its rational curtailment. How either one in his or her circumstance could have responded to passion in the way the Palmer recommends is difficult to discern.

If the reader recognizes that difficulty, he will be skeptical (many readers are) about the wisdom of giving Ruddymane to Medina. Since the child bears the parents' stain, there is no more cause to believe that measuring out a mean will benefit him than them, but that is the best Medina can do. Her very existence as a personification depends, paradoxically, on the passions which she controls: 'Conflict and division in [Medina's] society are the very lifeblood of her own personal excellence ... It is possible to see the extremities as existing for the sake of the mean'[7] (where would Medina be – *what* would she be – without Perissa and Elissa?). That is tantamount to saying that the passions exist for the sake of their moderation – a kind of *reductio ad absurdum* of the Aristotelian conception. Aquinas is certainly not guilty of the fallacy, but he does argue 'that moral virtues, which are about the passions as about their proper matter, cannot be without passions' because 'it is not the function of virtue to deprive the powers subordinate to reason of their proper activities, but to make them execute the commands of reason, by exercising their proper acts' (*ST* I–II, 59, 5).[8] Such an account of the control of passions presupposes their goodness when properly governed and serves as still another reminder of the difference in views of temperance between Aquinas and the Fathers – Anthony, Clement, and Basil would not likely agree that the passions have 'proper acts.' Since Medina personifies the belief that they do, we are not surprised that instead of observing an ascetical fast she 'attempered her feast' (italics added) and satisfied her guests' 'lust of meat and drinke' (II, ii, 39). The familiar tag may be supposed to call attention to its pagan origin and thereby to cast still further doubt upon the efficacy of Medina's economy. In any event, in a poem dominated by Acrasia, we can scarcely ignore *lust*, however innocent it may be in its Homeric context; and we suspect that a victim of lust like Ruddymane will not be benefitted by Medina's table. That Medina in this scene plays Dido to Guyon's Aeneas may also point to her pagan limitations and, in view of Dido's weakness, to the inadequacy of reason to withstand the assault of passion. Indeed Medina's response to the 'storie of the mortall payne, / Which *Mordant* and *Amauia* did rew' and of 'this their wretched sonne' (II, ii, 45, 44) appears to acknowledge that inadequacy. As though the very grimness of the tale had brought her to a recognition of the passions' destructive power and of the need for remedies more stringent than her own, she vows to 'learne from pleasures poyson to abstaine' (II, ii, 45). To characterize pleasure as, without qualification, poisonous is certainly alien to the conception of temperance as a 'golden squire' or measured mean; abstinence, moreover, is quite different from moderate indulgence. Were Medina more nearly a character than a personification, we should guess that she had suffered a conversion from a 'Christian humanist' to an ascetical view of temperance.

Still another reason for suspecting that Spenser is distancing himself from temperance as tempering and from regulation as opposed to mortification of passion is his placing a version of these conceptions in Phaedria's mouth. She wants 'louely peace, and gentle amitie,' but rather than seeking them in dispassion she espouses a balancing of passions: 'Mars is *Cupidoes* frend' (II, vi, 35). That parodies the Palmer's early recommendation for Mordant and Amavia – to measure out the mean between grief and pleasure. His motives are pure, Phaedria's corrupt, but their proposals are too close for comfort. By the same token, Phaedria parodies Medina, for both secure (or seek) peace by means of passion. In a perverse way Phaedria also signifies the mean:

she sails peaceably between the extremes of 'rocks and flats' (II, vi, 5). She stands in much the same relation to these classical conceptions of temperance as does the moderate climate of the Bower. In each instance the disreputable character or context casts serious doubt on ideas which in the Palmer or Medina seem, at least on first reading, admirable.

<h1 style="text-align:center">III</h1>

These are negative inferences, drawn from the apparent inadequacy in their respective contexts of versions of temperance-as-moderation. A more positive sort of evidence for Spenser's intending a more rigorous version of the virtue is that temperance conceived as mortification solves problems of interpretation which have hitherto proved obstinate.

For one, it makes sense of Guyon's personality. Many critics think him the least attractive hero in the poem – cold, indifferent to love and beauty, and except once, in the Bower of Bliss, to erotic attraction. To make matters worse, Spenser leaves no doubt that that one 'human' response is reprehensible. Is Guyon in all these respects not more nearly a starched Puritan than an exponent of temperance? Should a knight of temperance not be temperate rather than rigorous in his attitude toward beauty and pleasure? Should he not respond as Augustine, Aquinas, or Milton advise? By saying no, a patristic reading of the Book affords a convincing rationale for Guyon's manner and conduct and allows us to take him at face value. If *all* pleasures are obstacles to the recovery of divine ἀπάθεια and if that recovery is the purpose of temperance (or continence), the senses should be shielded from all access to pleasure, and all the passions which result from sensuous experience should be extirpated from the soul. If Guyon is singular among Spenser's heroes in his detachment from affairs of the heart, a patristic reading suggests that rather than censure him for indifference or priggishness we should applaud his 'perfect continence' and that we should recognize what many readers take for emotional frigidity to be a signature of the impassibility which crowns ascetic struggle.

Patristic temperance also allows us to conceive Guyon's virtue as, without qualification, Christian. We have already seen how the Fathers' emphasis on deification bypasses the distinction between nature and grace, which has bedeviled interpreters of Book Two. Since Woodhouse, no one has altogether gotten past the idea that temperance is less Christian than holiness. Even those critics who resist a clear-cut distinction between a Christian Book One and a Classical Book Two assume that temperance in contrast to holiness is a work rather than a grace, natural rather than divine, ethical rather than soteriological. Therefore Christian interpretations of the Book almost invariably treat temperance as a negative virtue which Guyon must transcend – Berger's and Hamilton's readings are representative.[9] Anthea Hume in her complete rejection of Woodhouse comes closest to assimilating temperance and holiness, and many of her quotations from Reformed theologians make at least a semi-patristic connection between virtuous conduct and salvation by grace. But because she conceives Spenser to be a thoroughgoing Protestant who believed salvation to be by grace *alone*, she never quite persuades her reader that a virtue concerned with works is as centrally and explicitly Christian as one that depends (in her judgment) wholly on grace. Therefore, though less radically than most of her predecessors, she persists in the thematic distinction between salvation, illustrated by Red Crosse, and 'the process of growth in moral virtue which necessarily *follows* it,' illustrated by Guyon.[10]

Even such a modified version of the nature-grace dichotomy belies the well-documented parallels which link Books One and Two – Maleger to the dragon, Arthur's victory to Red Crosse's, Guyon's ravaging of the Bower to Red Crosse's liberation of Eden. Many critics, Hamilton most prominently, have examined those parallels in detail,[11] but, almost certainly because they relegate temperance to a sub-religious category, they have not drawn what seems to be the obvious inference – that 'like race to runne' (II, i, 32) means precisely what it says: that Guyon's quest traverses the same theological terrain and reaches the same theological goal as Red Crosse's. The patristic conception of temperance as a divine-human work in which man's victory over passion is synonymous with Christ's victory over Satan allows us to understand exactly how that can be. Saint Anthony's kind of temperance is as eminently soteriological as Saint George's kind of holiness; their common term is deification. Such temperance, so far from being subordinate or subsequent to salvation by grace, *is* salvation by grace.

Another, and related, problem in Book Two is why Spenser should identify what is almost certainly an allegory of the Fall (Mordant, Amavia, Ruddymane) as the 'whole subject' of a legend of temperance. How can the rational government of passion serve as remedy for Adam's sin and its consequences? The antidote seems inadequate to the poison; original sin requires baptism, not moderation of the passions, as its remedy. Recognition of that difficulty may explain Hamilton's otherwise puzzling argument that temperance is not the subject of Book Two (that being, by Spenser's own profession, what Hamilton interprets as original sin) but 'the matter out of which Spenser creates his subject.'[12] If, however, we follow the Fathers in conceiving temperance as deifying mortification, the difficulty resolves itself immediately. Since the very meaning of the Fall is the obscuring of the divine image by the passions, what remedy could be more appropriate than the divine-human activity of mortification by which man recovers that image – washes away in the 'fountain of dispassion' from Christ's side (in baptism) the stains of lust and mortality? Regulation of passion is not synonymous with baptism and can scarcely effect the regeneration of fallen humanity; eradication of passion, because it is, can.

Another difficulty which a patristic conception of temperance resolves is how to account for Belphoebe; and Belphoebe so accounted for introduces new possibilities for interpreting the rest of Book Two. She is, I believe, our principal reason for believing that Spenser meant by temperance what the Fathers did.

IV

For most she has been a 'conspicuous irrelevance.' That Professor Quilligan in 1987 should praise Berger's 'heroic struggles' to make sense of her in 1957 indicates how little sense in fact anyone has made.[13] Belphoebe's irrelevance to the *action* of Book Two is undeniable; none of the principals – Guyon, the Palmer, or Arthur – ever sees her, and once she disappears from canto three the reader hears no more of her until Book Three. That she seems equally irrelevant thematically is probably owing to the persistent conception of temperance as a natural or secular virtue; Belphoebe is too obviously supernatural and holy to be pertinent. There can be no denying her a place among Spenser's deified figures; every detail of her description is redolent of a transfigured humanity. Her 'heauenly face' (as we have seen) is a 'glorious mirrhour of celestiall grace' (II, iii, 25) – suggesting that she has been 'transfigured' into the image of Christ, 'from glory to glory.' Her being 'borne of heauenly birth' (II, iii, 21) sustains the inference, and the claim is authenticated by what we learn of her conception and birth (a type of the virgin birth) in Book Three. The probable allusion is to Saint John's characterization of Christians as 'sons of God' – 'which were born, not of blood, nor of the will of the flesh, nor of the will of man, but of God' (John 1:13). These prove to be the very characteristics of Belphoebe's genesis and point to Christian *theosis*.

Since such glories seem alien to temperance as most readers have conceived the virtue, Belphoebe seems alien to Book Two. Hamilton's commentary is indicative of the difficulty: Belphoebe's being 'Hable to heale the sicke, and to reuiue the ded' (II, iii, 22) 'suggests that in the perfection of her nature she is the unfallen Eden watered and nourished by the Well and Tree of Life,' for, as Hamilton reminds us, she combines those two powers which restore Red Crosse in the Eden of Book One. Here, it would seem, is another of those parallels between the first two books which argue for a conception of temperance analogous to that of holiness, but Hamilton shuns that inference. He recognizes that Belphoebe by virtue of her sacramental and Edenic associations is 'the antithesis of Acrasia,' and her 'presence in the poem shows us that Nature must be redeemed,'[14] but he never hints that her presence may also illustrate the virtue by which redemption can be effected. On Hamilton's reading, Belphoebe stands apart from the balance of the allegory as a monitory but otherwise irrelevant image of perfection. Berger's analysis is to the same effect: Belphoebe is 'prelapsarian'; she is 'withdrawn from and untouched by the stain of sin'; she is therefore an idea which has no consequences for a virtue whose pertinence is to the fallen world and which derives from nature rather than from grace. Whereas temperance so conceived aims at a measure of goodness possible for unassisted mortals, Belphoebe 'represents a kind of perfection impossible to mortals.'[15]

The obvious question raised by a patristic reading is whether such perfection is in fact impossible – whether it is not a reasonable expectation for those who, by mortifying the passions, achieve ἀπάθεια. If temperance, like holiness, is a deifying virtue, may not the deified Belphoebe represent it? Instead of being prelapsarian, may she not rather be an image of mankind redeemed by ἐγκράτεια? Indeed, the allusions to Well and Tree, which signify to Hamilton Belphoebe's unfallen nature, are intimately connected with Red Crosse's redemption from the Fall; in the context of Book One the healing of the sick and raising of the dead signify man's return to Paradise rather than his original residence there. And in Scripture and Christian tradition such powers belong to the redeemed rather than the unfallen; no miracles are attributed to Adam and Eve but to the saints. When we are told that the mere sight of Belphoebe could heal and revive, we are probably supposed to recall that Saint Peter's shadow when he passed on the street or Saint Paul's handkerchief carried to the sick had similar virtues.[16] These are the *charismata* which Christ gives to men and women who are deified by His flesh, who, having become impassible, possess and transmit the virtues of the sacraments. The ascription of such powers to Belphoebe suggests that rather than being 'untouched by the stain of sin' and thus irrelevant to an allegory of temperance she personifies the condition of humanity when temperance (as ascetic mortification) has cleansed it of that stain and restored its original divinity.

That Spenser is indeed concerned in the portrait with temperance as ἐγκράτεια seems clear enough. Belphoebe's principal activity is hunting with her boar spear, quelling the 'saluage beastes in her victorious play' (II, iii, 29). Her subsequent use of this 'Iauelin bright' against the lustful Braggadocchio ('mistaken' a few stanzas earlier for a 'beast' [II, iii, 34]) suggests that the 'saluage beasts' are the passions. Like her practice, Belphoebe's theory is ascetic: 'Where ease abounds, yt's eath to doe amis; / But who his limbs with labours, and his mind / Behaues with cares, cannot so easie mis' (II, iii, 40). Therefore Belphoebe prefers forests to courts; in an allegory in which passions are beasts, her woods and waves become Anthony's desert. And her asceticism, like Anthony's, is integral to her *theosis*; the description of her face fuses the two motifs. 'Flesh it seemed not, / But heauenly pourtraict of bright Angels hew' (II, iii, 22). On first reading that seems merely to say that Belphoebe's countenance is divine, but the link between the angelic and the (apparently) fleshless recalls the common patristic association of ἀπάθεια with the incorporeal nature of angels. Mortification of passions takes man out of the flesh – 'even from the nature of man he is delivered ... and hath arrived ... at the very serenity of the angels.'[17] By achieving divine apathy Clement's gnostic not only becomes 'like to

God' but 'truly equal to an angel.'[18] To be angelic means both to be deified and to be impassible – conditions synonymous in patristic literature, as they seem to be in Belphoebe.

Belphoebe also illustrates the Fathers' oxymoronic active impassivity; her *theosis* is like the gnostic's, at one and the same time an achieved transfiguration and a struggle to achieve transfiguration in spiritual combat: the symbols of her deification are also her weapons of war. That her eyes are kindled 'at th'heauenly makers light' (II, iii, 23) signifies her beatitude and its source; it explains as well why a glance from those eyes can quell the passions. Their beams are 'So passing persant, and so wondrous bright, / That quite bereau'd the rash beholders sight' (II, iii, 23). Hamilton's gloss is astute: 'Belphoebe's eyes have the blinding power of the sun given to Arthur's shield (I vii 35.9) and Fidelia's face "That could haue dazd the rash beholders sight" (I x 12.8).' The shield is an obvious instrument of spiritual warfare, and Fidelia's another deified countenance; by combining the two, Belphoebe becomes the gnostic in both his active and apathetic aspects. And that the activity is warfare against passion is clear from the balance of the passage. *Rash*, as Hamilton remarks, 'signifies lustful,'[19] and in Belphoebe's case the 'rash beholder' is 'the blinded god' himself. Cupid tried to kindle his 'lustfull fire' at Belphoebe's eyes 'but had no might': 'She broke his wanton darts, and quenched base desire' (II, iii, 23).

V

Belphoebe so interpreted seems relevant to Book Two in several ways. Her asceticism, I suggest, illuminates Guyon's by manifesting the beauty and divine consequence of a virtue which in him seems to many negative – in something of the same way that Una's radiant face and white vestment afford a visible representation of Red Crosse's holiness. Belphoebe's κράτος anticipates Arthur's in his battle with Pyrochles and Cymochles and in his conquest of Maleger and Guyon's in the razing of the Bower. Had Belphoebe any part in the action of the allegory, it would certainly be in one or another of those violent episodes in which the lusts of the flesh are slain. Furthermore, interpreting her divine beauty as a signature of temperance should mollify the critics who think Guyon excessive and insensitive in his destruction of beauty. In effect she redefines beauty, showing that it belongs to the spirit rather than the flesh and therefore requires the mortification of the latter. When we witness Guyon effecting that mortification, recollection of Belphoebe should explain and justify his action. Finally her 'antithesis to Acrasia' (Hamilton) personifies very accurately Basil's vocabulary of the virtues in its application to man's fall and redemption and suggests that when Guyon completes his quest, he will have fulfilled the expectations raised by Belphoebe – the death of passion and man's consequent recovery of the divine image.

Belphoebe also redefines temperance, and at a crucial moment in the allegory: just after Guyon has committed Ruddymane to Medina's ministrations. Medina's learning 'from pleasures poyson to abstaine' anticipates by only twenty-two stanzas (and those constitute a comic interlude) the appearance of Belphoebe, who regards pleasure as poisonous and who practices abstinence. Of the many critics who find Medina wanting, I know of none who has noticed the close juxtaposition of the two ladies or asked what it signifies. A likely answer, I believe, is that Ruddymane should have been committed to Belphoebe; that he requires the ardor of the hunt and protection of the boar spear rather than a well-tempered feast.

Figuratively, perhaps, he receives that discipline, for Belphoebe sets Book Two on a new course: after she appears, temperance becomes more like her – more nearly rigorous and ascetical than before. Stephen Fallon uses Rosemond Tuve's theory of 'entrelacement' to explain why, when we get back to Guyon after the allegedly irrelevant digression in canto three, 'he is not where we left him ... but ... has been pulled by the events ... written about some one else.'[20] 'The Guyon we find walking to his meeting with Furor and Occasion in canto iv is a more developed character than the Guyon who set out from the Castle of Medina in canto iii.'[21] We should probably discard the notion of character development and say instead that another conception of temperance goes to meet Furor and Occasion. From the moment of Belphoebe's manifestation both Guyon and the Palmer become progressively more like her; they seem to come under her secret influence.

One evidence of that is Guyon's becoming, like Belphoebe, pedestrian. The allegorical significance of Braggadocchio's theft of Brigadore has been much discussed. Fallon introduces, only to dismiss, the possibility that Spenser refers to the identification of horses with passions in

the Phaedrus: 'The theft of the horse seems then to have been devised
... to point out the contrast between Guyon's reasoned restraint and
Braggadocchio's consequent license. But this can hardly be all there is
to it.' I agree that 'Spenser would not have required Guyon to trudge
on foot for three books merely to reinforce a contrast that is already
perfectly obvious,'[22] but he might have done so in order to associate
Guyon with Belphoebe and to transmit to him the version of temperance she signifies. Fallon clearly thinks of temperance as good mixture
or control of passion – 'reasoned restraint' – rather than passion's
removal. Is it not possible that the loss of Brigadore illustrates a transition from temperance as σωφροσύνη to temperance as ἐγκράτεια and
ἀπάθεια? Guyon horsed would indeed be a conventional symbol of
'reasoned restraint,' of what Medina represents; Guyon on foot would
signify Belphoebe's entire freedom from passion. Good horsemanship
– temperance-as-moderation – would be preferable to Braggadocchio's
lack of control, but want of a horse is arguably better than either – Belphoebe's speed on foot suggests a source of strength independent of
animal energy. Guyon as a pedestrian goes and fights more ploddingly
than she, no doubt because his exposition of temperance in canto four
is still in the making; but in his struggles on foot which follow, Guyon
exercises a greater measure of Belphoebe's κράτος than he has before. In
cantos one and two his temperance has shown itself only in restraint,
moderation, or in counsel thereto. Now, unhorsed, he becomes a warrior, and in his various encounters with Furor, Occasion, Pyrochles, and
Cymochles he behaves as Clement's gnostic wrestler, who fights
against passions as the martyrs fought literal beasts. That all these
struggles end indecisively and that the two principal exponents of passion remain to threaten Guyon further and to be slain by Arthur does
not so much disqualify Guyon's pedestrian achievements as point once
again to an as yet incomplete demonstration of temperance.

Belphoebe's influence seems also to be discernible in the Palmer,
who in canto four gives voice to a much more rigorous asceticism than
we could have anticipated from his earlier interpretations of temperance. These stronger statements are in response to Phedon's Othello-
like story and may be owing in part to its grisliness. The youth is
another 'image of mortalitie' in whom 'raging passion with fierce tyrannie / Robs reason of her due regalitie,' but this time the Palmer says
nothing of temperance's 'golden squire'; he offers sterner counsel. Phe-

don is a 'most wretched man' who has lent the bridle to affections (II, iv, 34), and the Palmer argues for more than a tighter rein. 'Contend' with passions, he admonishes, while they are still weak, 'For when they once to perfect strength do grow, / Strong warres they make, and cruell battry bend / Gainst fort of Reason, it to ouerthrow' (II, iv, 34). The preventative which the Palmer urges appears to be mortification: 'Wrath, gealosie, griefe, loue do thus expell' (II, iv, 35) – not moderate, discipline, or control, but *expel*. That is counsel to practice ἐγκράτεια of Saint Basil's sort, and it is the first such explicit counsel offered in Book Two.

The Palmer's inclusion of *love* in his list of passions is of particular interest, for it assimilates his theory to Belphoebe's practice and recalls once again the patristic identification of virginity with temperance. Phedon's initial love of Claribell seems blameless, but that is evidently beside the Palmer's point. We gather from the latter's admonition that eros by its nature is as reprehensible a passion as wrath, jealousy, and grief and as much in need of expulsion from the soul. Love even comes off worse than the rest; 'Wrath is a fire, and gealosie a weede, / Griefe is a flood' – all natural things – but 'loue a monster fell' a *lusus naturae*. Worse still, love is bred in 'filth' and to prevent love one must wipe the filth 'cleane away' (II, iv, 35). We can rationalize that the Palmer is talking about love of Acrasia's rather than, say, of Britomart's sort, but that is to evade the issue. There is no Britomart in Book Two, and it is scarcely fair to the allegory to import her. The only love affair in the Book is Phedon's and the only marriage Mordant's and Amavia's; both end in comparable disasters, both destroyed by passion. There is nothing in fact in Book Two to suggest that love is not precisely what the Palmer says; the filth in which it breeds is presumably the passions, and to wipe them 'cleane away' seems requisite for salvation. No set of ideas could be more thoroughly patristic, and if they seem just as thoroughly unSpenserian that may be because we have embraced too uncritically the prevailing assumption that Spenser is always and in all circumstances the champion of marriage. His conception of temperance, at any rate, seems to entail Belphoebe's perpetual virginity.[23]

VI

It is possibly to demonstrate that temperance requires sexual abstinence – 'perfect continence' – that Spenser makes eros so attractive in the Bower of Bliss and allows Guyon to be seriously tempted by it, showing thereby both how seductive the temptation is and how necessary the resistance. Spenser certainly could have done otherwise if he wished, for he does otherwise in various ways elsewhere. Eros in the Garden of Adonis is attractive but not titillating. Red Crosse is tempted by Duessa and yields to the temptation, but the reader is not involved – possibly because of the entirely unattractive personification of lust as a deadly sin and, retrospectively at least, because of what he learns about Duessa when Arthur exposes her. Sexual temptation in Books Three and Four is either comical (Paridell, Hellenore, Malbecco), diabolical (Busirane), or grotesque (Lust). Indeed there is no other place in *The Faerie Queene* in which the poetry involves the reader in the sexual excitement which tempts the hero – and indeed in sexual excitement that does not: the depiction of Verdant and Acrasia is by any measure heavily erotic. The naked bathing girls rear Guyon's 'courage cold' (II, xii, 68), and the whole presentation of the Bower seems calculated to raise the reader's.

A probable clue to Spenser's strategy is to be found at the beginning of canto six, as prelude to Guyon's first exposure to dalliance on Phaedria's floating island. Sexual pleasure, Spenser says,

> doth allure the weaker sense
> So strongly, that vneathes it can refraine
> From that, which feeble nature couets faine;
> But griefe and wrath, that be her enemies,
> And foes of life, she better can restraine.
>
> (II, vi, 1)

The contrast between what nature covets and 'foes of life' suggests that sexual sweetness is a friend of life, which is of course self-evident: erotic pleasure begets children. That Spenser understood that friendship and celebrated it elsewhere no reader of his poems need be reminded. In the Bower of Bliss, however, he is presenting the obverse of what appears so wholesome in, for instance, the *Epithalamion*. He is saying that erotic temptation is the most difficult to combat because it is a temptation to something good; to deny sex is to deny life, which one 'vneathes' can do. Indeed to do it is to die. To convince us of this paradox of desire Spenser needed to present the reader as well as

Guyon with sexual temptation – to make us feel the contradiction as well as understand it. Had he only wished us to understand, he could have personified lust unattractively, as he does when he demonstrates its ugliness and wickedness. But by doing that he could not have represented the cost and character of its mortification adequately. To do the latter he must make us feel ourselves that the sweetness which must be denied is one which nature herself covets.

But that it *must* be denied seems, in Book Two at least, unequivocal. However nearly impossible the feat may be and however destructive of life, the legend of temperance leaves little doubt that sexual desire like all other passions must be put to death – the Bower must be pulled down. The many fervent objections to Guyon's doing that surely reflect a recognition that he is in fact destroying life and beauty. Spenser's point in making the Bower so attractive and its demolition so rigorous is to make us see as much – that the only way to get rid of lust is to deny our vital energies, to be 'unnatural.' Efforts like C.S. Lewis's to represent the Bower as, contrary to our first impressions, sexually unattractive have missed the point and thus cheated us of the intense drama of the ascetic idea at work in canto twelve. Freudian critics and others like Stephen Greenblatt who borrow from Freud, who censure Guyon (and Spenser) for sexual repression, are closer to the mark, for Spenser seems to have known exactly what such repression entails and to have approved of it. Where Greenblatt goes wrong is in importing his contemporary, secular assumptions into the poem and supposing that his pejorative view of repression is universally applicable. When he says 'the threat of ... absorption [into the sensual] ... triggers Guyon's climactic violence,'[24] he is correct in his analysis of motive (Spenser's motive, not Guyon's) but incorrect in his moral judgment. The fear of absorption bespeaks for Greenblatt an inordinate (masculine) fear of the sexual, the primitive, and the feminine; for Spenser, we can be reasonably certain, it bespeaks an altogether ordinate recognition of the danger of eros, however good a friend of life, to the soul.

The soul is, finally, the issue. If the passions, even those which feeble nature covets, disfigure the divine image in which man was created, the justification for snuffing out natural instincts is obvious: to attain to a spiritual condition superior to the natural. That is a justification beyond the Freudians' and New Historicists' ken. 'Temperance,' says Greenblatt, which he defines as 'the avoidance of extremes, the "sober government" of the body, the achievement of the Golden Mean ... must be constituted paradoxically by a supreme act of destructive excess.'[25] If Spenser meant instead by temperance what the Fathers meant, there is no paradox, and no excess, in that 'supreme act.' Rather it is the only way to achieve ἀπάθεια in the battle with sexual temptation, the only way fallen man can recover his lost, original likeness to God, the only way Guyon can be conformed perfectly to Belphoebe or run 'like race' to Red Crosse. Were the compensation less perfect one would be foolish, perhaps as insane as the Freudians believe such people to be, to pay the price. No wonder secular critics think Guyon excessive; the only recompense they imagine for the destruction of life and beauty and 'sweetnesse' is 'avoidance of extremes, the "sober government" of the body, the achievement of the Golden Mean.' The Bower must be destroyed 'because its gratifications ... threaten "civility" – civilization – which for Spenser is achieved only through renunciation and the constant exercise of power.'[26] Were that so, only a person holding to a deformed (and again secular) conception of civilization (to which Greenblatt seems to believe Spenser held) would do what Guyon does. Conversely, if doing what he does restores men to the radiance and purity manifest in Belphoebe, the destruction of life and beauty is a spiritual necessity – a version of the central Christian paradox of dying in order to live.

VII

Still another version of that paradox, also in its ascetical manifestation, may account for Guyon's notorious faint at the end of canto seven. That much debated episode, like the figure of Belphoebe, makes new, and I believe better, sense when subjected to a patristic interpretation.

CHAPTER SEVEN

Temperance in the Cave of Mammon

I

There is very nearly a consensus that the Knight of Temperance in the Cave of Mammon is remarkable either for his personal or natural weakness or for the deficiency of temperance, and that his fainting indicates as much. Critics who follow Woodhouse emphasize the insufficiency of a pagan or classical virtue in a struggle with the powers of darkness. 'It is axiomatic in Book II,' says Alpers, 'that we cannot say, "Seke ye fyrst the kyngdome of God" ...'[1] Guyon can only respond, therefore, to Mammon in secular terms. Christianizing critics take much the same view because they believe Guyon comes to rely on grace only after he faints. The paradigm and principal source of that interpretation is Berger's reading, according to which the knight's collapse at the end of canto seven demonstrates the limitation, and exhaustion, of natural virtue and creates a spiritual vacuum which grace (in the persons of Arthur and the Palmer) can fill in the eighth and subsequent cantos. There are many variations on that thesis. Some critics, like Berger himself and Anthea Hume, believe Guyon to be personally at fault from the very beginning of the episode – guilty, says Berger, of curiosity or, says Hume, of a 'mistaken self-trust [which] may lead a human being into dangers from which only God's mercy can extricate him.'[2] Pride, in other words, cometh before the fall. Others blame the fall simply on the Fall; Guyon faints, not because he has sinned but because Adam sinned. That reading accounts for Guyon's impeccable conduct throughout the ordeal – his imperviousness to Mammon's temptations – and yet still explains the faint: 'The image of Guyon prostrate on the earth,' says Patrick Cullen, 'is an image of man's bondage to the flesh, to the old Adam within who is "of the earth, earthly."'[3]

Against these familiar – and repetitive – interpretations stands the evidence of Spenser's Christian typology and numerology. Interpreters have long recognized analogies between Guyon's temptations and Christ's in the wilderness, and more recently Hieatt and others have called attention to the forty stanzas required to narrate Guyon's three days beneath the earth.[4] An obvious inference, upon which Cullen builds his interpretation, is that Spenser is conflating the three days of the Harrowing with the forty days of Christ's fasting – an appropriate association for a legend of temperance. More recently still, Nohrnberg has reminded us that Red Crosse's version of the Harrowing also occupies forty stanzas. Nohrnberg attributes the numbering in both cases to a tradition that Christ was beneath the earth for forty hours between his burial and resurrection;[5] but that numerology need not exclude an allusion to the wilderness temptation, for the forty days of fasting translate liturgically into Lent and thus acquire paschal significance. Such associations suggest that withstanding Mammon is the allegorical equivalent both of resisting Satan's temptations in the wilderness and defeating him finally in Hell; yet even critics who take the numerology and typology seriously and draw what seems the likely conclusion that Guyon is in some way or other Christ, pull back from the identification. Their basis for hesitation is, once more, the faint. Hieatt is an instance; he goes so far as to compare Guyon with 'Milton's great abstainer' who 'comes through his long temptations triumphantly and is angelically ministered to' and to say that Guyon's 'imitation of the divine is licit' only to shy away from his own inference because Guyon collapses: 'That Guyon is not divine, but merely human, is no more a reproach to him than it is to Beowulf in his mortal dragonfight. Strong beyond most men, he yet faints ...'[6]

The argument is circular. Critics begin with the assumption that temperance is a secular and defective virtue or Guyon a secular and defective exemplar and therefore anticipate its, his, limitation. When Guyon faints, he presumably demonstrates that limitation and everyone is satisfied. But suppose we begin with another – the patristic – assumption about temperance (no more arbitrary a starting point than our usual classical or secular one): that temperance is every bit as Christian and

effective as holiness and is in fact a dimension of holiness. In that case
we clearly cannot attribute the faint to a deficiency in the virtue;
Anthony's *ascesis* will not prove lacking. Of course Guyon may prove
lacking, and those critics who think so may be correct. On the other
hand, as I have tried to show, a patristic conception of temperance and
its fruits accounts for what have seemed to be defects in his character.
More immediately, his impeccable conduct in the Cave suggests that
the faint is not to be taken as a measure of moral weakness and that we
should seek an explanation for it consonant with moral strength and
with the canto's Christian allusions.

   Curiously, inadvertently, Cullen suggests what that explanation
might be – a thesis which is the obverse of his own but also its mirror
image. Cullen's is the best interpretation of canto seven because he
believes the three days and forty stanzas mean what they say. He is
therefore compelled to assert that 'the faint of the hero is by no means
inconsistent with his ostensible *imitatio Christi*.'[7] On the other hand
Cullen is as hesitant in his affirmation as the syntax of his sentence; for
so considerable is the influence of the schools that he cannot relinquish
the notion of a flawed hero and a secular virtue. Guyon, he tells us,
makes a 'Christlike assertion of virtue' which he cannot live up to; the
abortive attempt 'reveals the Adamic limits of [his] virtue.' 'Only
through Christ can man be redeemed from the flesh, and only through
the intervention of Christ's grace can the devil ... be defeated.' Guyon
tries to defeat the devil – to play Christ – without access to that grace,
by means of a 'classical or purely human temperance' which 'can hold
the devil at bay, though precariously [Medina's role]' not vanquish him
as Christ did. The faint is the 'inevitable culmination of the Adamic
weakness he has manifested throughout the ordeal.'[8] The conclusion is
pure Berger, and if it be true, how can the faint *not* be inconsistent with
Guyon's *imitatio Christi*? How can the same event reveal Guyon to be
the old Adam and yet be consonant with his role as a type of the new?

   Cullen's solution – the inadequate thesis which prompts recourse to
its opposite – is to separate Christ's humanity from His divinity.
Guyon becomes Christ and thus fulfills the expectations of Spenser's
symbolism by an 'approximation' to Christ *as man* but not to Christ as
God. That means that Guyon imitates Christ adequately in the wilderness but not in the Harrowing, for in Cullen's formulation 'the wilderness provides the locus for the ultimate reaches of classical or natural

ethics.' 'In the wilderness, Christ as the new Adam demonstrated Himself as the perfect man, *without the assistance of His divinity*' (italics added). 'But in the Harrowing of Hell, Christ performed a supernatural mission, one that could be accomplished only by the sufficient sacrifice of the *deus homo* on the cross.'[9] Guyon 'as *homo*' but not *deus homo* can imitate the former role but not the latter. That is in effect to say that during the forty days of fasting and temptation Christ was in roughly the same circumstance which most critics attribute to Guyon – dependent on natural virtue rather than on grace. Therefore, to the extent that natural virtue sufficed for Christ's victory, Guyon can be Christ. But since Christ performed the Harrowing divinely, Guyon, without grace, cannot be Christ in that venture. When he tries, he faints. 'Christ's resistance in the wilderness can be approximated by man without grace, but only His resistance and not the full debelling of the devil.'[10]

What Cullen has done is to introduce the Woodhousean distinction between nature and grace into the theology of the Incarnation, and he admits as much: 'The conflation in the Cave of the Temptation in the Wilderness with the Harrowing of Hell is ... an outgrowth of the central distinction drawn in Book II' between 'classical or purely human temperance [which] can restrain the flesh' and the grace of Christ by which man 'can ... be redeemed from the flesh.'[11] That conception allows Guyon to be Christ without being deified – without, presumably, even being a Christian. Guyon can be natural man practicing a 'classical or purely human temperance' without the assistance of grace and still imitate Christ because Christ, *as man*, allegedly did the same so long as he merely resisted the devil rather than sought to overthrow him. That is an ingenious way to have one's cake and eat it too, but does the thesis really satisfy the expectations generated by the Christian symbols? If Guyon imitates only Christ's humanity, does *imitatio Christi* mean anything *essentially* different from what Cullen calls *imitatio Adamis*? I stress *essentially* because Christ as man was obedient to God and resisted the temptation to which Adam yielded; but if an 'approximation' to Christ cannot issue in a transcendence of the 'purely human,' does it have an *essential* meaning? If not, does it justify Spenser's symbolism and numerology?

A further reason for questioning Cullen's interpretation is that Spenser's holding such a view of the Incarnation is historically

improbable. Even if his theology was determined entirely by the
Church of England, he would have been unlikely to isolate Christ's
humanity from His divinity or to have suggested that in one of the
great soteriological mysteries Christ acted only as man and in another
as both God and man. The second of the Thirty-nine Articles says
explicitly and firmly that the 'two whole and perfect Natures ... were
joined together in one Person, *never to be divided*' (italics added). That
teaching is transconfessional and antique. Aquinas quotes Cyril of
Alexandria's anathema against anyone who '*believes that some* [things
said of Christ] *are to be applied to the Man*, and ... *some to the Word alone*';
and Aquinas adds, 'Of the Man may be said what belongs to the
Divine Nature ... and of God may be said what belongs to the human
nature' (*ST*, III, xvi, 4).[12] There can obviously, therefore, be no such
thing as an *imitatio Christi* which pertains only to the Lord's humanity,
for in the Incarnation not only is God man but Man is God. Though
'the two natures are preserved in [Christ] after the union,' says John of
Damascus, 'we do not hold that each is separate and by itself, but that
they are united to each other in one compound subsistence.' 'The Word
appropriates to Himself the attributes of humanity: for all that pertains
to His holy flesh is His: and He imparts to the flesh His own attributes
by way of communication in virtue of the interpenetration of the parts
one with another ... For the Lord of Glory is one and the same with
Him who is in nature and in truth the Son of Man.' Therefore, 'When
He is called Man and Son of Man, He still keeps the properties and glories of the divine nature.'[13]

Not only is this orthodox Christology the one most likely to have
recommended itself to so orthodox a Christian as Spenser seems to
have been; this is the only Christology which in fact allows us to conceive of any man as *microchristus*. Without it, the term becomes – as it
does in Cullen's interpretation of it – merely a figure of speech. With it
we can take seriously what the three days and forty stanzas imply –
that like Red Crosse in the dragon fight, Guyon in Mammon's Cave is a
true type of the Harrower, the *miles christi* become 'Christ himself.' For
it is precisely because the Word 'imparts to the flesh His own
attributes' that man can be deified: 'the unmixed unity of preserved
oneness of the Hypostasis ... in the preserved duality of natures'
effects, says John of Damascus in the Homily on the Transfiguration,
'the incomprehensible theosis of mortal flesh.'[14] By taking Spenser's

numerology and typology seriously, Cullen brings us to the very edge of a coherent interpretation of Guyon's descent. We need only take just as seriously the theology which historically underlies that numerology and typology in order to grasp their full meaning and to understand why Guyon's 'imitation of the divine is licit.'

If, however, we do that, we are brought back immediately to the problem of the faint, the motive for Cullen's appeal to an improbable Christology in the first place; for how can a genuine *microchristus* faint? The answer may be simpler than it seems; in fact we might ask, can a genuine *microchristus* do other than faint? If the *Christus* was subject to death, should we not expect the *microchristus* to be also? (Spenser treats Guyon's faint as though it were a literal death.) Is it in fact possible to speak of *theosis* through participation in Christ without speaking of participation in His death? Baptism, which deifies, is into that death (as Red Crosse's descent into the Well of Life makes clear) because deification derives from the union of divine and human natures, not solely through the strength of the former but also through the weakness of the latter; because God became frail and mortal, frailty and mortality become the means to – even the signature of – man's becoming God. Although Christ's 'divine nature never endured the Cross,' says John of Damascus, nevertheless because of its union with humanity, 'the Lord of Glory is said to have been crucified.'[15] Man must therefore be 'crucified with Christ' in order to be united with 'the Lord of Glory.' To speak in terms closer to the allegory of canto seven, to win the victory over Satan (or Mammon) through Christ's all-powerful divinity, man must conform himself to the weakness of Christ's humanity. A Byzantine matins hymn says, 'By [His] *divine strength* ... Christ, through *weakness of the flesh* ... didst lay low the mighty one' (italics added);[16] the *microchristus* must lay him low by the same paradoxical means. And for a knight of temperance, what could be a more appropriate symbol of participation in Christ's divinely empowering weakness and His life-giving death than a faint (a 'death') induced by watching, fasting, hunger, and thirst?

The Church's principal models for these ascetic labors are the early monks who sought solitary lives of abstinence in the Egyptian desert, and Guyon's ἐγκράτεια in Mammon's cave recalls stories of their rigorous self-denial. Anthony is the most famous of these, but Spenser could have learned the legends of other famous fasters from one or another of the collections of lives and sayings of the desert fathers which circulated in the West.[17] (An especially likely source would have been the *Collationes S.S Patrum* and the *Eremitae Monasticarum Institutionum* of John Cassian.)[18] These accounts celebrate lengthy watchings and the most rigorous fasting as means to achieving *theosis*. Spenser could also have known the legend of Mary of Egypt, which appears in the *Legenda Aurea* and is alluded to on several occasions in the *Triodion*. Mary's fame (in Eastern Christendom) is second only to Anthony's, and she is honored liturgically as a symbol of Lenten abstinence. She lived forty-seven years in the desert, alone, naked, and without shelter, on three loaves of bread which she purchased when she began her fast. During the first seventeen years 'the desires of my body ... came in my thought'; thereafter she achieved (received) the peace of ἀπάθεια: 'I have been delivered of all temptations.'[19] At the end of her fast (and of her life), in the paschal season (on Holy Thursday night, the night of the Passion), she walked on the waters of the Jordan to receive the sacrament. Having died to the flesh through ἐγκράτεια, she lived miraculously in the Spirit – and very specifically by means of the suffering and deified body of Christ in whose power over nature she participated. 'By thine excellent [or, perhaps, 'extreme'] way of life on earth, O Mother, thou hast attained to heavenly dispassion (ἀπάθεια)'; 'by thy strange way of life thou hast astonished all, [both] ranks of angels and assemblies of men, having lived bodilessly and having surpassed nature; being as one without matter, O Mary, walking on thy feet thou hast crossed over Jordan.' We have already seen that to be 'as one without matter' – which is to say, as an angel – means for the Fathers to have 'attained to heavenly dispassion.' Mary's legend makes very clear – and liturgically in the context of the forty days – that such freedom is the fruit of the most extreme denial of the flesh. Another Lenten hymn invokes Mary's intercessions with Christ, 'for whom thou hast caused thy flesh to waste.'[20]

Guyon faints when he has caused his flesh to waste by traditional ascetic practices. In view of the numerology of canto seven, his three foodless, sleepless days recall the ancient discipline of fasting and watching during the *triduum sanctum* so as by the mortification of passion to be united to Christ's Passion and thereby attain His Resurrection. Much has been made of Guyon's motives for entering Mammon's cave, and those critics who believe him culpable regard the faint as a poetic justice. In view, however, of the Lenten and Paschal numerology, we may just as reasonably argue that he entered the cave precisely *in order to faint* – like Anthony or Mary in a 'desert wildernesse' (II, vii, 2) to exhaust himself for Christ. What seems to Anthea Hume and others spiritual presumption, Guyon's excessive confidence in himself which the faint serves to mortify, can as legitimately be interpreted as a version of the desert monk's quest for radical self-denial. Or even of Christ's: according to John Chrysostom, Christ went 'not into a city and forum, but into a wilderness' (seeking both hardship and solitude) because He was 'minded to attract the Devil'; Christ fasted forty days so as by being hungry to give the Devil 'a handle.'[21] That sounds like presumption, and Chrysostom admits that Christ's example is a dangerous one for fallen men; but apparently not for His saints, His knights of temperance. A boast of ancient Christians and an astonishment to their persecutors was that thousands who might have escaped torture nevertheless flocked to martyrdom, deliberately putting to the ultimate test the achievement of their *ascesis*. And Athanasius tells us that Anthony chose to sleep in tombs so as to be more easily accessible to demonic assault.[22] He did not merely endure suffering heroically when it was imposed upon him but went in search of it so as by it to be united with Christ who did the same. Such conduct may seem presumptuous (and intemperate) by classical and even by some sets of Christian standards, but it is wholly in accord with a desire to become divine in Christ by putting the passions to death. A Lenten hymn praises the desert monks for having deliberately 'forced nature.'[23] If Guyon's faint can be conceived as owing to such forcing, so far from revealing flaws in him or his virtue his collapse becomes a signature of his playing to perfection the role to which the numerology of canto seven points.

II

Another possible signature is another facet of the canto which has been puzzling to interpreters – what Alpers calls Guyon's 'chilly self-assurance,' his indifference to Mammon's offers.[24] That Guyon is not tempted seems certain, and though many critics acknowledge this, few have explored its significance. Lest there be any doubt of Guyon's immunity to temptation, Spenser tells us that had the knight 'inclined

... at all' to any of Mammon's offers (II, vii, 64), the attendant fiend
would have rent him into a thousand pieces. Guyon does not, apparently, resist temptation; he does not suffer it. Inclination transcends
action; passion may demand what the will refuses. Presumably Guyon
would have been torn asunder had he even so much as for an instant
desired either Mammon's gold or Mammon's daughter. That he
emerges intact, to Mammon's and the fiend's dismay, guarantees his
perfect purity of motive and proves the adventure is not a *psychomachia*
in the usual sense. Berger attributes Guyon's indifference to his playing the part of the Aristotelian *megalopsychos*: 'Guyon is not the Christian relying upon God but the megalopsychos relying on himself.'[25]
An alternative explanation, one consonant both with the Christian elements in the canto and with a faint induced by watching and fasting, is
that Guyon's freedom from temptation manifests the principal fruit of
watching and fasting – the ἀπάθεια of the gnostic.

The Fathers depict the great martyrs and ascetics as Spenser depicts
Guyon – indifferent and self-assured in the face of temptation and
demonic assault. They can afford to give the devil 'a handle' because
they have achieved independence of the passions through which alone
the devil can assail them. A definitive characteristic of *theosis* is the
ability to reject lust without experiencing temptation to lust and to
engage in the warfare against all spiritual adversaries without wrath.
To be passible, to be even partially in subjection to the passions one
fights against, would be to be less than wholly effective as a soldier in
spiritual warfare. Such residual passibility, it goes without saying, is
the circumstance of everyman, but the saint, 'the *true* wrestler' – the
knight of temperance – is in a different spiritual category. For him victory is certain because he fights with Christ's dispassion. There is no
suggestion that Christ in the wilderness desired what Satan had to
offer. Though after forty days He was 'an hungred' (Matthew 4:2), his
readiness of response suggests that He did not desire to turn a stone
into bread. Nor is there any indication that He desired the kingdoms of
the world or to present a dazzling display of His divinity. In each of the
temptations He manifests a self-assurance commensurate with His
divine ἀπάθεια. Had Christ desired – 'inclined ... at all' – He could not,
presumably, have delivered man from desire; refusal in spite of desire
would have been insufficient to have won for flesh (and in flesh) the
independence of passion which He bestows on His saints. Though

Christ's encounter with Satan in the Harrowing is not recorded in Scripture, the Fathers and the liturgies insist that in Hades as in the wilderness the Lord was impassible in His humanity as well as in His divinity. Patristic exegesis and many hymns interpret 'free among the dead' (*Septuagint*) in Psalm 88 (87) to signify the Savior's perfect freedom from desire – that in the three days as in the forty He was wholly without passion.[26] One of the Sunday hymns for the Resurrection goes so far as to set up a cause-and-effect relationship between ἀπάθεια and the Harrowing, saying in effect that Christ was able to conquer Hell because He did not desire what the Devil could offer Him: 'Thou hast destroyed Hades, for Thou wast not tempted by it.'[27]

Since the saints re-enact Christ's victory, we should not expect them to be tempted either. George in his martyrdom is not represented as being in agony and therefore in danger of consenting to his torturers. When Dacian requires George to drink 'strong venom,' the Saint 'took it and made the sign of the cross on it, and anon drank it without grieving him any thing.' Then Dacian commanded 'that they should put him in a caldron full of molten lead, and when S. George entered therein, by the virtue of our Lord it seemed that he was in a bath well at ease.'[28] Such ease is likely to disappoint modern readers in much the same way that Guyon's imperviousness has disappointed – or at least puzzled – some critics; but that is almost certainly because in the Western Christian tradition, especially in its Protestant version, we expect the saint to be an everyman. The point of George's legend (and I believe of Guyon's) is not how much the saint suffered and how sorely tempted he was on account of suffering but that as a man deified by Christ's suffering he was impassible. The martyrs are not characteristically presented as men and women whose steadfastness is hard won against the assaults of passion but as being, on account of their asceticism, impervious to pain. Three ancient 'common' hymns for martyrs make the point precisely: 'Thy victorious martyrs O Lord, imitating the ranks of the angels, endured the tortures as though they were bodiless'; 'Seeing clearly the severing of your limbs, glorying, ye did rejoice in the streams of blood'; and 'in the fountain of fire, as upon a water of rest, the holy martyr rejoiced.' Behind the imagery of the third passage lies the account of the Three Holy Children refreshed by dew in the Babylonian furnace, whose watching and fasting had made them indifferent to temptation and impervious to torture: 'Once in Babylon, fasting, having hardened the children, made them stronger than the fire.' We hear an echo of the same motif in another Lenten martyrs' hymn: 'Burning in the divine love of Christ, the blessed martyrs, praising Him, walked upon coals of fire as upon dew.'[29] A similar emphasis informs the legends of ascetics. When Athanasius tells us that Anthony won victory over a 'spirit of fornication,'[30] we are not supposed to understand that Anthony desired to fornicate and struggled success-fully to resist but that he was subjected to demonic assault (compara-ble in its physical severity to what Dacian imposed on George and Nebuchadnezzar on the children) because he did not desire. At no point in the *Life* does Athanasius suggest that Anthony was pervious to lust and wrath. Had Anthony 'inclined ... at all' (even though he had resisted the inclination), the devils would presumably have had him and rent him. Self-confident in his impassibility he emerges from their torments fresh and unscathed.

Guyon's responses to Mammon reflect such self-confidence. Some of these are difficult to interpret on any reading of the canto – ill-gotten gains, the requirements of chivalry, a mistress not mentioned before or after (who may but just as easily may not be Gloriana) – but whatever else they mean, they suggest that Guyon is 'free among the dead.' They read like polite evasions, ways of putting Mammon off until the three-days' ordeal is done – the sort of evasions which would only be possi-ble for a man who not only did not want at all what he saw but who was fully confident of his spiritual resources. The question which per-sists, of course, is why not overtly Christian responses, something comparable to George's making the sign of the Cross when he was plunged into the cauldron? If Guyon has been assimilated to Christ by the grace of *ascesis*, why should he not respond theologically, as Christ did in the wilderness; or, as Alpers asks, why not say to Mammon what Christ commands: 'Seek ye first the kingdom of God?' A possible answer lies in the evasiveness of Christ's responses to Satan. These are indeed theological but not explicit, and from the Fathers to Milton they were customarily interpreted as Christ's means of keeping the devil mystified as to who the 'Son of God' is. They are not, in other words, adequate responses to Satan's proffers – no more than Guyon's are to Mammon's – but, as Guyon's seem to be, means of teasing the demon. Interpreting 'Man shall not live by bread alone,' Chrysostom does not so much emphasize the theological import of the statement as that by it

'Christ signifies Himself not to have consented' – which seems to be exactly what Guyon's enigmatic answers signify. Christ's followers should learn from such a rejoinder what Guyon seems to know – that 'whatever we may have power to do, yet to do nothing vainly and at random.' Instead of revealing Himself, Christ 'for a while discourses' with Satan 'as one of the many';[31] something close to that may be Spenser's intention in allowing Guyon to present himself as just another knight-errant committed to a code of 'derring-do' and in the service of a lady to whom he is pledged. (In the chivalric context of *The Faerie Queene* no responses could be better calculated to disguise Guyon as one of the many.) Chrysostom's commentary may also shed light upon the most puzzling facet of these answers – that Guyon is actually polite to Mammon when the demon offers Philotime. Instead of scorning the daughter as he has scorned the gold, Guyon humbly thanks the father and protests himself unworthy. Chrysostom says Christ responds to Satan with 'extreme gentleness ... teaching us that we must overcome the Devil, not by miracles, but by forbearance and long-suffering'; we should learn from that gentleness not to be 'troubled, nor confounded, but answer with meekness.'[32] The saint's ἀπάθεια must manifest itself not only in indifference to temptation but in his attitude toward the tempter. Evasive and polite responses come easily to the man who is not only not 'troubled' by what the demon has to offer but not even by the demon himself. That such ease of resistance does not itself come easily goes without saying; we recall Mary of Egypt's seventeen years of warfare against lust and Anthony's twenty-five years of fasting before he vanquished the demon of fornication. But the rigor of ascetic preparation is one thing; the rigor of resisting temptation another. The faint suggests that Guyon suffers the former; his nonchalance, that because he suffers the former, like the saints he is free of the latter.

A clue to the meaning of that freedom is the contrast between Guyon and Tantalus. Both are hungry and both are presented with golden apples which cannot nourish. Guyon's refusing them seems, if nothing else, merely sensible; they cannot do him any good. That Tantalus desires them with his whole being, though they can do him no good either, suggests that he represents the polar antithesis of ἀπάθεια and defines that virtue by contrast. Tantalus is desire pure and simple, desire for its own sake without reference to need. (That Guyon is free

from desire even for what he needs is an inference from his refusal of
the silver stool: the apples could not have satisfied his hunger, but he
could presumably have rested on the stool in his extremity of
fatigue.)[33] The apples are fantasies of satisfaction, stones to be turned
into bread, images which might inspire craving in a hungry man
despite his knowing better – provided that hungry man was still passible. They are like those 'desires of [the] body' which tormented Mary
of Egypt for seventeen years until she was 'delivered of all temptations.' Tantalus has not been delivered. Guyon's refusing the apples
(and the stool) ratifies his independence of desire, while Tantalus'
grasping for them serves as foil to Guyon's strength: if Guyon had
'inclined ... at all,' he would be in the spiritual condition of which Tantalus is a grotesque but revealing parody. Tantalus is what passibility
ultimately means.

Canto seven affords no mean between these extremes – complete
impassibility and desire for its own sake. There is no Medina to provide a moderate satisfaction of the 'lust of meat and drinke.' As one
who feasted Jove, Tantalus had means at his disposal to satisfy his
appetite, but his discovery seems to have been that appetite cannot be
satisfied. His eating and drinking made him all the more ravenous.
Guyon's eating and drinking nothing at all have made him by contrast
impervious to appetite. Man's life, Spenser seems to be saying, is either
passion or spirit; one is either Acrasia or Belphoebe, and Tantalus
reveals the torment of being the former. Cullen is correct that the Cave
is 'not simply a figure of Hell' but 'a real, psychological Hell of the self-
torment and frustration of desire that, through the Fall, has become ...
uncontrollable. It is a Hell in which fallen desire becomes its own punishment.' I suggest only the deletion of *fallen*, for if Guyon's virtue is
the Fathers' ἀπάθεια, 'fallen desire' is a tautology; all desire is fallen,
for all desire is the consequence of the passible condition of the soul
induced by Adam's eating. The sheer insanity of Tantalus' longing
argues that that patristic point is also Spenser's; a starving man's insa-
tiable hunger for metal fruit is not an excess (and in that sense a 'fallen
desire' correctable by temperance-as-moderation) but a madness
which only the extirpation of desire could cure. Cullen interprets
'Mammon's offer to Guyon of the apples and the stool' not as 'a temptation to satisfy desire so much as ... a temptation to desires that can
never be satisfied.'[34] That is entirely true, but the last phrase implies

that some desires can or should be satisfied. The point of Tantalus' negative example seems rather to be the Fathers' – that desire by its very nature is a disease of the soul which efforts to satisfy only exacerbate. Spenser appears to be saying that temperance is not the refusal of excess or of unsatisfying objects of desire; rather to be temperate – or at least to be a knight or hero of temperance – is to refuse the very act of desiring.

The only way to do that is the only way to deny eros – to die. Because Adam sought to satisfy his desire for an apple, all Adam's children live to want; the energy of fallen life is desire. Therefore to cease to desire is to cease to be. Tantalus, because his very definition is desire, cannot therefore die: he 'daily dyde, yet neuer throughly dyen couth' (II, vii, 58); forever wanting he lives forever, yet that life is itself death. Guyon's 'death' from not desiring an apple suggests conversely that the way to real life is through the death which Tantalus cannot die – the death of wanting, mortification of a will subjected in Adam to the tyranny of passion. That is, of course, the death which the New Adam died in His passionless Passion and in which the saint participates by his ascetic labor. Its fruit is a life wholly different in kind from Tantalus', one whose motive power is divine energy rather than desire. No wonder it baffles Mammon, who thinks Guyon a 'fearfull foole' for not resting on the silver seat, for it assumes a definition of man as deified rather than as natural. Such a man, having ceased to want, is dead by the world's definition of life. He lives instead in the Resurrection, as Guyon does when Arthur as Christ raises him in canto eight. The faint so conceived is not merely the consequence of *ascesis*, the side effect of the medicine for curing the passions, but the very cure itself.

Why then did Guyon enter Mammon's Cave to 'feed his eyes' (II, vii, 24)? His doing so is to some interpreters evidence of an intellectual lust more culpable than simple physical desire.[35] If we are correct, however, in comparing Guyon with the desert monks, we may reasonably argue that his wish to see is comparable to Anthony's sleeping in tombs to attract the devil – or, for that matter, to Christ's making himself vulnerable to Satan. What would be evidence of a blameworthy *curiositas* in everyman is for the saint a necessary means of exercising himself in dispassion. Not desiring when there is no object of desire is less a virtue than an aspiration, a potency rather than an act. Unless one sees the image of lust which a demon of fornication presents to the eyes of the mind, one cannot *not* lust. The test or proof of ἀπάθεια is *both* to see and not want – to feed the eyes and not the body. Impassibility renders curiosity not only innocent but positively virtuous.

That Spenser intended such a meaning is suggested by his not allowing what Guyon feeds his eyes upon to tantalize the reader.[36] Had Mammon's wealth appeared to us so beautiful as it evidently appears to Mammon himself or as palatable as the golden apples seem to Tantalus, we should find Guyon's innocence of desire difficult to credit. But since we do not desire what *we* see through Guyon's eyes, we readily believe he does not either and that he can afford to feed upon such sights with spiritual impunity. Spenser is encouraging us to see as the saint sees: to the man who has achieved impassibility, what is desirable to Adam's unregenerate progeny is unappealing, even repellent. When Mammon says, 'Behold, thou Faeries sonne, with mortall eye, / That liuing eye before did neuer see: / The thing, that thou didst craue so earnestly' (II, vii, 38), the demon speaks more wisely than he knows. Were Guyon (and we) to behold 'with *mortall* eye,' we should indeed 'craue ... earnestly'; but Spenser lets his hero and his reader see with 'liuing eye' that what mortality desires, what Tantalus craves as the means of his 'life,' is death. Mammon sees 'the worldes blis' (II, vii, 32), but we see smoke and darkness, scattered bones and skulls. Even the riches themselves are unattractive to the sight: 'massy gold' which embosses the vaulted ceiling threatens 'heavy ruine' (II, vii, 28) – which means quite simply that it is about to fall and crush Guyon (and us) at any moment. Not only are the golden floors and walls 'ouergrowne with dust and old decay' but 'hid in darkenesse, that none could behold / The hew thereof' (II, vii, 29). In the Garden of Proserpina, 'hearbs and fruits' are 'direfull deadly blacke both leafe and bloom / Fit to adorne the dead, and decke the drery toombe' (II, vii, 51) (are they beautiful to Mammon and Philotime?). They are fit, too, as foil for golden apples which feed the eyes of Tantalus but which in their setting and because of Spenser's associating them with strife and discord are as unattractive to the reader as to Guyon. We do not require Guyon's aloofness toward Mammon to persuade us that he does not want such things, for we do not want them either. By virtue of the poetry if not of our own sanctity, we participate in the health of impassibility and see for what it is the disease of desire in Mammon and Tantalus. Having fed the eye, we too would rather faint than feed the body.

III

If we interpret temperance, then, as the Fathers do and place it as they do in the context of Christ's temptation, passion, and death, neither the beginning nor the end of Guyon's venture, neither his motive for entering Mammon's Cave nor his faint upon leaving it, need disqualify him for his role as *microchristus*. The persistent obstacles to believing in Guyon's sanctity show themselves instead as evidences of it: he seeks temptation as Christ did and as heroic ascetics and martyrs do, not presumptuously and not even to prove himself capable of resisting (what Berger belittles as 'muscle flexing'), but so that by seeing the desirable as not desirable he may participate in Christ's victory over the devil, whose only access to the soul is through desire. Guyon does not collapse through an excess of self-assurance but because he has achieved by watching and fasting a divine measure of assurance. Instead of fainting from the strain of resisting temptation by merely human means, he faints so as to participate in Christ's divine capacity not to be tempted.[37]

For anyone who remains in doubt about Guyon's having achieved that capacity, Spenser offers an almost certain confirmation – a hint that Guyon, like Red Crosse, has become Christ the Harrower. I refer to the last two verses of stanza sixty-four: 'Ne suffred lust his safetie to betray; / So goodly did beguile the Guyler of the pray.' The first line summarizes what we have been at pains to demonstrate – that Guyon's safety is owing to his not desiring. The second makes a causal connection between that lack of 'lust' and a familiar trope which no one, surprisingly, seems to have recognized. Judith Anderson comes close when she remarks that 'in a manner very familiar to readers of *Piers Plowman*' canto seven becomes more Christian as it develops, until, at the end Mammon is 'no longer just the world but now the traditionally Satanic "Guyler."'[38] She does not however seem to recognize that Spenser echoes instances of this motif in Langland's account of the Harrowing:

> So shall thys death fordo, I dare my lyfe lygge
> Al that death did fyrst, throughe the deuils entisynge
> And as throughe gyle, man was begiled
> So shall grace that began, make a good sleyght.[39]

In other words grace, which is to say Christ, will use guile against the beguiler. I quote the B-text in Crowley's edition, which is presumably the only one to which Spenser had access. It is nonetheless interesting that the C-text at this point contains the very figure which Spenser employs:

> So shal grace, þat bigan al, maken a goed ende
> And *bigile þe gilour*, and þat is a goed sleythe.[40]

We need not wonder whether Spenser could have seen that version in manuscript (it was not in print), for variations on the figure appear elsewhere in the B-text Harrowing. Gobelyn reminds Satan that 'God wil not be begiled,'[41] with the obvious inference that Satan will be (or has been). Christ says to Satan, 'Thefely thou me robbest, the olde lawe graunteth / That gilers be bigyled, and that is good reason.'[42] Later in the same speech Christ returns to the trope and expands it:

> Thou Lucifer in lykenes of a luther edder
> Gatiste by gyle, tho that God loued
> And in lykenes of a leode, that Lorde am of heauen
> Graciously thy gyle haue quite, go gile agaynst gyle
> And as Adam and all, throughe a tree dyed
> Adam & al through a tree, should turne againe to life
> And gile is gyled, and in hys gyle fallen.[43]

Spenser's probable debt to such verses strengthens Professor Anderson's (and Hamilton's)[44] case for Langland's influence on *The Faerie Queene* and argues for Guyon's as well as Red Crosse's assimilation to Piers in the role of Christ the Harrower.[45]

Langland is probably not, however, Spenser's only source for the trope. Beguiling the beguiler is proverbial in middle English poetry, appearing even in so unlikely a context as the Reeve's Tale.[46] It usually applies, however, as Langland applies it, to the Harrowing and probably has for its ultimate source a similar turn of phrase in Psalm 68: God 'led captiuitie captiue.' Patristic and later Catholic exegesis, taking Saint Paul's reference to the verse in Ephesians as its point of departure, interpret it as an Old Testament Prophecy of the Harrowing.[47] Spenser employs the phrase in his Easter sonnet – not by accident, one suspects, the sixty-eighth of the *Amoretti*. The trope appears as well in the paschal, liturgical context which seems to inform the last two cantos of Book One; in a hymn for Holy Saturday we encounter, 'Beguiled is the beguiler; the beguiled one [Adam, man] is ransomed by Thy wisdom, O my God.'[48] Fortunatus employs the figure in his famous paschal hymn, *Pange lingua gloriosi*, from which Langland quotes. The Latin tag which follows 'So shall grace that began, make a good sleyght' (or in the C-text, 'And bigile þe gilour, and þat is a goed sleyth') is Fortunatus' *Ars ut artem falleret*, 'that guile might beguile guile.' Langland varies the original slightly by substituting *ars* for *arte* and thus altering the subject of the clause. In the hymn it is Christ by guile, not guile hypostatized, who does the beguiling:

> *Hoc opus nostrae salutis ordo deposcerat,*
> *multiformis perditoris arte ut artem falleret.*

> Justice demanded this work of our salvation,
> That by guile He should beguile the guile of the
> multiform [or guileful] destroyer.[49]

In view of the frequency of such passages in representations of the descent into Hell, Spenser's applying the trope to Guyon as he emerges from three days in the depths of the earth hints that at this juncture he is as much the Harrower and vanquisher of Satan as Red Crosse is at the beginning of canto twelve of Book One.

IV

But does canto eight of Book Two not belie that claim? Does not Guyon's helplessness and entire dependence on Arthur and the Palmer prove correct the critics who believe either the knight or his virtue inadequate? Not if we assume that Spenser was conceiving temperance in the way that Athanasius, Clement, or Basil conceived it – as a virtue which is both achieved by ascetic labor (canto seven) and given entirely by grace (canto eight). That the same knight of temperance who has become Christ and walked 'free among the dead' is in need of being raised from the dead *by* Christ is fully consistent with that paradox.

That Spenser intended Guyon's strength and weakness as corollaries rather than contradictions is suggested by the extension of the paschal motifs of canto seven into eight. The very numbering is probably intentional: on the seventh day Guyon, as Christ, both descends into Hell and rests from his labors in a death which is also a sleep; on the eighth day Arthur, as Christ, raises Guyon (now Adam) from the dead. Like Philip in Clement's exegesis, Guyon rises when Christ has 'killed his passions,' Pyrochles and Cymochles (in fact Guyon revives upon the very instant of the second brother's death).[50] Spenser's calling the faint both a sleep and a death sustains that reading and recalls as well the common New Testament characterization of those who have died in hope of the Resurrection as 'asleep in the Lord,' awaiting His return when the seven ages of this life are done. Another possibly applicable text is a passage from Colossians appointed in the Sarum Missal for the first Mass of Easter. When catechumens prepared by forty days of watching, fasting, and mortification of passion arise from the tomb of the font at the beginning of the eighth day, the first Scripture they hear is, 'For ye are dead, and your life is hid with Christ in God. When Christ, who is our life, shall appear, then shall ye also appear with him in glory.'[51] By their descent into the font, those catechumens have participated, as has Guyon, in the Harrowing. Appropriately, therefore, he like them should be dead and in expectation of Christ's intervention from above to raise him up.

Parallels to Book One sustain this interpretation. Red Crosse, whose role as Harrower most interpreters acknowledge, also sleeps; he lies in the Balm from the Tree of Life 'as in a dreame of deepe delight,' from which he rises on the day of Resurrection (the third in the typology of Book One) and 'did himselfe to battell readie dight' (I, xi, 50, 52). That Red Crosse rises in his own strength and becomes the triumphant Christ whereas Guyon is raised by Arthur in the latter role is more nearly a variation on a theme dictated by the terms of the respective allegories than a theological difference between the two episodes. Furthermore, to say that Red Crosse rises in his own strength is not entirely true, for at the ends of the first two days of his ordeal he is fully as helpless as Guyon and, like Guyon, 'dies' in order to be raised up by the grace Christ gives him in the Well and the Tree. One might reasonably argue that the sacraments of baptism and chrismation play in Book One the role that Arthur plays in Two. (Belphoebe's eyes' possessing such virtue prepares us for Arthur's doing so.) Nor is that to suggest that Spenser excludes those sacraments altogether from Two; there is no representation of chrism, but Spenser hints that Guyon's 'death' or 'sleep' is baptismal: 'all [Guyon's] senses [are] drowned in deepe senselesse *waue*' (II, viii, 24; italics added), an odd way of characterizing a swound unless *waue* conveys more than a literal sense. If Spenser in fact intends a version of the Well of Life appropriate to a legend of temperance, he has chosen his words with characteristic care: to drown the senses rather than Guyon himself is presumably to effect the impassibility which is synonymous with deification and the principal fruit of temperance; and the wave's being itself 'senselesse' reminds us that the font, like its source in Christ's pierced side, is a 'fountain of dispassion.'

Spenser also hints that the sleeping Guyon plays Christ's role. That Guyon 'dyde entire' (II, viii, 15), is possibly to remind us that 'A bone of him shall not be broken' (John 19:36). When Pyrochles and Cymochles attempt to 'spoile the dead of weed' (II, viii, 16), we recall that 'They parted my raiment among them' (John 19:24; Psalm 22:18). The Palmer calls Guyon's weeds 'relicks' (II, viii, 16), which Christ's garments became. The angel who comes to Guyon's aid at the very beginning of the canto, though on one hand a minister of grace to a helpless man, reminds us also of the angel of the Resurrection. It is almost certainly to convey this latter significance that Spenser describes the heavenly messenger as 'a faire young man, / Of wondrous beautie, and of freshest yeares, / Whose tender bud to blossome new began' (II, viii, 5). That characterization expands Saint Mark's account of 'a young man ... clothed in a long white garment' (16:5) to incorporate images of regeneration and deification appropriate to a personification of resurrected humanity. That such was Spenser's intention is rendered the more likely by his bestowing on this youth the radiance of countenance which elsewhere in *The Faerie Queene* he reserves for deified ladies; the young man's face, like Una's, Belphoebe's, Britomart's, and Dame Nature's is 'adornd with sunny rayes' and shines 'diuinely' (II, viii, 5). By virtue of that similarity the young man's being angelic takes on a second significance: it recalls the 'bodiless' character of men and women who by *theosis* have become impassible. In all those respects the angel recapitulates the theme of deification and transfers what Belphoebe represents to Guyon at the very moment when Guyon to all

appearances is least angelic and least divine. For such symbolism
Spenser had liturgical precedent: the angel at the tomb is an epiphany
of the resurrected Christ, whose personal appearance, like Guyon's,
remains inglorious or obscure (Mary Magdalene mistook Him for a
gardener). The angel manifests the glory which Christ revealed in the
Transfiguration but hid in His Resurrection appearances. Saint Mark's
young man reveals 'by [his] form the brightness of the Resurrection.'[52]
Spenser's, by intimating that revelation, suggests that Guyon by fainting, so far from failing, has led captivity captive.

                                    V

The Fathers' understanding of passion and its discipline, their identification of ascetical mortification with Christ's passionless Passion and
of impassibility with the resurrected flesh, and their consequent identification of the death of passion through watching and fasting with baptism into Christ's death thus allow us to interpret Book Two as the
complement to Book One which the many parallels suggest it is supposed to be rather than the secular parody which it has seemed to
modern readers. And there is still another – and closely related –
dimension of the legend of temperance (and indeed of *The Faerie
Queene* as a whole) upon which another dimension of patristic theology affords a new perspective – Spenser's representation of sin. To that
we now turn.

PART THREE

SIN

CHAPTER EIGHT

Spenser and Original Sin

I

An allegory which presents images of man and nature in a redeemed condition and leads the reader through dramas of redemption (the dragon slaying, the destruction of the Bower) presupposes, of course, the need for redemption and thus some version of the Fall. Both the dragon's imprisonment of Una's parents and Acrasia's seduction of Mordant appear to signify the original transgression; but the reader witnesses neither, and Spenser does not elaborate. In Book Seven, however, by way of introducing Mutabilitie, he gives us a more explicit allegory of the Fall. Its terms are surprising. Though critics have paid them scant attention, they should be as startling to Western, post-Augustinian readers as *theosis* and *impassibility*, as Spenser's interpretations of Easter baptism and the Transfiguration. The Mutabilitie Cantos give us a version of the Fall in which sin is not so much as mentioned.

Change and death, which is to say Mutabilitie, do sin's work. As a 'daughter by descent / Of those old *Titans*, that did whylome striue / With *Saturnes* sonne for heauens regiment' (vii, vi, 2), Mutabilitie is intimately associated with the primaeval rebellion. In a dramatic presentation such as Milton's, that is Satan's role; but in an allegory, in which virtues and vices rather than subjects are represented, we should expect a personification, Sin, to be the agent of revolt. Mutabilitie makes '*wrong* of right, and *bad* of good' (vii, vi, 6; italics added), but Spenser seems to go out of his way to avoid the very word and conception his readers would presumably have expected in this context. We can argue, of course, that rebellion is tantamount to sin and that 'bad' and 'wrong' are virtually synonymous with it, but we normally think of sin as more nearly a condition than an act (rebellion) and more nearly the cause of 'bad' and 'wrong' than their equivalent. Sin is an entity or hypostasis, something which, as Saint Paul says, 'entered into the world' (Romans 5:12) as a person or power might – something easily personified, as Milton's Sin, sprung from Satan's head, indicates. There is no hint of such an hypostasis in Spenser's allegory. Furthermore Spenser violates another of our expectations by revising the relationship between sin and death. 'The wages of sin is death' (Romans 6:23), and 'sin entered into the world, *and death by sin*' (Romans 5:12; italics added). Accordingly Milton's much more conventional allegory depicts Death as Sin's offspring. Spenser appears to be saying instead that death (Mutabilitie) entered into the world and sin (at least 'bad' and 'wrong') by death – not that we die because we sin but that we sin because we die, because we are subject to mutability and its ultimate consequence.

For that seemingly topsy-turvy relationship, as for holiness as deification and temperance as deifying mortification, Spenser had well established patristic precedents: the major pre-Augustinian Fathers did not believe in original sin. All Christians of orthodox persuasion believe, of course, that Satan's and Adam's sins caused the aboriginal calamity, but that 'in Adam's fall, we sinned all' is not an ancient conception. Before Augustine (and in the East after) there is little evidence of the belief that all men inherited Adam's sin and consequent guilt. The pre-Augustinian and Eastern Fathers taught instead that man inherited death from Adam and that man's mortal condition causes him to make 'wrong of right, and bad of good.' They taught, in other words, what canto six of Book Seven seems to – that Mutabilitie rather than sin breaks the laws of nature, of justice, and of policy (VII, vi, 6) and causes the only kind of sin which the Fathers countenance, the individual sins of individual men and women (what Western theologians call 'actual sin').

The contrary, Western, conception is an innovation upon earlier doctrine. It seems to have originated with Ambrosiaster, but its full development comes in Augustine's anti-Pelagian writings. In *On Forgiveness of Sins, and Baptism*, for instance, Augustine says that in Adam 'was constituted the form of condemnation to his future progeny, who should spring from him by natural descent; so that from one all men were born to a condemnation, from which there is no deliverance but in the Saviour's grace.' In *On Marriage and Concupiscence* Augustine connects the transmission of guilt to the lust which attaches to procreation even in Christian marriage, and in *On Original Sin* he insists that 'the fault of our nature remains in our offspring ... even when the guilt of the self-same fault has been washed away in the parent by remission of sins.'[1] These teachings became central ingredients of medieval, Latin Christianity and were taught and believed with remarkable unanimity by Western Christians of all persuasions until well beyond the sixteenth century. Though the Schoolmen differed with Augustine in some respects, making greater allowance for natural goodness and free will in fallen man, they did not deny the central tenets of Augustine's teaching. Aquinas's formulation of it states the conviction of the Church for a millennium: 'According to the Catholic Faith we are bound to hold that the first sin of the first man is transmitted to his descendents, by the way of origin. For this reason children are taken to be baptized soon after their birth ... The contrary is part of the Pelagian heresy, as is clear from Augustine in many of his books.' Aquinas is explicit about the inheritance not merely of sin in some general sense (such as spiritual debility or a propensity for wrongdoing) but specifically of guilt: 'Guilt is transmitted by the way of origin from father to son'; this guilt is 'not actually in the semen [as some theologians taught], yet human nature is there virtually, accompanied by that guilt' (*ST*, I-II, 81, 1).[2] Although the principal Reformers differed with Catholics as to the effectiveness of baptismal grace in remitting this guilt, there was no significant difference between them as to the guilt itself. Indeed Luther and Calvin (or an English Puritan like William Perkins)[3] are more Augustinian than Augustine in their insistence on man's congenital sinfulness and liability for Adam's trespass.

The radical difference between the Augustinian and more ancient conceptions is easily obscured by a common vocabulary – words like *sin* and *justification* can mean different things in different theological contexts, and a person acquainted with only one of those contexts, as most of Spenser's readers are, will not likely recognize the existence of the other. If one assumes that the Greek and early Latin Fathers mean by these terms what Augustine taught his successors to mean, recognition of the earlier and oriental doctrine of the Fall and its consequence becomes difficult if not impossible. Before, therefore, we examine Spenser's representation of the curse of Adam, we need to discover exactly what the Eastern and pre-Augustinian Fathers intend when they speak of the Fall. Cyril of Alexandria illustrates the need for doing so, for he sounds Augustinian but is not. He says, 'We have been condemned to death through the transgression in Adam, the whole of human nature suffering this in him'; or, 'from one and through one the condemnation of Adam spread to all'; or, in Adam 'many were made sinners.' Read from the point of view of Augustinian teaching, such statements seem to say that all men sinned in Adam and became guilty in him; but when we examine the context in which Cyril makes these remarks, it becomes clear that he means something quite different. When he says that the 'condemnation of Adam spread to all,' he adds, 'according to his likeness.' Cyril's apparent meaning is that we suffer Adam's penalty, death, not because we were born guilty of his sin but because we bear the same nature which Adam corrupted (Migne's Latin version reads, *propter generis similitudinem*). Cyril explains 'many were made sinners' in Adam accordingly – '*not as having transgressed in Adam, for they did not exist*, but as being of his nature, they fell under the law of sin.'[4] The second clause saves Cyril from the charge of Pelagianism; he does not simply say that we die because we repeat Adam's transgression but that we repeat Adam's transgression because being of one nature with Adam, and that nature being corrupted by Adam, we fall under the law of sin inherent in that nature. But the 'law of sin' obviously does not entail guilt, for Cyril has just denied that Adam's descendants transgressed in him.

What it does seem to entail is what all the early and Eastern Fathers attribute to Adam – *mortality. Mortality* means more than physical death; it signifies all that attends on death – change, decay, corruption (everything Mutabilitie personifies), and the soul's subjection to the passions (which ascetic temperance must undo). That subjection leads, of course, to sin, so one can say that to become mortal is to be placed in a circumstance in which the enslaved intellect and will cannot but sin. Hence 'many were made sinners' in Adam not because, as Augustine taught, they participated in his transgression (being in his loins) but because many were made mortal in Adam and thus became subject to the law of sin, which is to say the passions' domination of corrupted flesh. Adam, says Cyril, 'was created for incorruption and life ... But ...

he has fallen under sin and has slipped down into corruption ...
Nature, therefore, has become sick through the sin of disobedience of
one, that is, Adam.'[5] Death (mortality) on that showing is not, as later
Latin theologians taught, the penalty for inherited guilt (in that sense,
the 'wages of sin') but a congenital ailment conducive to personal sin; a
nature weakened by such sickness lacks the stamina to live without
sin. David Weaver understands Cyril to be saying that 'Adam's sin
may be truly the source of corruption and mortality,' not in the Augustinian, juridical sense, but because 'it has altered the actual physical
nature which is transmitted by sexual generation.'[6]

Unfortunately for a demonstration of influence, Spenser is not likely
to have read the passages which I have quoted; they come from Cyril's
homilies on Romans, which were not published in the West until the
nineteenth century.[7] But patristic treatises and Eastern liturgical texts
available in sixteenth-century editions repeat Cyril's arguments in a
variety of contexts. Theodoret of Cyrrhus (of the Antiochene school
and at a further theological remove from Augustine than the Alexan-
drian Fathers) insists even more strongly than Cyril that sin is a consequence of the passions, which is to say, of inherited mortality, rather
than being itself an inherited condition: a nature made subject to the
vicissitudes of change and death by Adam's transgression 'is in need
of many things, of food, and of drink, and of clothing, and of shelter,
and of various crafts. The need of such things often provokes to intemperate passion, and the intemperance gives birth to sin.'[8] Irenaeus
habitually associates death rather than sin with Adam, life rather than
remission or justification with Christ. Christ 'exhibited a new sort of
generation: that as by the former generation we inherited death, so by
this generation we might inherit life.'[9] (Patrick Grant has argued persuasively for Irenaeus' anti-Augustinian influence on conceptions of
sin in later Renaissance literature, especially in Traherne.)[10] Tertullian,
in the same treatise on baptism in which he attributes physical healing
to the font and deification to chrism, asks, 'Why should innocent
infancy come with haste to the remission of sins?' 'Let them come,
when they are growing up ... when they have become competent to
know Christ.'[11] Since Augustine and his successors considered infant
baptism imperative on account of inherited guilt, Tertullian's opposite
notion seems a clear indication that he meant the phrase 'innocent
infancy' literally. Also he speaks of the 'remission of sins' rather than of

sin, suggesting that he means personal or actual rather than original sin. In his *Exhortation to Chastity* Tertullian speaks of a will contrary to God's will in our 'seed' and ascribes that circumstance to Adam, the 'head both of the race and of sin.'[12] Such language, like Cyril's, can be construed in an Augustinian fashion, but Tertullian probably refers to something like Cyril's 'law of sin' – the enslavement to sin of a nature made mortal in Adam. Jaroslav Pelikan, commenting on the characterization of Adam as 'head both of the race and of sin,' remarks that Tertullian would not have spoken of infants as innocents and discouraged infant baptism, if he meant that Adam transmitted sin and guilt to his 'seed.'[13] In other passages, Tertullian places heavy emphasis instead on the transmission of death from the father of the race: 'Now all are perishing who have not known any green field of Paradise.'[14]

Athanasius is even more explicit in ascribing death rather than sin to the Fall. So far from teaching that all men inherit Adam's transgression, he teaches that man can live entirely free of sin and that Jeremiah and John the Baptist did. They nevertheless inherited Adam's penalty and were subject to corruption and death, even though they resisted the enticements of the passions which attend upon mortality.[15] Like Tertullian, Gregory of Nyssa teaches that newborn children are innocent; man's moral deficiencies are owing to Adam but rather by way of inherited weakness than of inherited depravity.[16] Accordingly Gregory interprets the tunics of skin in which God clothed Adam and Eve after the Fall as indicating that Adam's sin made man subject to animal lusts and thus to personal sin.[17] In that way, but apparently not through an inheritance of original sin, the Fall affected man's moral nature. That is evidently Gregory's meaning when he says that the humanity which Christ assumed and deified was 'sinful' (ἁμαρτητικήν) and that sin is 'congenital to [lit., produced together with – συναποτικτομένη] our nature.'[18] If he had meant by *congenital* what Augustine and Latin Christendom meant – that Adam's guilt was transmitted through procreation – he could not consistently have taught that infants are innocent. Gregory's language, like Cyril's or Tertullian's, means something different when read backward through an Augustinian medium from what it evidently meant to Gregory and his contemporaries.

Except for Augustine, Chrysostom was the most widely read of the Fathers in the sixteenth century, and Chrysostom's doctrine of the Fall is explicitly unAugustinian. If Spenser had read the homilies on

Romans in any one of the several editions in which they appeared – perhaps in the 1530 Erasmian edition in the Pembroke library – he would have discovered that the most famous of the Eastern Fathers denies in almost so many words what the most famous of the Western Fathers taught. In Romans 5:19, Saint Paul says that 'by one man's [Adam's] disobedience many were made sinners.' That could easily be interpreted as stating a doctrine of inherited transgression, but Chrysostom interprets 'many were made sinners' in a wholly different way, deliberately rejecting innate depravity as unreasonable and substituting for it the conception of inherited mortality:

> For that one having sinned became mortal, and
> that they who are from him are in the same
> condition is nothing unlikely. But that from
> the disobedience of that one another is made
> a sinner – how would that follow? For if one
> does not become a sinner of his own will,
> such a one is not found to deserve
> punishment.[19]

Chrysostom is saying in effect that Saint Paul cannot have meant literally that Adam's disobedience made his descendants sinners: that would be unjust. He must have meant that Adam's disobedience made his descendants mortal: that would be 'nothing unlikely.' Chrysostom in effect substitutes death for sin and reads Saint Paul to say that 'by one man's disobedience many were made *mortal*.' 'A more explicit rejection of original sin,' remarks David Weaver, 'would be hard to find.'[20]

That it has not appeared so explicit to Western Christians – and that interpreters of Spenser's theology have never taken this ancient interpretation of the Fall into account – is owing to more than ignorance of the Fathers. There has been a persistent tendency among Catholic theologians to read Eastern and pre-Augustinian formulations in terms of Western and post-Augustinian conceptions. Quasten's account of original sin and inherited guilt is indicative: Chrysostom according to Quasten believed in these doctrines, but the Greek Father's mode of stating the belief 'does not coincide exactly with the ideas and *better terminology* of Augustine. Though Chrysostom repeatedly avers that the consequences or penalties of Adam's sin affect not only our first parents, but also their descendants, *he never states explicitly that sin itself was inherited by their posterity and is inherent in their nature*' (italics added).[21] As we have just seen, Chrysostom evidently does not believe that; when he 'avers that the consequences ... of Adam's sin affect ... [his] descendents,' he means that those descendants became mortal, not guilty. What Quasten takes to be a failure to state a doctrine as precisely as Augustine, appears to be the precise statement of a doctrine contrary to Augustine's. Only within the past few decades, in the work of such scholars as Romanides, Meyendorff, Pelikan, and Kelly, have these distinctions been set forth clearly in a Western theological context. Thanks to these recent analyses, Renaissance scholars are now in a position to recognize differences hitherto obscured.[22]

II

But would a sixteenth-century reader have recognized them? Would not Spenser have been predisposed by his theological milieu to read Chrysostom as Quasten does? Both Trent and Geneva reaffirmed the Augustinian doctrine of original sin, and both Catholic and Protestant polemicists quoted from the Fathers to support their positions, even when those positions were unpatristic. Theological polemicists were not, however, the only Renaissance scholars interested in the Fathers; there were the humanists as well, who though Christians and in some instances theologians, were not using patristic documents as proof texts. Their motive was the very opposite, not polemical but critical. They sought to return *ad fontes*, not to confirm such established teachings as inherited sin but to go behind those beliefs to the meaning of 'original' Christian texts. The Renaissance editions of the Fathers which Spenser could have known were inspired by that motive and frequently reflected it in their introductions and *scholia*; and one of the doctrines which was subjected to such scrutiny was the one in question. No less a figure than Erasmus had called Augustine's teaching into question, and his address to the issue was sufficiently controversial that it could easily have come to Spenser's attention.

Erasmus' initial challenge was lexical. At issue was a proper translation of Romans 5:12: 'Wherefore, as by one man [Adam] sin entered into the world, and death by sin; so death passed upon all men, *for that*

all have sinned.' I quote from the King James translation which is ultimately owing to Erasmus' attack on the Vulgate's version of the verse:
'Through one man sin entered into the world, and death by sin, and so
death passed upon all men, *in whom* [or *in which*] all have sinned' (*Per
unum hominem peccatum intravit in mundum et per peccatum mors, et ita in
omnes homines mors pertransiit 'in quo' omnes peccaverunt*). I emphasize
in each version the phrase which Erasmus contested. The Greek original is ἐφ' ᾧ, a contraction of ἐπὶ ᾧ. Jerome had rendered it pronomi-
nally, as equivalent to ἐν ᾧ, but when Erasmus translated Romans in
1516, he replaced *in quo* with *quatenus*, meaning 'because,' and in a
brief annotation explained that in Pauline usage ἐφ' ᾧ had the force of
a causal conjunction, that ᾧ does not presuppose a person or thing as
its antecedent, and that no adequate translation can render the expres-
sion other than causally. As an alternative to *quatenus* he suggested *in
eo quod* – 'in so far as' or the King James 'for that.'[23]

That reasoning and retranslation constituted a direct challenge to the
doctrine of inherited sin, for Augustine, whose knowledge of Greek
was slight, had relied on the Vulgate translation of Romans 5:12 for his
authority. Jerome's *quo* seemed to require either *hominem* (Adam) or
peccatum (Adam's sin) for its antecedent; Augustine allowed for both
possibilities and drew the same theology from each: 'If you understand
that sin to be meant which by one man entered into the world, "In
which [sin] all have sinned," it is surely clear enough, that the sins
which are peculiar to every man, which they themselves commit and
which belong simply to them [actual sin], mean one thing; and that the
one sin, *in and by which all have sinned*, means another thing' (italics
added). 'If, however, it be not the sin, but that one man that is understood, "In which [one man] all have sinned," what again can be plainer
than even this clear statement?'[24] Since all men were in Adam, all
sinned in him or in his sin. The implications of Erasmus' argument
were inescapable: if ᾧ could refer neither to Adam nor his sin, there
was no foundation whatsoever for Augustine's enormously influential
exegesis; the universal Western understanding of original sin for a millennium was the issue of a faulty translation.[25]

Erasmus was promptly taken to task for both translation and commentary, accused of being a Pelagian, and strongly admonished to read
his Augustine.[26] To defend himself he expanded his annotation into a
treatise (1535) in which he argued (with copious illustrations) that Paul

consistently used ἐν rather than ἐπί with the dative to express the figurative presence of one person in another; and Erasmus repeated his previous argument, with further citations, that ἐπί with ᾧ could not be rendered other than causally. He specifically attacked Augustine's 'in which' and the derivative doctrine that all men sinned in Adam's *sin*, demonstrating that the Greek gender would not allow that interpretation. Jerome's *peccatum*, a neuter noun, translates ἁμαρτία, a feminine; ᾧ cannot therefore refer to sin, and Saint Paul cannot be translated to say that all men sinned in Adam's *sin*. Augustine's alternative exegesis, that all men sinned in Adam himself, entails no difficulty with pronoun reference since ᾧ can be masculine as well as neuter; but against that reading Erasmus repeats his argument for the causal meaning of ἐφ᾽ ᾧ.[27] The *adnotatio* did not persuade Erasmus' adversaries, and his literary works, including the New Testament translation, were put on the Index of 1559. As Jerome Bentley remarks, 'Medieval theologians had invested much Catholic doctrine in the precise language of the Vulgate,' and many Renaissance theologians were obviously loth to question that language.[28]

Spenser could easily have learned of this controversy; he could have read Erasmus' translation and annotations, and if he paid attention to English biblical translations, he would have discerned that except for the Rheims New Testament every sixteenth-century Bible followed Erasmus rather than the Vulgate.[29] In 1568 Peter Martyr published (in English) a series of commentaries on Romans which rehearsed Erasmus' arguments in detail; from these Spenser could have apprised himself of the doctrinal issues concerning original sin.[30] So even if he had not read any of the patristic texts from which we have quoted, he could have learned from Erasmus (directly or indirectly) that the pre-Augustinian Church did not believe in inherited sin and guilt.

He could also have learned that Augustine's predecessors and Eastern contemporaries did believe in inherited mortality – though less easily from Erasmus' exegesis than from his citations. Erasmus is so intent on linking death to actual sin that he pays little attention to Cyril's 'law of sin'; Erasmus implies (though he never actually says) that man enters life unencumbered by any Adamic liability. In that emphasis Erasmus comes very close to the Pelagianism he disclaimed, and, ironically, he quotes Pelagius (mistakenly, as pseudo-Jerome) against Augustine. Since most of the Fathers limit sin to actual sin (witness Tertullian and Chrysostom), Erasmus enlists them on his side in the contest, but much of what he quotes from them works against the quasi-Pelagian grain of his argument. The emphasis on inherited mortality is so nearly universal in patristic literature, that one can scarcely find a discussion of the Fall in which that doctrine is not manifest, and frequently paramount. The *adnotatio* contains, therefore – whether or not Erasmus intended that it should – plentiful evidence of belief in the legacy of Adam's death. No one reading the note (without a doctrinal bias or polemical motive) would likely be persuaded of the Augustinian position, but anyone who attended to Erasmus' citations as fully as to Erasmus' reasoning might well be persuaded that 'death passed upon all men' not only because all had sinned individually but because they inherited the nature which Adam had infected with death.

This is precisely Origen's argument in passages which Erasmus quotes: '"all men who are born and have been born in this world were in the loins of Adam when he was yet in Paradise. And all men with him or in him were expelled from Paradise when he was expelled thence."' Since Paradise is the locus of eternal life, to say that all men suffered Adam's expulsion is tantamount to saying that all inherit his mortality or that all died in him. Origen proceeds to say that (and Erasmus to quote it) in so many words: '"Death, which came upon [Adam] through transgression consequently passed also to them who were held in his loins; and therefore the Apostle speaks correctly: *For in Adam all die, just as in Christ all will be made alive.*"' Erasmus' motive for the citation is to underscore the difference between Origen and Augustine: that though both believed in the solidarity of the human race in Adam and that all men were in Adam when he sinned, Origen did not teach that all men sinned in Adam: 'Origen,' says Erasmus, 'does not speak here properly of original sin.'[31] That Origen *does* speak here of what we might call 'original death' is equally, indeed more clearly, evident; and though Erasmus pays little attention to that matter, anyone reading the quotation is likely to be as much impressed by it as by Erasmus' more nearly Pelagian point.

The centerpiece of Erasmus' patristic evidence is Chrysostom on Romans 5:12, and the passages quoted in the *adnotatio* emphasize as fully as any we have examined man's inheritance of Adam's mortality. Chrysostom addresses ἐφ' ᾧ directly, asking its meaning, and Erasmus quotes the discussion in full: '"But what is ἐφ' ᾧ πάντες ἥμαρτον?"' Chrysostom does not answer his question by explaining the grammar or exact meaning of the contraction. What he does, however, is to interpret the entire clause so as to place all his emphasis on death rather than sin. 'Εφ' ᾧ πάντες ἥμαρτον means '"That one [Adam] having fallen, even those not eating from the tree became mortal from him"' – mortal (θνητός), not sinful.[32] Chrysostom seems to be doing here precisely what he does in the exegesis of Romans 5:19 – assuming that when Saint Paul says *sin* he in fact means *death*. There he interpreted 'by one man's disobedience many were made *sinners*' to mean, 'by one man's disobedience many were made *mortal*,' and here he says in effect that Paul's 'death passed upon all men because all have *sinned*' really means that 'death passed upon all men because all have *died* (in Adam).' Such an interpretation seems more nearly to contradict than support Erasmus' contention that Paul is talking here exclusively about death as a penalty for actual sins. Chrysostom is obviously less concerned with that relationship than with the curse of Adam, which Erasmus comes close to denying.

Another citation argues to the same effect. In Romans 5:13 Saint Paul says that 'until the law sin was in the world: but sin is not imputed when there is no law.' Erasmus quotes Chrysostom asking why, if there was no law to disobey and therefore no sin, men nevertheless died: '"if ... death drew its root from sin,"' and if '"when there is no law sin is not imputed, how did death prevail?"' A Christian in the Augustinian tradition would presumably respond by pointing to Saint Paul's first clause, that even before the law 'sin was in the world' – the sin and hence the punishment of Adam. But Chrysostom answers himself in characteristically pre-Augustinian and Eastern fashion – that death, not sin, comes from Adam: '"Death reigned from Adam to Moses, even over them that *had not sinned*."' My emphasis illustrates Erasmus' interest in the statement; Chrysostom is obviously assuming that all sin is actual rather than original – that when there was no law to disobey and therefore no occasion for actual sin, there simply was no sin. But Chrysostom's emphasis is not on that matter (which he seems merely to take for granted) but on the dominion of death even over those who are innocent – from Adam to Moses, from the Fall to the Law and the commencement of actual sin. In this instance Erasmus acknowledges Chrysostom's point, if only in passing: that 'corporeal death spread abroad amongst them, just as if they had eaten with Adam their progenitor from the forbidden tree.'[33]

III

From such commentary, even without going beyond the *adnotatio*, Spenser could have informed himself of the differences between Augustinian and earlier (and Eastern) doctrines of the Fall. Once we recognize those differences ourselves, we see how much more closely Spenser's allegory resembles the latter theology than the former. In the whole of *The Faerie Queene* there is not in fact a single reference to the Fall which demands to be interpreted in Augustinian or Lutheran-Calvinist terms and only two which could so be construed.[34] One occurs in an unlikely, because non-theological, context, which excludes certain exegesis – the dating of Kimbeline's reign in the chronology of kings in the House of Alma (II, x, 50): 'What time th'eternal Lord in fleshly slime / Enwombed was, from wretched *Adams* line / To purge away the guilt of sinfull crime.' The 'guilt of sinfull crime' may be inherited from Adam, and Adam's line may be 'wretched' because of that inheritance; but nothing in the passage compels us to assume that. 'Sinfull crime' could as easily signify actual as original sin, and the guilt attaching to it, that which the individual sinner incurs. The wretchedness of Adam's line may be owing to mortality rather than inherited sin, and the phrase 'fleshly slime' strengthens that possibility. The characterization of mutable, mortal flesh as slime is not uncommon among the Fathers and probably has its source in exegeses of Exodus. The children of Israel, in Egyptian bondage, made bricks of slime, signifying according to Gregory of Nyssa (and others) bondage to the mortal and passible body. From that slavery, inherited from Adam, they were released by Christ – by a type of baptism (in the Red Sea) – and restored to life in Paradise (the Promised Land).[35] John of Damascus almost certainly alludes to that typology when, in the Homily on the Transfiguration, he says that man ceased to be 'a citizen of Eden and a companion of angels' when he 'darkened and confounded the likeness of the divine image with the *slime* of the passions.'[36] By washing away the slime in baptism, Christ set man free from the inheritance of death.

The second Spenserian passage can also be read in two ways. Contemplation shows Red Crosse the New Jerusalem, 'built / For those to dwell in, that are chosen his, / His chosen people purg'd from sinfull guilt, / with pretious bloud, which cruelly was spilt / On cursed tree, of that vnspotted lam, / That for the sinnes of all the world was kilt' (I, x, 57). If we come to this statement with Augustinian (or Calvinist) assumptions, we are likely to read 'chosen people purg'd from sinfull guilt' as a reference to the doctrine of election to salvation by virtue of Christ's atonement for inherited sin; but nothing in the language demands that reading or excludes the contrary. The Church as the New Israel is God's 'chosen people,' and the sinful guilt from which He purges them may just as easily be their own as Adam's. That interpretation seems, indeed, the more likely in view of the subsequent plural 'sinne̲s of all the world' for which Christ was 'kilt.' If original sin were the issue, we should expect the singular. If in reading either of these passages we take the Augustinian conception of sin for granted (as most of Spenser's readers probably do), we shall neglect the possibility that another theology, more consonant with the rest of *The Faerie Queene*, was Spenser's intention.

Most of the other references to sin and guilt in the poem (of which there are surprisingly few considering its length and theological subject matter) are unmistakably to actual sin. Only a few (all in Book One) require comment. When Una tells Arthur that many knights have failed to slay the dragon and release her parents 'For want of faith, or guilt of sin' (I, vii, 45), the link between infidelity and guilt could signify an unbaptized condition in which the guilt of Adam remains in the soul – lack of faith meaning specifically the infidel condition of non-Christians. But obviously the passage need not mean that and indeed seems much more likely to refer to the personal weaknesses of Una's former champions. Why ever would she have chosen heathen warriors for such a quest? In the House of Holinesse Red Crosse is purged of 'Inward corruption, and infected sin' (I, x, 25); 'original sin' is a conventional gloss, but we have abundant evidence that Red Crosse is infected by sin of his own commission. The reference is more likely to misdirected wrath toward Una and lust for Duessa than to the inherited sin of Adam – a presumption strengthened by the remedy administered. Sackcloth, ashes, fasting, and continuous prayer would presumably avail nothing for the healing of man's inherited guilt (I, x, 26); *Amendment* (personified) is to no purpose where the sin of Adam is concerned, from which Christ's suffering alone can deliver man. But for actual sins such as Red Crosse has committed these traditional means of cleansing are entirely appropriate (as they are, of course, for the passions which induce the sins). Furthermore, if Red Crosse's 'infected sin' were original, Spenser's characterization of the Well of Life primarily as deifying rather than purgative (and thus more effective as a remedy for mortality than for sin) would present a discrepancy in the allegory. So too would the fact that it washes away the 'guilt of sinfull crime_s' (I, xi, 30) rather than of 'sinfull crime.' In the parallel description of the Tree of Life, Adam is the man whose 'fault hath doen vs all to dy' (I, xi, 47; italics added); he did not, apparently, make us sinful but mortal. Appropriately, therefore, the Balm, like the Well, heals mortality; there is no mention of remission or justification in the account of its effects:

> Life and long health that gratious ointment gaue,
> And deadly woundes could heale, and reare againe
> The senselesse corse appointed for the graue.
>
> (I, xi, 48)

When Red Crosse receives this unction, it 'did from death him saue.' Had Spenser intended the Augustinian conception of original sin, he would surely have made clear that the Well and Balm saved Red Crosse from death by remitting his inherited guilt. Finally the description of Red Crosse in his fallen condition as infected with 'corruption' may point directly to Eastern influence. Corruption (φθορά), like slime, appears with remarkable frequency in the Greek Fathers' characterization of Adam's and his descendants' mortal circumstance. Though the word so used includes moral delinquency, that is by no means its exclusive or primary significance. Rather it means the dissolution of the body that attends upon death and which, like death itself, is a cause of sin.[37] Spenser's sequence, 'Inward corruption, and infected sin,' suggests that relationship and links sin directly to mortality rather than isolating inherited, original sin as a single or predominant evil. Only once is Red Crosse characterized in such a way as to suggest that he is innately sinful or guilty: Despair calls him a 'man of sin' (I, ix, 46). Even that characterization could refer to Red Crosse's personal transgressions, but if the reference is more radical, we must consider Despair's intention.

Spenser's closest approximation to a statement of inherited guilt comes not from *The Faerie Queene* but from the 'Hymne of Heavenly Love': 'In flesh at first the guilt committed was, / Therefore in flesh it must be satisfyde'; Christ's blood flows to 'clense the guilt of that infected cryme, / Which was enrooted in all fleshly slyme' (*HHL*, 141–2, 167–8). The terminology of guilt and satisfaction is characteristically Augustinian (or Calvinist), but the heavy emphasis on the flesh qualifies the phrasing. Were Spenser's assumptions strictly those of Latin and Protestant theology, he would have been more likely to ascribe the guilt of original sin and its residual infection to the *will* than to the flesh. By doing the opposite, he establishes a close association between inherited culpability (if that is in fact his meaning) and inherited mortality. Here again, moreover, we encounter *slime* and its association for anyone who knows patristic theology with inherited mortality; 'fleshly slyme' certainly balances and perhaps outweighs 'the guilt of ... infected cryme.' But even if we grant that Spenser is being Augustinian in the 'Hymne of Heavenly Love,' we need not assume that the theology of the Hymns is identical with that of *The Faerie Queene* or that because Spenser states a doctrine of inherited culpability (if he does) in these almost certainly later poems he intended such a conception of the Fall in the earlier work. Robert Ellrodt has shown that the Hymns differ from *The Faerie Queene* in being more consistently and self-consciously Neoplatonic;[38] why should they not differ theologically (if they do) as well as philosophically? Spenser's eucharistic imagery in the 'Hymne of Heavenly Love' reminds us more pointedly than anything in *The Faerie Queene* of the sacramental language of the Counter-Reformation: we hear 'Of loues deepe wound, that pierst the piteous hart / Of that dear Lord with so entyre affection, / And sharply launching euery inner part, / Dolours of death into his soule did dart'; the wound in Christ's side is a 'bleeding sourse' whose 'streames yet neuer staunch, / But stil do flow and freshly still redound, / To heale the sores of sinfull soules vnsound' (*HHL*, 156–9, 164–6). Such imagery has a distinctly continental and Catholic character; in English poetry it more nearly anticipates Crashaw (or some of Herbert) than looks back to *The Faerie Queene*. If Spenser did indeed come under a measure of Counter Reformation influence in the Hymns, we should not be surprised if he gave voice there to a conception of original sin characteristic of Tridentine theology (and Trent reaffirmed Augustine's doctrine with vigor).[39] The apparent absence of that conception in *The Faerie Queene* suggests that Spenser's major poem ought to be measured by another theology.

For positive statements of the latter, for two allegories which seem to mirror Chrysostom's conceptions of sin and death rather than Augustine's, we return to Book Two.

CHAPTER NINE

Two Images of Mortalitie

I

Why are Ruddymane's hands indelibly stained? Because the stain signifies 'the sin of the flesh which is inherent and cannot be removed by any earthly means.' That is Professor Winstanley in 1914, and later interpreters have followed her lead.[1] Though she does not say in so many words that Ruddymane has inherited the guilt of original sin, that seems to be her meaning, and A.C. Hamilton in 1958 adopted that account without qualification: Ruddymane represents 'mankind which from its infancy has been infected by original sin.'[2] On that showing, Mordant and Amavia are Adam and Eve who leave the blot of their transgression on their progeny, and Hamilton glosses 'Pittifull spectacle of deadly smart' (II, i, 40) accordingly: 'the dead father, the dying mother, and the living, yet stained, offspring present a brief allegory of the human condition.'[3] Alastair Fowler (1961), taking Hamilton's interpretation as his point of departure, develops a fully Augustinian account of the episode. Ruddymane is 'sad witness of [his] fathers fall' (II, i, 37) 'in that his stains testify to the fall of the old Adam: the blood is Amavia's, but the indelible filth goes back to Acrasia's poison.'[4] Ruddymane cannot be washed because though baptism justifies man by taking away the guilt of original sin from his soul, it leaves the flesh subject to death and concupiscence. Fowler quotes from Ficino a passage which makes that Augustinian distinction with great precision: baptism '"does away the guilt and the bond of sin in the mind [soul] of him who is by baptism cleansed; but the proclivity to sin, inherent in the natural body, it does not extirpate."'[5] Hamilton argues to the same effect, though with a more heavily Protestant emphasis;

the spring's failure to wash Ruddymane is owing to 'the limits of baptism: while man, born in sin, may be "borne anewe of water" (baptismal service), the inner corruption of original sin remains.'[6]

An obvious difficulty with such explanations is that Ruddymane, though physically stained, seems to be neither sinful nor guilty; phrases like 'born in sin,' 'the inner corruption of original sin,' and the 'proclivity to sin, inherent in the natural body' belie Spenser's emphasis. Ruddymane is a 'sweet Babe,' 'a louely babe' (II, i, 37, 40), and Spenser even describes him as 'innocent' (II, ii, 1). Hamilton argues that 'the syntax restricts the meaning in the next line': 'innocent / Of that was doen' (italics added);[7] but we might as easily argue that the placement of *innocent* at the end of a line restricts the syntax, placing greater emphasis upon the condition than the qualification. Furthermore since what 'was doen' is the destruction of Mordant and presumably an allegory of the Fall, Ruddymane's being innocent of *that* seems equivalent to his being innocent of Adam's transgression. Fowler recognizes this innocence but attributes it, oddly, to baptism: 'the bloody babe ... is as innocent ... as the baptized are imputed to be, who plays unharmed amid tragic death, and who is compared with the phoenix, a traditional resurrection symbol.'[8] I say 'oddly' because Ruddymane's innocence precedes and seems to have nothing to do with his abortive washing. There is no suggestion that the spring bestows his innocence; it has no effect on him whatever – a phenomenon which Fowler himself attempts subsequently to explain. Ruddymane appears to be stained but innocent simply by virtue of his birth, like those infants for whom Tertullian discourages baptism – marked or cursed with mortality but without sin or guilt.

There are several indications that Spenser means us to understand the mark or curse in that pre-Augustinian way. Mordant is not 'sin-giving' but 'death-giving,' and Amavia insists upon his fleshly, which is to say his mortal, weakness. Acrasia's enigmatic charm contains the same emphasis: '*giue death to him that death does giue*' (II, i, 55); and, however we interpret Amavia's name, she is a lover not of sin's but of death's antithesis. Also Ruddymane is nurtured in death rather than in sin: 'in *dead* [not sinful] parents balefull ashes bred' (II, ii, 2: italics added), and Guyon does not grieve because the child will be morally tainted but because, through his parents' demise, he too will die: 'As budding braunch rent from the natiue tree, / And throwen forth till it be *withered'* (II, ii, 2; italics added). Finally, when Guyon surveys the scene – dead parents and bloody babe – he admonishes the Palmer to 'Behold the image [not of *sin* or *guilt* but] of *mortalitie'* (II, i, 57; italics added).

That Spenser intended a pre-Augustinian allegory of the Fall is also suggested by Guyon's 'diuerse doubt' (II, ii, 3) when Ruddymane's hands fail to wash:

> He wist not whether blot of foule offence
> Might not be purgd with water nor with bath;
> Or that high God, in lieu of innocence,
> Imprinted had that token of his wrath,
> To shew how sore bloudguiltinesse he hat'th;
> Or that the charme and venim, which they druncke,
> Their bloud with secret filth infected hath,
> Being diffused through the senselesse truncke,
> That through the great contagion direfull deadly stunck
>
> (II, ii, 4).

Fowler recognizes here two conjectures about original sin. The first he calls the *'reatus* theory,' which 'rests on a forensic metaphor of guilt'; the second employs 'a medical, not a forensic, metaphor [and] describes the effect of Adam's fall upon his posterity as a hereditary disease in the human constitution.'[9] Although Fowler does not draw the doctrinal parallels, we can see that the former is very close to the Augustinian and Lutheran-Calvinist understanding of original sin and the latter to the doctrine of the early and Eastern Fathers. Carol Kaske reads the stanza with precisely those referents: 'The Greek view of original sin [i.e., the pre-Augustinian, which she calls Greek because since Augustine it has been identified with the Eastern Church] is illustrated by Guyon's second conjecture, while the Augustinian, Western, distinctively Protestant view is illustrated by the first.'[10] Certainly to say that 'God, *in lieu of innocence,* / Imprinted had that token of his wrath, / To shew how sore bloudguiltinesse he hat'th' (italics added) states a doctrine of transmitted guilt. One can scarcely interpret such language to mean anything other than that the child is born guilty – either guilty of blood or, as by carnal conception, in his blood. (The latter reading would accord exactly with Augustine's understanding of the transmission of guilt from Adam to his line.) The medical language of the second conjecture is less explicitly Greek than the former is Augustinian, but many of the Fathers speak of human nature's being *infected* with death by Adam's sin, and metaphors of disease suggest the inheritance of mortality.[11] Furthermore, references to sin and guilt are conspicuously missing from the second conjecture. Professor Kaske thinks that Spenser like Guyon vacillates between the two theologies, but Ruddymane's innocence and Spenser's heavy emphasis on mortality and human frailty rather than guilt in his depiction of Mordant and Amavia suggest that the allegory adopts the second.

If that is so, how are we to interpret the occasion for Guyon's doubt – the failure of the spring to wash away the stain? Since the pre-Augustinian and Eastern Fathers interpret baptism as the catechumen's participation in Christ's destruction of death and renewal of *theosis* in Paradise, an allegory of the sacrament so conceived ought to be one in which its effect is both complete and manifest. If Spenser is writing such an allegory and if the child's stained hands signify the inheritance of mortality, we should expect the water to wash the stain away. A residual blemish, as both Fowler and Hamilton have shown, is consonant with Western conceptions of baptism – especially with the Lutheran and Calvinist – but the pre-Augustinian and Eastern understanding is much more accurately represented by the immediate and complete regeneration of Red Crosse in the Well and Balm. No wonder Guyon vacillates between two conceptions of sin and grace; since he believes that what lies before him is an 'image of mortalitie' (rather than of inherited sin), he presumably expects from baptism the washing away of that image; and he does not get it.

We do not know what conclusion, if any, Guyon comes to, for the Palmer interrupts him with an explanation – an etiological myth to account for the spring and its failure to wash.[12] The story raises as many questions as it answers, but it seems to make one point very clear: that Guyon (and the critics) erred in conceiving the spring as baptism. The water, we learn, is a nymph's tears; she was a member of Diana's train, and there is nothing about her characterization to associate her with the source of baptismal water. The usual allegory of the font's origin is Christ's pierced side, from which flowed both the blood of the eucharist and the water of baptism. There is no hint of any such imagery here, and the nymph, though virtuous, is not Christlike in her virtue. Her metamorphosis is a means of securing her virginity, but the Palmer's story of her desperate flight from Faunus and her ultimate liquification as a last and equally desperate resort is contrary in emphasis at every point to the image of Christ enduring in perfect charity the passion which his persecutors inflict upon Him and freely pouring out water from his wounded flesh for the salvation of those very persecutors. Furthermore the nymph is not only liquified but petrified 'With stony feare of that rude rustick mate' (II, ii, 8), and Spenser associates the stoniness with her virginity – 'Transformd ... to a stone from stedfast virgins state' (II, ii, 8). Virginity is virtuous, but this nymph's virginity is negative (one anticipates by contrast the wholly positive presentation of virginity in Belphoebe, in the next canto). The waters that transmit her virtue are 'chast and pure' but also 'cold through feare' (II, ii, 9). Small wonder that unlike the water of baptism, poured out freely in fervent charity, this spring will not heal the wound of man's nature.

It seems, in fact, to exacerbate it. This same stream which will not wash Ruddymane is, if not the cause, the occasion of Mordant's death.[13] Guyon (and the critics) should have remembered that and, even before the Palmer told his story, recognized that the water could not possibly be the font; there is no theology – patristic, Catholic, or Protestant – in which the 'laver of regeneration' kills. Fowler tries to avoid this difficulty by interpreting Mordant's death as the baptismal 'dying into life,' and he quotes Saint Paul's '"We are buried ... with [Christ] by baptism into his death ... our old man is crucified with him."' 'What,' asks Fowler, 'is the burial of Mordant-Amavia but a burial of the "old man"?' That interpretation depends, however, from Fowler's apparently groundless assumption that Ruddymane's innocence derives from his washing in this very stream which caused his father's death: 'Since the death of the old man is the beginning of a new life free from the domination of sin and death, Spenser has set over against the image of mortality an image of rebirth. This is the bloody babe, who is as innocent ... as the baptized are imputed to be.'[14] If the bloody babe is not innocent by virtue of his washing but, as Spenser seems to indicate, before it, interpreting the father's death as baptismal seems much less plausible than Fowler's reading suggests.

Furthermore none of the details of Mordant's death suggest baptismal symbolism; he is not 'buried with Christ' as Red Crosse is when he goes down into the Well of Life. Mordant is not immersed; he drinks. And so far as Amavia is concerned, the incident is wholly lamentable; there is nothing in her account (which is all Spenser gives us) to suggest that her mate's demise is regenerative. The effect of the spring is nothing more nor less than to fulfill Acrasia's charm: 'Till comming to this well, he stoupt to drincke: / The charme fulfild, dead suddenly he downe did sincke' (II, i, 55). We surely strain even against the halting staccato of the alliteration to read that event as a regenerative death in Christ. Furthermore, since Amavia's suicide, which stains the child, is the immediate consequence of the stream's lethal effect on Mordant, we can reasonably argue that so far from being an antidote to Ruddymane's stigma, the water is its efficient cause. Amavia's staining the spring as well as the child (II, i, 40) strengthens that argument, suggesting that this water is implicated in the original transgression and its consequence. For unless we are to insist more strongly than the allegory warrants on Amavia's innocence (for all her virtuous intentions, we cannot forget that she dies the very death to which Despair tempted Red Crosse), we are constrained to regard the mixing of her blood with the stream as indicative of a further spreading of the taint of death.

If the spring then is not the font, what is it? Hamilton suggests temperance (as well as baptism), but, as Fowler remarks, that is improbable: 'Spenser would hardly wish to show the ineffectuality of the virtue he is celebrating.'[15] Fowler's alternative (one of them) seems much closer to the mark – that the stream signifies the Mosaic law;[16] for the Law, unlike temperance and indeed unlike any of the virtues (powers), is negative or prohibitive by nature.[17] Furthermore the Law in Christian theology is the traditional antithesis of grace and thus a foil to, and parody of, baptism, just as the nymph's well seems to be. Guyon's effort to wash away the inherited consequence of Adam's transgression in this water suggests that he mistakes it for baptism, just as one mistakes a parody for the real thing. Fowler's analysis of the symbolism is persuasive (and how, two pages later, he can reidentify the stream as baptism is not clear from the logic of his essay). Saint Paul says, 'I had not known sin, but by the law: for I had not known lust [or concupiscence], except the law had said, Thou shalt not covet ... For I was alive without the law once: but when the commandment came, sin revived, and I died' (Romans 7:7, 9). Fowler quotes this passage and

draws the obvious parallels: Mordant lusted but did not perish in his
sin until he drank from the pure well; 'He, too, was alive in sin so long
as "he knew not ... his owne ill" ... it was only when he reformed that
he died. His death, too, appeared to be caused by something good –
the pure well – though in reality it was Acrasia who slew him, taking
occasion by the well.'[18]

Such an interpretation is fully consonant with an allegory of sin as
the pre-Augustinian Fathers understood it, for their denial of *inherited*
guilt did not preclude – in fact entailed – ascription of guilt by the
Mosaic law; man is not born a sinner, but the coming of the Law made
him one. That, as we have seen, is because the only sin is actual, not
original, and without a prohibition, there is no occasion for actual sin
(precisely Chrysostom's point in his exegesis of Romans 5:13).[19] 'Sin is
not imputed when there is no law,' and when sin is not imputed, there
is no condemnation, no guilt, and no penalty. With the coming of the
Law, men were condemned for their own sins, not Adam's, and became
subject to Adam's punishment – death. Death, therefore, must be considered under two aspects – as a postlapsarian circumstance which pre-
ceded the Law and which 'reigned from Adam to Moses' over those
who were without the Law, and as a penalty for the actual sins of individual men and women occasioned by the Law. Death, in other words,
is both congenital and penal, becoming the latter, however, only when
the Law imputed sin. Chrysostom seems to be saying (though not in so
many words) that the coming of the Law transformed an inherited condition into a punishment; sin, given strength by the Law, gave death its
sting. Therefore all mankind can say with Saint Paul, 'I was alive without the law once' – alive because, though mortal, uncondemned – 'but
when the commandment came, sin revived, and I died' (Romans 7:9).

Spenser's allegory seems sensitive to these complexities. As giver of
death and cause of his child's stain, Mordant almost certainly signifies
Adam; but as recipient of death he can reasonably be interpreted as
Adam's historical extension, fallen humanity.[20] The death, moreover,
which he receives seems to be both congenital and penal; we infer the
former from Amavia's 'For he was flesh: (all flesh doth frailtie breed)'
(II, i, 52) as well as from the close (and sinister) link between eros and
death in Mordant's sexually attractive corpse (II, i, 41) and the latter
from the spring's effect upon him. Lust, represented by Acrasia's
charm, taking the commandment as its occasion, gives '*death* [as pen-

alty] *to him* [fallen humanity] *that* [as Adam] *death* [as inherited mortality] *does giue'* (II, i, 55). The spring on that reading is Mordant's Moses, and his drinking its water is the imputation of his sin, the consequent acquisition of guilt, and therefore the occasion of his death. Ruddymane is one of those men sprung from Adam over whom death reigns but who because of his infancy – perhaps the pre-Mosaic infancy of the race – is free of law, guilt, and *penal* death. Obviously, therefore, the stream can have no effect on him, for the Law cannot take away inherited mortality, which is his only liability. He requires the water of baptism, which, at least in this episode, is not forthcoming. What he gets instead is the pagan complement to Mosaic law – classical temperance in the Castle of Medina – and there is little reason to anticipate more from that remedy than from the spring.

II

If this reading of the Ruddymane episode is correct, the 'whole subject' of the Legend of Temperance must be man's inheritance of Adam's death (not his guilt), the ineffectuality of the Law to take away mortality, the instrumentality of the Law in imputing sin and transforming death into a punishment, and the inaccessibility (at least at the outset) of baptism. At the opposite end of Book Two and serving (along with the destruction of the Bower) to complete the action which the Ruddymane story initiates is Arthur's defeat of Maleger. That episode is also conventionally glossed as an allegory of original sin and the 'standing lake' into which Arthur ultimately plunges Maleger as the font. We now need to ask whether the pre-Augustinian understanding of the Fall and its remedy applies to Maleger as well as to Ruddymane and, if it does, whether the 'standing lake' is in fact the regenerative baptismal water unavailable in cantos one and two.

Though commentators now take the identification of Maleger as original sin for granted, the idea is relatively new. It seems to have begun with Woodhouse, who called the monster very explicitly 'original sin or human depravity, the result of the fall.'[21] That language as well as the whole context of Woodhouse's essay leaves no doubt that he intends original sin in the Augustinian and Calvinist sense; he even characterizes Maleger as man's 'inherited taint.'[22] Hamilton developed Woodhouse's thesis in much the same way he developed an Augustin-

ian interpretation of the Mordant-Amavia-Ruddymane allegory, and
what we now take to be conventional wisdom about Maleger is owing
largely to that development: 'Maleger is the state of sin, both actual
and original; it is that state of sin from which the Red Cross Knight
must be purged before he may slay the Dragon, and which must be
slain before Guyon may overthrow the power of Acrasia.'[23] According
to that reading, Arthur's victory is comparable to Red Crosse's and the
'standing lake' to the Well of Life. In each instance (each in the eleventh
canto of its respective book) the hero relies on baptism to deliver him
from original sin.

But if we are correct that the Well of Life does not in fact deliver Red
Crosse from original sin (which is never mentioned) but only from
'sins' and that its principal effect is not to justify a sinner but to bestow
life and deification upon the moribund, and if Hamilton is correct (as
he almost certainly is) that Spenser intended parallels between the two
eleventh cantos, will it not follow that Arthur's defeat of Maleger is
also a deliverance (presumably of Alma) from death? Spenser's
description of the monster suggests precisely that. Maleger's being
'vnsound' and of 'subtile substance' hints at physical decay, and his
other attributes identify him even more explicitly with mortality. He
looks 'like a ghost ... whose graue-clothes were vnbound' (II, xi, 20); 'As
pale and wan as ashes was his looke'; 'His bodie [is] leane and meagre
as a rake, / And skin all withered like a dryed rooke' (II, xi, 22). Hamilton glosses *meagre* as 'emaciated; fleshless like the skeleton Death';[24]
the comparison is exact, for Maleger reminds us – and surely is supposed to – of the traditional, skeletal figure of death. A 'rooke' is a hay-
stack, and that detail along with Maleger's belt of twisted bracken
associates him with autumn or the death of the year. His withered skin
suggests that he is a corpse, as does his being 'cold and drery as a
Snake' (II, xi, 22); (Spenser may also wish to remind us that the Serpent
is author of death). Presumably Maleger has a face, but we never see it;
it is masked by 'a dead mans skull,' which he wears for a helmet (II, xi,
22). Maleger, like the dead, is bloodless; though Arthur runs him
through, 'Ne drop of bloud appeared shed to bee' (II, xi, 38), and
Spenser calls this active and very dangerous adversary a 'dead corse'
(II, xi, 37) and 'carkasse' (II, xi, 38). Arthur concludes in amazement that
the monster is a 'wandring ghost, that wanted funerall' (II, xi, 39).
Finally there are the frequently quoted riddles of stanza forty. What is

'Flesh without bloud, a person without spright'? What can 'doe harme, yet could not harmed bee'? What cannot 'die, yet seem'd a mortall wight'? And what is 'most strong in most infirmitee'? Anyone who had read the canto without reference to the schools would surely answer, 'death,' and would conclude that when Arthur slays Maleger we witness the death of death, not of original sin. Hamilton's argument that Maleger is thin because 'worn out by evil' or Woodhouse's that 'the marks of physical disease and death are the symbols of the inherited taint' seem rather strained attempts to impose a meaning extraneous to the symbolism and required by a theology alien to the allegory.[25]

Maleger's relation to the passions, his being 'the Captain of the Lusts of the Flesh,'[26] is fully as consonant with his being death as with his being sin. That is so according to either Western or Eastern, Augustinian or pre-Augustinian theology, but in different ways; and the Eastern, pre-Augustinian way is both the more immediate and the closer to Spenser's allegory. Again the difference is between a juridical and an organic metaphor. Augustine conceives possibility (which means for him, as we have seen, the disordering of inherently good impulses) as a punishment, like mortality, inflicted on Adam for his guilt and which Adam's progeny inherit along with the guilt. Baptism takes the guilt away, but passibility, like mortality, remains. For the pre-Augustinian and Eastern Fathers, as we have also seen, passibility and mortality are virtually synonymous (and by effecting deification, baptism takes both away) – not comparable but distinct punishments for Adam's transgression but that transgression's very constituents and the constituents of each other. To be fallen is to be mortal is to be passionate. To die in Adam is to live in desire – as Tantalus does. When the deifying image of God is corrupted by passion, passion becomes the life of man – carnal and chthonic energies displace divine energies. Death so conceived is not a cessation – or at least not an immediate cessation – of spiritual and physical activities but an inversion of the source and end of those activities. Death, therefore, paradoxically, has life, and that life is the life of the passions.

Maleger appears to embody that paradox. That he is attended by impatience and impotence suggests that passion and death coinhere in him; and he is himself a personification of death who is passionately alive. Arthur is 'amazed' that though he fights against a 'lifelesse shadow,' he nevertheless sees life 'and felt his mightie maine.' Arthur must devise new ways 'to take *life* from that *dead-liuing* swaine' (II, xi, 44; italics added) and squeeze from Maleger's 'carrion corse / The lothfull life' (II, xi, 46). That the old way, throwing Maleger on the ground, has not worked indicates that death's life is chthonic and carnal; like the old Adam Maleger is 'of the earth, earthy.' Earth is his mother, and his revivifying falls signify his return to the source of death's life. The parallels between Red Crosse's and Arthur's battles on which Hamilton bases (in part) his interpretation of Maleger as original sin testify more convincingly to his significance as a carnally vital death, for his falls parody Red Crosse's returns to the sacramental sources of divine life. George is also a 'man of earth' (γεωργός), as all unbaptized men are – a member of the old Adam whose life is lust and death. But when he falls it is not upon earth (Adam) but into the Well and Balm, which is into Christ. He is therefore renewed by Christ's deifying victory over lust and death; Red Crosse ceases to be the old Adam by participation in the new – George becomes Saint George. Maleger returns instead to the dust from which the first Adam was formed and to which all who are in the first Adam, both in literal death and in carnal affection, return. Maleger's falls, in effect, repeat the Fall and thus renew the dead (which is to say, passionate) life which the Fall inaugurated. Red Crosse's falls repeat Christ's victorious descent into the grave and Hell whereby the mortal and passionate consequence of the Fall was undone.

Still another compelling reason to believe that Spenser conceives the relation between death and passion in pre-Augustinian and Eastern terms is that the passions perish with Maleger, setting Alma free from their assaults. Maleger's death by water – in the 'standing lake' – presumably signifies Alma's baptism; and its obvious effect, and indeed the motive for Arthur's combat, is her entire deliverance from the lusts which attack her battlements. Such an effect is radically inconsistent with the Latin Catholic and Protestant doctrine of the lust's persistence after baptism, to which interpreters of Ruddymane's stain appeal. Just as the Fathers speak of death as already destroyed by baptism, even though the fact of physical death remains, they emphasize Christ's definitive victory over passion and the soul's freedom from the lusts, though of course the lusts too remain. In the second circumstance as in the first, the perspective is eschatological; because the baptized Christian has become a partaker of the Resurrection and lives already in the age to come, his flesh has been delivered from concupiscence. Christ 'dost anoint the mortal substance [with chrism] *perfecting it'*; He 'changes [it] into life without end' (italics added). Christ was baptized in Jordan, 'healing the passion of the cosmos.' Such liturgical exclamations (both from the Byzantine Epiphany liturgy with its heavy emphasis on baptism)[27] are indicative of patristic attitudes; mystically and liturgically, if not phenomenally, baptism confers Christ's own impassibility upon both soul and body. If Mordant had in fact received baptism, if the spring had been the font, Acrasia's poison would have been purged. Such a theology accounts convincingly for Alma's happy circumstance at the end of canto eleven, and there seems no equally convincing way to reconcile that circumstance with the medieval and Reformation doctrine of residual concupiscence.

Nor will Western teaching allow for Alma's righteousness *before* Arthur's victory. If we interpret Maleger as the 'inherited taint' and Alma as the soul, he must be her taint and his destruction her justification. That means before Arthur buries Maleger in the lake Alma must be guilty of original sin, and in effect, a lost soul. If we go further and take a specifically Calvinist view of the matter as Woodhouse encourages us to do, we shall be forced to argue that she is in a condition of total depravity when she entertains Guyon and Arthur in cantos nine and ten. Such a reading clearly violates the poem; nothing in Spenser's presentation of Alma or her house suggests that she is other than good and wise. She is assaulted by the passions but resists them. They pose a threat (evidently a steadily increasing threat)[28] to her and to the continuity of her establishment, and she obviously needs the help which Arthur affords; but there is no suggestion that she is unrighteous or culpable. The only way to reconcile her characterization with the Augustinian understanding of original sin and redemption is to make the effect of Maleger's death retroactive – to assume that Alma has received justifying grace prior to the action which procures her that grace. She would then be understandable as the soul which according to Augustine is righteous by virtue of baptism but still, in this life, subject to concupiscence. But, if we take that view of the matter (and to do so strains against the sequence of the fiction), how are we to explain Alma's being righteous and besieged according to one conception of baptism (applied retroactively) and delivered from the siege, after baptism, according to another? To save Woodhouse's and Hamilton's thesis we should have to assume that Spenser took liberties with the baptismal theology which is germane to that thesis (adding to justification deliverance from concupiscence); we should also be forced to respect the poem's chronology in explaining one element in the allegory and ignore it in order to explain another. That is rather like multiplying epicycles to save appearances when the wiser course is to discard the old theory and adopt a new one.

If we do the latter, if we lay aside our Augustinian or Calvinist ideas both of original sin and of the limits of baptismal grace, the difficulties resolve themselves. The doctrine of inherited death allows, as we have seen, for the soul's innocence prior to baptism; man inherits no taint. So long therefore as the soul fends off the assaults of the passions, to which its legacy of death subjects it, and commits no personal, actual sin, it remains righteous. In practice, this condition of original but mortal and besieged innocence cannot be sustained past the age of accountability, for the strength of man's living death, of the chthonic energies which have become the motive forces of fallen nature, is too great to be withstood by merely human means. But since Alma is the soul in a generic sense and since this is allegory rather than realistic fiction, there is no inherent contradiction in Spenser's depicting her as entirely righteous before she receives the benefit of baptism. She may be regarded as signifying the fallen condition of humanity as it were in its essence rather than in its historical accidents. If so, she represents precisely what Ruddymane appears to, the way Adam's offspring are born – innocent of their father's sin but subject to its mortal consequence. Arthur – Christ – delivers her from that consequence. Or Spenser's context may be in a measure historical, as it may also be in the Ruddymane episode: both Alma and Ruddymane appear to be pre-Christian souls. He has the Law but evidently lacks access to baptismal grace; she has the classical complement to the Law, temperance-as-moderation (which Ruddymane is also offered), but until Arthur's advent she also lacks grace. Perhaps we should conceive Alma as the soul of the archetypal noble pagan, the sort Dante puts in Limbo, who has relied successfully upon the pagan virtues to keep the house of the body in order and secure itself against the passions' encroachments. (Such a reading would explain the conspicuous absence of Christian symbolism in Spenser's depiction of Alma's otherwise exemplary economy.) If so, she is another 'image of mortalitie, / And feeble nature cloth'd with fleshly tyre' (II, i, 57) but more fortunate than Ruddymane in that she ultimately receives grace. Or perhaps, since neither is a character in a fiction, we can say that Alma is simply Ruddymane in another allegorical context – Ruddymane, let us say, after he has been taught by Medina. Maleger then unfolds the meaning of Ruddymane's stain, and when Alma receives the benefit of Arthur's victory, we may reasonably argue that Ruddymane has at last been washed and the 'whole subject' of the Legend of Temperance resolved.

III

Finally, pre-Augustinian conceptions of the Fall and its remedy shed fresh light on Arthur's battle with Maleger and on the meaning of the 'standing lake.' That Arthur is here (as elsewhere) a type of Christ and that his ordeal is an allegory of the Passion has been suggested by a number of commentators and carries conviction. We should expect, therefore, if Maleger were original sin, some hint of the theology of atonement and justification. What we get instead is a fierce battle and wrestling match (one of the most strenuous struggles in *The Faerie Queene*), and that is what anyone who had read the Fathers and ancient liturgies would expect. Lacking a doctrine of inherited guilt, antique soteriology largely excludes juridical considerations; Christ did not atone for inherited sin (there being no such thing) but conquered inherited death – hence the persistent patristic characterizations of Christ as soldier, warrior and even (Chrysostom) wrestler. But Christ, as we have learned – as the Easter hymns say repeatedly – conquered death *by death*, and Arthur's experience seems to reflect that paradox. Not only is this battle hard fought; there are few if any in the poem which take so heavy a toll upon the victor. Arthur bleeds and almost dies as a consequence of his struggle. Indeed we should be taking no undue liberty with the allegory to say that Arthur dies symbolically, in a type of the Passion. That that is how Spenser intended the episode to be interpreted is suggested by Arthur's subsequent unction with 'balme and wine and costly spicery' (II, xi, 49), recalling the preparation of Christ's body for burial. The unction (the balm) suggests in turn the Resurrection (just as it effects Red Crosse's resurrection and *theosis*) and thus reminds us that with death's death (through the agency of

Christ's death and burial) man is delivered from the curse of Adam. This hint of something beyond the end of canto eleven, something comparable to Red Crosse's Christification and regaining of Paradise at the corresponding moment in Book One, completes the pattern of parallels to which Hamilton has called our attention.

That Arthur wrestles Maleger to death rather than drowning him brings us to the debated question whether (as I have been assuming) the 'standing lake' in fact signifies the font. More than one interpreter has questioned the symbolism and for good reason: the lake's static quality, especially in contrast with Arthur's vigorous activity, raises doubts; one would expect a symbol of baptism to be actively involved in the destruction of death, but the standing lake *merely* stands, acting as a receptacle for Maleger's corpse. Hamilton, while interpreting the lake as baptism and as a symbol corresponding to the Well of Life in Book One, acknowledges the difficulty, and Anthea Hume specifically denies the correspondence: the lake 'lacks the vitality which Spenser unerringly gives to images of present spiritual power,' the most obvious being Red Crosse's 'liuing well.'[29] One simple reason for identifying the lake as the font is lack of a plausible alternative (Professor Hume's suggestion that it represents Arthur's memory of his baptism seems strained and rather arbitrary.)[30] Furthermore, the lake, however passive, is the final and decisive means of Maleger's overthrow; had Arthur not cast him there, Death would have revived yet again to 'lothfull life.' Moreover, though baptism according to patristic theology and liturgy destroys death, the meaning of course is that Christ destroys death by means of baptism, and that is precisely what Arthur does by means of the lake. Furthermore, in traditional typology baptism follows Christ's victory over death *by death*, just as the lake's reception of Maleger follows Arthur's; only after Christ dies on the cross does the water of the sacrament flow from His side, and only after Arthur has killed Maleger by what appears to be a type of the Passion does the lake present itself as the means of death's destruction.

But the water of baptism does *flow* from Christ, and in most Scriptural and liturgical symbols of the sacrament, baptismal water is 'living.' Why then should the lake be passive? A possible explanation is that Spenser intended a specific contrast with the activity of the 'liuing well,' to which the lake in its principal signification corresponds – that he is representing here a different facet of baptismal grace from that

which informs Book One. In Red Crosse's immersion we see the positive effects of the sacrament – regeneration and deification – on a
Christian soul; in Maleger's, on the contrary, we witness the negative,
the destruction of a Christian soul's chief impediment to regeneration
and deification. We should remember in this connection that while Red
Crosse is baptized, Maleger is not. Rather the latter's death by water is
one of the effects of the Well of Life on the former; Maleger is what Red
Crosse (or any catechumen) leaves behind in the depth of the baptismal pool when he rises to a passionless and divine life. In other words
the Well and the lake may be intended as the convex and concave of
the same sphere, the one signifying the consequence of the other.
Maleger is as it were George's inherited earth (passion and death)
which must be destroyed by water before Saint George can arise from
the Well as the 'signe of victoree.' Static as opposed to living water is
fitting for such an allegorical significance – a negation reflecting a
negation – and the stasis corresponds nicely with Arthur's symbolic
death, the means by which a dead lake puts death to death. The furi-
ous action of canto eleven winds down to a theologically appropriate
stillness in which we await the allegorical complement to Red Crosse's
victory on the morning of the third day. That of course is Guyon's
destruction of the Bower.

PART FOUR

EPILOGUE

Reverberations

I

Is there evidence of patristic influence elsewhere in *The Faerie Queene*? I detect several muted repetitions of the motifs we have discussed. In Book Six, for instance, grace collapses into nature (or nature into grace) in a fashion that anticipates the personification of a deified *natura* in Book Seven. Tristram, who has been nurtured by nature, is praised for his grace. (The fact that neither here nor elsewhere in the Book – on Mount Acidale for instance – can we distinguish precisely between grace and Grace sustains the point.) In Tristram's 'face appeares ... gratious goodlyhead' (VI, ii, 25); is he another instance of the deified countenance, another mirror of celestial grace? Not so explicitly as Belphoebe, whom he resembles, but the very resemblance prompts the question. So does Calidore's near infatuation with the youth's beauty, making us wonder whether we are to hear 'Godhead' for 'goodlyhead.' Book Six is also concerned with the destructive power of the passions. The Blatant Beast captures Serena when she is 'loosely wandring,' 'as liking led / Her wauering lust' (VI, iii, 24, 23); *lust* here is not explicitly sexual (Serena desires flowers for a garland), but in conjunction with 'loosely wandring' and with the obvious allusion to Proserpina, we can scarcely ignore the sexual implications. And when, as remedy for her wound, the Hermit counsels her 'To rule the stubborne rage of passion blinde' and 'learne your outward sences to refraine / From things, that stir up fraile affection,' (VI, vi, 7), he appears to be prescribing ἐγκράτεια rather than σωφροσύνη.

Book Six also contains a version of the Harrowing – Calidore's breaking into the robbers' cave and bringing Serena back from the underworld to light. The emphasis is less exclusively Christian than in

Book One or than in Guyon's beguiling of Mammon (we hear echoes of classical descent myths as well); but the robbers being 'brigants,' or devils, points toward the Harrowing, and when Calidore 'with huge resistlesse mighte, / The dores assayled, and the locks vpbrast' (VI, xi, 43), we are surely supposed to recall that Christ entering Hell broke the gates of brass and smote the bars of iron. Just as Spenser may intend Belphoebe and the theology of deification to enhance our understanding of Tristram, so here Red Crosse's becoming Christ the Harrower may be our point of reference for Calidore's victory. 'Huge resistlesse mighte' suggests a strength beyond the human, and his singlehandedly slaying all the large crowd of 'brigants' sustains that inference. He is like a lion in battle (the lion of Judah?) and his effect upon Pastorella is like Christ upon the dead: 'So her vneath at last he did reuiue, / That long had lyen dead, and made againe aliue' (VI, xi, 50). Of these lines Hamilton remarks, 'The resurrection is rendered as though entirely natural'[1] – just as we should expect it to be in a book which treats nature as divine. Meanwhile the less 'natural,' more specifically theological treatment in Book One may be supposed to guide us here.

And elsewhere – the motif is recurrent: in Mammon's Cave (as we have seen); in the three-day, forty-stanza journey to the Bower of Bliss; in Marinell's rescue of Florimell, imprisoned 'most neare' to 'lowest hell' (IV, xii, 6) for seven months by 'yron barres' and 'brasen locke' (IV, xi, 3); and (this instance has gone unrecognized) in Britomart's rescue of Amoret from Busirane. Amoret's confinement, like Florimell's, has lasted seven months (also like Alma's imprisonment by the besieging passions; is Arthur's destruction of Maleger still another Harrowing?); the number probably signifies the seven ages or 'days' between the creation (the Fall) and the Resurrection, during which the faithful await deliverance from the enchanter's power. Amoret is also bound with iron and brass, 'with yron bands, / Unto a brasen pillour' (III, xii, 30), and Scudamour tells us that she has been 'pend / In dolefull darkenesse from the vew of day' (III, xi, 11) – a description which answers less accurately to what we see of her circumstances (darkness as such is not the principal emphasis) than to conventional representations of Adam's confinement in the depths of the earth where 'the sun is silent.' When Britomart penetrates this kingdom of darkness, she passes through three rooms, entering the third, where she wins her victory and releases a soul from bondage, at midnight of the second night of her venture, which is at the beginning of the morning of the third day. Finally, in the original version of Book Three, canto twelve ends with stanza forty-seven, a number uniting the seven ages of the fallen world with the years of the Exodus and the days of Lent (or of fasting in the wilderness). The implication is that Book Three ends with the end of bondage or of ascetic preparation. Recollection of the end of Book One should then remind us that just ahead lies the freedom of recovered Paradise and the festival of the mystical eighth day. The last two verses of the stanza suggest as much: 'Now cease your worke, and at your pleasure play; / Now cease your worke; tomorrow is an holy day.'

II

There may be other such echoes of the themes we have explored, but there is another and ultimately more interesting reverberation from patristic conceptions of holiness and temperance. Interpreting the former as *theosis* and the latter as the ascetic means to *theosis* calls our conventional understanding of Books Three and Four into question.

The issue at stake is eros and Spenser's attitude toward it. His ostensible thesis is clear: that, since chastity is nubile, eros, when properly directed, is an ennobling emotion, a 'most sacred fire' (III, iii, 1), a 'kindly flame,' and the root of 'honor and all vertue' (IV, Proem, 2). Most critics take Spenser at his word, concentrate on his celebration of married chastity, and perhaps underestimate the complexity of the poem. Hamilton's comparison of Books Two and Three is characteristic: 'In ... the adolescent state of temperance, the feminine appears only as the virgin Belphoebe or the whore Acrasia, that is, the rejection of sexual love or its abuse. Though Guyon is the servant of the "heauenly Mayd", he never sees the one and only spies on the other as a peeping Tom. He may respond to Acrasia only by binding her. Such repressive action cannot be Britomart's ... the yoking together of affection and chastity is the central task of her legend.' Hamilton concludes in effect that the resolution of Book Two is only tentative and that 'a central concern of the allegory in Books III and IV is to establish the conditions under which Acrasia may be released.'[2] Most interpreters pursue one version or another of that idea and place a heavy emphasis on the

goodness of eros; preference of the (at least theoretically) nubile Britomart to the virginal Belphoebe has become a critical commonplace. A
patristic interpretation of holiness and temperance necessarily casts
doubt on that preference, for if temperance entails the complete rejection of eros in order to achieve dispassion and thus to 'make man God'
by restoring in him the divine Image, there can be *no* 'conditions under
which Acrasia may be released.' If such conditions do exist (and if the
allegory is theologically consistent), my patristic interpretation comes
into question. Conversely, if the critics have found conditions which
are not in fact in the allegory and if Books Three and Four cast more
doubt on the goodness of eros and of marriage than they are thought to
do, conceiving holiness as *theosis* and temperance as 'perfect continence' may give us more convincing ways to understand chastity and
friendship than those to which we have become accustomed.

The poetry itself must always be the measure, and if we look at the
allegories of these central Books without the usual assumptions, we
find reasons to call those assumptions into question. Though sexual
love properly directed (which is to say, to marriage) may be all the
good things which Spenser (and the critics) say it is, there are in fact
very few instances of proper direction and many of improper. Indeed
for the author of the House of Busirane and the Cave of Lust to call
eros a '*kindly* flame' (in either sense of the adjective) approaches irony.
On the evidence of the poetry (as opposed to that of the commentaries)
we should have to say at the very least that the danger of a perverted
and perverting sexuality impinges as forcefully on Spenser's imagination as his belief in the goodness of 'wedded love.' We find many more
instances of destructive passions than of happy marriages. *Amoretti and
Epithalamion* may embrace wedlock as unreservedly as received opinion believes Spenser always does, but in the legends of chastity and
friendship – and for that matter in *The Faerie Queene* as a whole – 'affection chaste' seems more often a paradoxical aspiration than a practical
possibility. In all seven books there is only one consummated marriage
(among the principals) – Marinell's and Florimell's – and in Books
Three and Four sex in marriage is typically frustrating and destructive.

The obvious instance is that of Amoret and Scudamour; not only are
their nuptials never consummated (in the poem as we know it), eros
seems itself to be the obstacle to consummation. That is very odd in
view of Spenser's offering Amoret as his principal personification of

married love, counterpart to her twin sister's virginity. Why should Amoret's marriage not be happy and an emblem of chaste affection? The answer on the literal level of the allegory is that Busirane stole her away from her husband between the wedding and the bedding, but what does that mean? There are, as we know, numerous answers from the critics, none in my judgment entirely convincing; but two contradictory things seem certain: Amoret's imprisonment is the main obstacle to her marriage but also the consequence of that marriage. Had Amoret not been a bride, had she been virginal like her sister, nurtured by Diana rather than Venus, she would not have become prey to Busirane. We need not psychologize Scudamour and Amoret, which is surely a mistaken approach to allegorical figures, nor decide exactly what Busirane and his house signify, to recognize what Spenser is saying: that marriage – yes, even chaste, Christian marriage – releases dangerous passions which threaten the institution itself and the souls of man and wife. How then can eros be a sacred fire or a kindly flame, and where do we look for that flame burning brightly in marriage?

Not even, surprisingly, to Britomart. Though she is supposed to unite affection with chastity, enfolding the (supposedly) nubile Amoret and the virginal Belphoebe, she resembles the latter so much more strikingly than the former that we tend to forget that she is not simply a symbol of virginity. Nowhere is that more true than in the culminating episode of Book Three, the rescue of Amoret from Busirane; for there Britomart's superior strength, her ability to part the wall of flame (sexual passion) and in general to do what neither Scudamour nor Amoret can do is to all appearances owing to her independence of eros – like Guyon in Mammon's Cave – she sees and is not tempted. By the measure of *married* chastity, Amoret is no whit less chaste and should therefore be no less strong than Britomart, but Britomart here has Belphoebe's virginal strength, which is clearly greater than the strength of Belphoebe's marriageable (and married) sister – just as it proves to be in Book Four when Belphoebe herself rescues the nubile, and again helpless, Amoret from Lust.

In the original ending of Book Three, Britomart feels a pang of jealousy at the happiness of the reunited Amoret and Scudamour – reminding us that Britomart too is in love and therefore subject to erotic attraction and called to marriage. But the very fact that we require reminding is indicative of where the poem's center of gravity lies. The momentary jealousy surprises us, especially on the heels of the victory over Busirane, and seems out of character. So too does Britomart's initial infatuation and adolescent lovesickness, all the more so in that it is an isolated event narrated in a flashback, *after* we have seen her in action with her chaste and invincible spear. The martial maiden who by sexual purity unhorses even the temperate (and chaste) Guyon is consistent with the maiden who rescues Amoret; first impressions are enforced by final, and the other Britomart, the one destined for sexual experience in marriage, recedes from the surface of the poem. All Spenser's reminders of that destiny come as jolts, for they violate our sense of verisimilitude: the trite (intentionally trite?) Petrarchan lament in Book Three and the jealousy of Artegall in Five are instances. Both episodes interfere with our exalted estimation of a heroine whose strength is apparently owing to independence of such passions.

Even her relations to Artegall are less than entirely convincing. When in Book Four she finally meets him, Spenser says, 'Her hart did leape, and all her hart-strings tremble' (IV, vi, 29). We have bountiful evidence that Spenser can do better than that – both the language and the sentiment are trite (deliberately so or not) and out of character, especially in view of Artegall's response to Britomart – which does not seem erotic at all but entirely proper for an exalted personification of purity. He discerns in her face 'so diuine a beauties excellence' that he believes 'some heauenly goddesse he did see' 'and of his wonder made religion.' That is the kind of response we have come to think appropriate for her, a 'celestiall vision' to be worshipped rather than a lady to be wooed (IV, vi, 22, 24). Of course courtly lovers worship as they woo, but when Artegall falls humbly on his knees, he seems more convincingly a Christian than a Petrarchan suitor. He seems so, moreover, because throughout the episode Spenser goes out of his way to emphasize Britomart's holiness; she becomes a saint before our eyes: hers is an 'angels face,' she is a 'heauenly image of perfection' before whom Scudamour 'blest himselfe' (crossed himself?), and, most telling of all (and as we know), she resembles 'the maker selfe' (IV, vi, 19, 21, 24, 17). This language is theological; it exceeds 'sonnet talk' and insists on being taken at its face value rather than as conventional hyperbole. We are therefore not likely to be convinced that this sacred lady's heart strings trembled (really now!), and we are scarcely surprised that the ensuing account of Artegall's courtship seems perfunctory and anticlimactic:

'She yeelded her consent / To be his loue, and take him for her Lord, / Till they with marriage meet might finish that accord' (IV, vi, 41). The poetry here, altogether unlike that which deifies Britomart in the preceding stanzas, seems to be in the service of plot rather than of the poem's emotional commitments. Those commitments, I suggest, are to Britomart as 'Magnificke Virgin' (V, vii, 21), which is how the prophetic priest in the Temple of Isis later describes her, rather than to Britomart as chaste wife. To the possible objection that had Spenser lived to finish *The Faerie Queene* he would have found poetry sufficient for Britomart's marriage, one can only reply that the *prospect* of that marriage does not engage either the poet's or the reader's imagination in Book Four. Red Crosse's betrothal to Una – not an erotic union but a symbolic one, of holiness and truth, of Christ and the Church – is an indication of what Spenser might have done for Britomart and Artegall. That he did not suggests that marital chastity does not make so definitive a claim upon him as holiness did. It is indeed Britomart's holiness rather than her nubility that yields the greatest poetry of Books Three and Four.

Another case in point – which is to say another reason for believing that Spenser even while ostensibly celebrating marriage is imaginatively more engaged by virginity – is the lamentable history of Florimell. Like Britomart she is destined for marriage, and unlike Britomart she does marry, but in poetry as perfunctory as that in which Britomart and Artegall are betrothed. The ceremony is postponed to Book Five, takes place offstage, and strikes the reader rather as an afterthought, as a means of tying up loose ends of the story. (Would Britomart and Artegall in fact have fared better had Spenser written their nuptials?) Spenser declines in so many words 'To tell the glorie of the feast that day ... worke fit for an Herauld, not for me' (V, iii, 3) – an unconvincing disclaimer coming from the author of Book One, canto twelve. A reasonable surmise is that Spenser was more interested in Florimell as virgin, on whom he lavishes a great deal of fine poetry, than in Florimell as wife, whose nuptials he declines to describe. And, like Britomart, Florimell sticks in our imagination as a maiden, specifically as a maiden in distress on account of her maidenhead, defending her purity from various attacks by fleshly lusts – by the foresters, the witch's son, the fisherman, and Proteus. She seems rather like a romance version of the virgin martyr, prepared to suffer imprisonment

(which she does) and, if necessary, death to save her purity. Florimell
seeks to save it, of course, for Marinell, but since he has little part in the
action we forget that, just as in the course of the story we tend to forget
Britomart's nubility. When Marinell returns to the scene at the end of
Book Four to discover and rescue Florimell, his advent seems a *deus ex
machina* rather than a thematically inevitable development.

III

These apparent doubts and hesitations about eros come into focus
where we would expect them to – at the allegorical core. Canto six of
Book Three begins with an episode radically at odds with an allegory
of married chastity; Chrysogonee's marvelous begetting and birthgiv-
ing seems carefully designed to exclude eros from procreation and to
celebrate virginity rather than marriage. It celebrates in fact a virgin
birth and almost certainly alludes (as Roche has recognized) to the conception and nativity of Christ.[3] When Spenser tells us that Chrysogonee 'bore withouten paine, that she conceiued / Withouten pleasure'
(III, vi, 27), he gives us as concise and accurate a statement as one could
wish of the ancient Christian understanding of Mary's parturition.
Mary alone among women, and according to a tradition centuries
older than the doctrine of the Immaculate Conception, is free of the
inherited slavery to sexual passion that descends from Adam and of
the curse of childbearing placed on Eve. That is to say she is the
supreme instance of humanity deified by impassibility. She conceived
Christ miraculously, without carnal knowledge, as Chrysogonee conceives Belphoebe and Amoret, and bore him, as Chrysogonee bears,
without pain or corruption. That parallel, if Spenser intended it, makes
the highest possible claim for a mode of generation which excludes
sexuality, and there are reasons to believe he did intend it. One is his
employment of a familiar bit of typology: not only does a birth 'of the
wombe of Morning dew' (III, vi, 3) recall the prophecy of Psalm 110 –
that the dew of Christ's birth 'is of the wombe of the morning' – but
also the venerable association of the Annunciation with the falling of
dew upon Gideon's fleece, a liturgical commonplace repeated with
variations in medieval lyrics. Furthermore Richard Berleth has pointed
out that Chrysogonee's conceiving being 'of the ioyous Prime' places it
sometime after 21 March, which, given the other Christian allusions,

points to the feast of the Annunciation on the 25th (though Berleth
stops short of that conclusion and shuns what seems a very likely
Christian reference).[4] Such symbolism suggests that even as Spenser
was writing a legend of married chastity, he was not only countenanc-
ing but perhaps giving spiritual priority to a chastity which knows
nothing of marriage and to a mode of procreation innocent of eros.

What then are we to make of his setting the Chrysogonee episode
side-by-side with the Garden of Adonis? We still lack an interpretation
of the latter which accounts for all its details, but whatever view we
take of Spenser's ideas about form and matter, there can be little question that the generation and regeneration which take place in the Garden entail sexual union and erotic pleasure and that these are good.
Love here fulfills all the expectations generated by Spenser's praise of
eros – it is a 'gentle fit,' to which no shame attaches: '*Franckly* each par-
amour his leman knowes' (III, vi, 41; italics added). Spenser may be
referring directly to coitus when he declares himself to know '*by tryall*,
that this same / All other pleasant places doth excell' (III, vi, 29; italics
added). In view of the subsequent image of the *mons veneris* as the
place of Venus' and Adonis' sexual play, we will not go far wrong if we
identify the entire pleasure of this paradise as that of orgasm. And that
we are to regard that pleasure as an unmitigated good seems clear in
view of the equally heavy emphasis on procreation; the opposition of
the fruitfulness of the Garden to the sterility of the Bower of Bliss is a
valid commonplace. In enjoying themselves sexually the denizens of
the Garden also respond to God's original procreative command to
'increase and multiply' (III, vi, 34). Not even the destructive power of
time in the Garden (of which more shortly) is sufficient to mitigate
very seriously this pleasure and fruitfulness, for the generative process
conquers time in its own way: there is continual spring and harvest,
'both meeting at one time' (III, vi, 42), and at the Garden's center, Adonis is 'eterne in mutabilitie' (III, vi, 47).

Here then we seem to have an allegory of that attitude toward eros
which Spenser announces as his theme (and upon which the critics
have focused most of their attention) but which we do not see realized
elsewhere – which in fact we see contradicted elsewhere – in Books
Three and Four. That the other principal allegory of canto six also
seems to contradict it raises a question of consistency: how are we to
explain the transition from a virgin birth (probably alluding to *the* vir-

gin birth) to sexual play on the *mons veneris*? Does the Garden where Amoret is raised contradict the implications of her conception and birth? The possibility of a theological allusion, of a meaning behind the image of the Garden, reinforces the impression that it does.

I refer to the belief that had Adam and Eve not fallen they would have enjoyed a guiltless sexuality in Paradise and have begotten children by carnal union – and with carnal pleasure – but without sin. This teaching probably originated with Jovinian (d.c. 405), but its classic formulation is owing to Augustine, to the ninth book of the *Commentary on the Literal Meaning of Genesis* and the fourteenth book of *The City of God*. In the latter Augustine tells us 'We must never allow ourselves to believe that God's blessing, "Increase and multiply and fill the earth" would have been fulfilled through ... lust by the pair who were set in paradise.'[5] Instead, there would have been marriage and conception without sin and yet with pleasure: 'Marriage would have been worthy of the happiness of paradise ... and yet would not have given rise to any lust to be ashamed of.'[6] In unfallen Eden, in a way fallen man cannot imagine, the pleasure of coitus would have been without corrupting passion. Furthermore this unfallen sexuality would have been consonant with the preservation of virginity: 'the male seed could have been dispatched into the womb, with no loss of the wife's integrity, just as the menstrual flux can now be produced from the womb of a virgin without loss of maidenhead' (there, if ever, we have '*chaste* affection'). The impossibility of such a mode of union between a fallen man and woman is owing to lust, to the violent activation of the penis 'by the turbulent heat of passion.'[7]

Everyone knows where this conception impinges most strikingly on English literature. Milton's Raphael is being thoroughly Augustinian when he admonishes Adam that 'in loving thou dost well; in passion not, / Wherein true Love consists not' (*PL*, VII, 588–9). Since the context makes clear that the 'true Love' at issue is sexual, the admonition embodies Augustine's paradox – sexual pleasure without sexual passion. Of course Milton goes Augustine one better, eliminating the subjunctive – not saying there *would* have been marriage in Eden but that there *was*. To attribute that variation to the Protestant preference of marriage to celibacy is conventional and no doubt correct. Since Spenser is usually credited with being Milton's predecessor in the celebration of that preference, it is surprising that no one except Ellrodt (and he only in passing)[8] has brought forward Augustine's conception of prelapsarian intercourse as a gloss on the Garden of Adonis. What more convincing theological precedent (and in Spenser we expect one) are we likely to find for the innocent sexual pleasure of the Garden? Certainly the place has strong Edenic associations; it is situated 'in fruitfull soyle *of old*' (III, vi, 31; italics added), and we learn from the Elfin Chronicle of Book Two that the 'gardins of Adonis' (II, x, 71) are the fairy counterpart to Eden.

The temporal character of the Garden may seem to some an obstacle to that interpretation; if its inhabitants are subject to time's scythe, can the place be Edenic? Is being 'eterne in mutabilitie' the same as enjoying the freedom from mortality which Christianity attributes to Adam and Eve before the Fall? Obviously not; but if we are correct that the whole is an allegory of sexual union, we should expect its pleasure, however innocent, to be temporal. To state the matter another way, we might say that the Garden is not simply Eden but an Edenic allegorical place signifying the sexual facet – and *only* that facet – of prelapsarian existence. On that reading the Garden is what happens in Adam and Eve's marriage bower (or what, according to Augustine, would have happened had they not sinned), and we should not expect even such unfallen sexuality to be, *in itself*, independent of time and change. There is no difficulty in conceiving unfallen man as immortal and yet recognizing that his unfallen generative function is temporal. It is Adam and Eve, not their sexuality, who would have inherited the 'immortall blis' (III, vi, 41) inaccessible to the Garden's denizens; and to say that unfallen man's procreativity would be no obstacle to that inheritance is not the same as saying that in itself it would achieve immortality. Augustine does not make the distinction in so many words, but his exegesis seems to presuppose it. Spenser appears to be making it when he tells us that of the 'Infinite shapes of creatures' bred in the Garden some are 'fit for reasonable soules t'indew' (III, vi, 35), others for beasts, birds, and fish. That limits the meaning of the Garden to physical procreativity, to sexual intercourse for the making of *bodies* – an entirely temporal process. The 'indewing' of some of those bodies with 'reasonable soules' would lift them out of the temporal and, in an unfallen world, bestow immortality, but Spenser is clearly saying that that development will come later and is not a part of the Garden's meaning – a part of what it means to live before the Fall in Paradise but not of the innocent sexual pleasure which unfallen man would have enjoyed there. As though to reinforce this distinction Spenser is careful to distinguish between the Garden's mutability and the death which, outside the Garden, is a consequence of sin. Within the walls, time is the *only* 'troubler,' and there is no hint that it is *spiritually* destructive. Outside, mortality is inseparable from sin; Genius clothes the naked babes 'with *sinfull* mire,' and sends them forth 'to liue in *mortall* state' (III, vi, 32; italics added). *Sinful* is not applied to any facet of life in the Garden, nor does Spenser at any point use *mortal* to characterize the Garden's temporality. Sending the babes forth may, in fact, signify the Fall, for they make a choice (a point largely ignored by interpreters): Genius clothes and sends only those 'that to come into the world *desire*' and 'which doe require, / That he with fleshly weedes would them attire' (III, vi, 32; italics added). There may be a pun on *desire*, and both *world* and *fleshly* have, obviously, their pejorative, Christian connotations.

There is therefore nothing in Spenser's allegory to contradict Augustine's conception of unfallen eros and a great deal to encourage our reading the Garden in terms of that conception. If we do so, moreover, we introduce a possible point of contact between the two parts of canto six. Augustine's theory of unfallen sexuality is revisionist; it innovates upon a prior and contrary doctrine which Chrysogonee's sexless child-bearing adequately represents. That doctrine, moreover, is Greek and patristic and theologically of a piece with an ascetic understanding of temperance.

Among Augustine's predecessors and Eastern contemporaries, only Clement of Alexandria seems to have entertained what was to become the Augustinian teaching, and he only guardedly.[9] For the rest, including Augustine's own mentor, Ambrose, procreation by coitus between unfallen man and woman was a contradiction in terms. The Fathers did not make Augustine's (and Milton's) distinction between love and lust: sexual love necessarily involves the passions, and because the passions obscure the divine image which was manifest in unfallen man, unfallen man could not have known sexual union. We have mentioned in another context (the Fathers' preference of virginity to marriage) what has come to be regarded as the classic statement of that position – Gregory of Nyssa's argument that had man and woman remained in Paradise, they would not 'have needed the assistance of marriage' but would have begotten offspring in whatever manner the bodiless angels do.[10] Gregory argues to the same effect from eschatology: since, in the resurrection, men and women '"neither marry, nor are given in marriage"' but '"are equal to the angels"' and since 'the resurrection promises us nothing else than the restoration of the fallen to their ancient state,' 'it is clear that the life before the transgression was a kind of angelic life.' Procreation in Paradise would have been therefore after an angelic manner: 'whatever the mode of increase in the angelic nature is ... it would have operated also in the case of men.'[11] (Milton's angels appear to copulate [*PL*, VIII, 618–29]; we can rest assured that Gregory's do no such thing.)

If Chrysogonee's miraculous childbearing alludes to Mary's, it attaches itself as firmly to Gregory's teaching as the innocent sexuality of the Garden of Adonis appears to attach itself to Augustine's. The Greek Fathers did not regard the engendering and nativity of Christ simply as an isolated, miraculous means of bringing God into the world as man. That, of course, it was, but it was also God's means of taking away the curse on procreation – pleasure and pain – which descended upon Adam and Eve. Because Christ, like Chrysogonee's children, was conceived without the former and born without the latter, He undid the legacy of the Fall. Maximus the Confessor explains that 'because Adam disobeyed, human nature has come to be generated through sensual pleasure; banishing such pleasure from human nature, the Lord had nothing to do with engendering by means of seed.' Because of the Fall 'the generation of human nature begins in pain; expelling this from human nature through His birth, the Lord did not allow her who bore Him to lose her virginity.' He was born as He was so as 'to expel from human nature both pleasure deliberately sought and the resulting unsought pain.'[12] 'The pains of our mother Eve have been destroyed. For escaping pain, Thou [Mary] hast without wedlock [i.e., without sexual pleasure] borne child.'[13] Such statements are recurrent in patristic theology and Eastern liturgy. They say in effect that Christ's conception and birth reinaugurated the 'angelic' mode of procreation which Gregory says would have obtained in Paradise. We see, therefore, that the mode of procreation depicted in Chrysogonee is not only at odds with what follows in the Garden but, by way of Chrysogonee's Marian associations, symbolizes a theology which is at odds.

And it should by now be becoming clear what is at odds with what –
that these points of theological reference for the two allegories of canto
six are versions of teachings with which we are by now familiar. Gregory and Augustine confront each other across the divide between
Eastern and Western, patristic and post-Augustinian beliefs about the
passions and about nature. One can easily see why Augustine would
reject Gregory's argument: if the passions are good when the love is
good, what love could be better than that between unfallen man and
woman, in whom reason controls the passions completely? Aquinas
draws out the difference with specific reference to nature, endorsing
Augustine and rejecting Gregory. To the latter's argument from the
angelic condition of man in the Resurrection Aquinas responds that 'in
paradise man would have been like an angel in his spirituality of
mind, yet with an animal life in his body. After the resurrection man
will be like an angel, spiritualized in soul and body. Wherefore there is
no parallel.' Augustine's position is therefore the correct one, for 'what
is natural to man was neither acquired nor forfeited by sin. Now it is
clear that generation by coition is natural to man by reason of his animal life, which he possessed before sin' (ST, I, 98, 2)[14] It was obviously
not 'clear' to Gregory of Nyssa that an 'animal life' is 'natural' to man.
Rather what is natural to man is the *imago dei*, which passion – 'animal
life' – defaces and to which man is called to return by the mortification
of that life. If I am correct that that ascetical soteriology informs the legends of holiness and temperance, Spenser's setting an allegory of one
of its recognizable emblems, the Virgin Birth, side by side with an allegory of its antithesis, appears to invite a confrontation. On that showing, the purpose of canto six is to give theological definition to the
tension between the ascetical and the connubial which manifests itself
so frequently in Books Three and Four.

IV

How are we to assess that tension and what are we to conclude about
the relation of affection to chastity? Was Spenser deliberately offering
his readers a choice of theologies, presented as a choice of myths, and
refraining from a judgment of his own? Or is the allegory exploratory?
Is Spenser finding his way as he goes, discovering meaning – and contradiction – in the very process of symbolizing meaning? My sense of

the poetry is that the latter is more likely than the former – that he was much less certain of the ostensible theses of Books Three and Four, the easy reconcilability of chastity with marriage and the goodness of eros, than we have taken him to be; that coming to these subjects from the Greek Fathers' different understanding of the passions and from their belief in *theosis* with which he was engaged in Books One and Two, he was unable to make the imaginative accommodation necessary to champion sex and marriage unequivocally. In canto six of Book Three he was very possibly testing the relative claims of the two theologies which he recognized to be at issue, attempting to mediate between them, and discovering difficulty in doing so.

Amoret would obviously be the means of such mediation and her difficulties owing to that discovery. The myth of Chrysogonee suggests deification through the achievement of impassibility and man's restoration to his paradisal and angelic state. But Spenser places Amoret in a paradise hospitable to an animal rather than angelic life. Was he attempting to shift his theological ground so as to justify a connubial as opposed to a celibate conception of sanctity, only to find that he was too deeply committed to Belphoebe to make allowance for her sister? The prelapsarian and therefore hypothetical character of Augustine's eros may have been intended as a mediating or extenuating circumstance: might not Belphoebe's sister – might not Belphoebe herself – be able to participate in *unfallen* erotic activity and remain a mirror of celestial grace? Quite possibly; but Spenser may have discovered that prelapsarian eros is *only* hypothetical – that Augustine is describing what eros is *not*. If what happens in the Garden of Adonis is what might have happened in paradise but for the Fall, then the Garden's activity is only a conjecture. Even if we imagine Spenser taking Milton's view that Adam and Eve actually enjoyed innocent orgasm before they sinned, such innocence is no less hypothetical after sin than if, as according to Augustine, they did not. The garden walls which protect an innocent eros from the world just as surely prevent the world's access to innocent eros, and that appears to be Amoret's discovery – or Spenser's discovery in Amoret – when she leaves the sacred enclosure. The 'sinful mire' outside spawns Busirane and Lust. That is in effect to ratify Basil's and Gregory's teaching that unfallen eros is a contradiction in terms because eros involves the passions and passions are a consequence of the Fall – to enjoy sexual experience is by definition to be fallen. That too seems to be Spenser's discovery – that having given Amoret an 'animal life,' he cannot preserve that life unfallen. She ceases to be the image of Christ and mirror of grace which her sister, nurtured as well as conceived and born angelically, remains and becomes instead a child of fallen Eve, plagued by passion. In Books Three and Four, at least, the choice between Belphoebe and Acrasia will not seem to go away. The Augustinian alternative – good passion in the service of good love, an animal life innocent of sin – does not appear to be imaginatively accessible except as a theologian's paradox. Affection only proves to be chaste within the precincts of an hypothesis.

                                    V

A patristic interpretation of holiness and temperance prompts such reflections on Books Three and Four and on the whole subject of eros in Spenser's allegory. Despite his intention to depict sex in marriage as kindly and sacred, Spenser seems not yet ready to relinquish an ascetical and mystical theology which contradicts that intention. That by the time he wrote *Amoretti and Epithalamion* he had relinquished it seems clear, for there, well outside the Garden, Spenser convinces us that eros as fallen man knows it can, in the context of 'endlesse matrimony,' become divine. Is there any evidence of that shift of perspective within *The Faerie Queene*, any point at which the transition which may have been supposed to occur in canto six of Book Three actually does occur?

We should look, I suggest, to Mount Acidale where for the first time an epiphany is not reserved for the transfigured. There the cosmos dances not around a deified virgin with luminous countenance whose context is explicitly theological but around a 'countrey lasse' with whom Colin, a shepherd boy, not a type of Christ the Harrower, is amorously, not theologically, in love. That Colin cannot tell whether his lass is 'a creature, or a goddesse graced / With heauenly gifts from heuen first enraced' (VI, x, 25) encourages us on first reading to identify her with Una or Belphoebe; but the very fact that Colin rather than the narrator says this allows us to interpret the statement as hyperbole inspired by eros. And Colin identifies her with the unmistakably Venerean Graces; since she is now 'Another Grace,' we infer that her 'Diuine resemblaunce' and 'Firme Chastity' are reconcilable with eros in a way that Belphoebe's are not. What Colin seems to be offering us (and Calidore) is the very kind of union of affection with chastity, nubility with virginity, which the critics ascribe to Britomart. The 'countrey lasse' appears to be what Amoret might have been had it not been for the counteracting pressure of an ascetic theology.

Spenser's famous 'Pardon thy shepheard' (VI, x, 28), though undeniably political in its implications, gains resonance from this interpretation. The Queen is the archetype of all the deified virgins of the poem, and she has been upstaged by a theologically as well as socially inferior symbol. That the lass who displaces her may also be named Elizabeth is a fascinating possibility, for the deified lady of the *Amoretti* is convincingly nubile. The title of the sonnet sequence may signal an extension and completion of the meaning of Amoret, which could not be completed in those parts of *The Faerie Queene* in which Belphoebe's virtue remained dominant. Furthermore the Lenten numerology of the *Amoretti* and the explicit identification of eros with the Harrowing and Resurrection in sonnet sixty-eight translate the paschal symbolism of Book One into an amorous context, suggesting that the physically consummated marriage of *Epithalamion* can replace the heavenly nuptials (and postponed consummation) which complete the legend of holiness. For such a 'suggestion Spenser may be begging pardon not merely of his patroness and Virgin Queen but of his principal symbol of a contradictory vision.

Mount Acidale has seemed to many readers a proper consummation of Spenser's poem and to manifest a recovery of the momentum of the early Books which many feel Spenser loses in Four and Five. And most of those who take that view ascribe it to Spenser's return to the pastoral and the erotic. Richard Helgerson is characteristic in saying that Spenser 'comes home' at the end of his career 'to the pastoral, the personal and the amorous,'[15] and to agree with that is tempting. It is also tempting to regard Mount Acidale and *Epithalamion* as more complete symbols of human experience than any that precedes them. But the metaphor of homecoming implies a finality which the poetry does not sustain, and our preference for a vision which includes eros may be owing to assumptions of our own time. There is no certainty that Spenser was any more completely at home on Mount Acidale than on the Mount of Contemplation or Mount Tabor. The fabric of Colin's vision melts into thin air, and, in the poem's next epiphany (and last), the deified virgin returns in her most magnificent representation, as an hermaphroditic and therefore transsexual symbol of deification. Dame Nature may include all procreative energies, but she just as surely translates them into Christ's immutability. With her the theology of Books One and Two reasserts itself and becomes Spenser's last word. The poem which achieves one of its finest moments in Colin's departure from what I believe I have shown to be a patristic vision of a passionless and deified humanity ends, as it begins, with a celebration of that vision.

Tabernacles

Patristic interpretations of the Transfiguration may account for another detail in the depiction of Dame Nature in the Mutabilitie Cantos. John of Damascus rebukes Peter for wishing to build three tabernacles and remain on Mount Tabor – not because the desire is inherently wrong but because it is premature. 'If Adam had not sought theosis before the due time, he would have attained his desire. Do not seek the good before its time, O Peter. There will come a time when thou wilt receive that vision [and keep it] forever.' That time, John proceeds to explain, is when Christ harrows Hell, rises from the dead, and renews creation. Then Peter, as the chief apostle, will be 'a governor [not] of tabernacles but of a pancosmic Church' (Homily on the Transfiguration, 21–2). (The advice, incidentally, resembles Nature's to Mutabilitie, who has 'sought theosis before the due time,' not recognizing that in due time she would have attained her desire – 'time shall come that all shall changed bee.')

At issue here is the typology of the tabernacle. The contrast between Sinai and Tabor is central to the exegetical tradition, and John of Damascus relies heavily upon it: 'For the Law had a shadow of things to come, not the truth itself' (John is paraphrasing, and he duly cites, Hebrews 10:1). In the Transfiguration, the shadow has been replaced by the truth (the veiled Moses by the unveiled Christ), 'for the mystery hidden from the ages and generations has been unveiled ...' (22). (It is in this context that John introduces the Pauline reference to Moses's veil in Second Corinthians.) On Sinai God commanded Moses to construct a tabernacle, but Christ came 'an high Priest of good things to come, by a greater and more perfect Tabernacle, not made with hands' (Hebrews 9:11) – which is Christ's body – 'the true Tabernacle, which the Lord pitched, and not man' (Hebrews 8:2). John does not refer directly to these two verses, but he is probably alluding to them in his advice to Peter: the material tabernacles which Peter proposes to pitch bear the same relation to the 'pancosmic Church' as Moses's tabernacle, delivered on Sinai, bears to the 'Taber-

nacle, not made with Hands' revealed on Tabor. Peter runs the risk of
substituting the type for the antitype, the prophecy for its fulfillment. To build
a man-made tabernacle in the presence of the 'Tabernacle, not made with
hands' is tantamount to preferring the Law to Grace, the Old Covenant to the
New.

Is this typology responsible for Spenser's placing Dame Nature in a tabernacle not made with hands – 'in a pauilion; / Not such as Craftes-men by their
idle skill / Are wont ... to fashion' (VII, vii, 8)? If we can assume that Spenser
read the passages from Hebrews and from the Damascene commentary in
Greek, *pauilion* presents no difficulty. There can be no question that *tabernacle* is
more common in a religious context, but either word translates σκηνή as accurately as the other; and Spenser had biblical precedents for both. All sixteenth-
century Bibles render the 'more perfect σκηνή, not made with hands' and the
'true σκηνή, which the Lord pitched, and not man' as *tabernacle*, but *pavilion*
appears in other contexts. In Second Samuel, for instance, Coverdale says God
'made darkness his *pavilion*' (22:12) while the Geneva, Great, and Bishops'
Bibles all say He made darkness his *tabernacle*. In a variation on that verse in
Psalm 18 (11), however, all the translators choose *pavilion*: 'He made darkness
his secret place, his *pavilion* round about him.' In Psalm 27 (5), all the sixteenth-
century Bibles say that 'in the time of trouble he shall hide me (hath hid me) in
his *tabernacle*,' while the King James translators, only a decade later, chose
pavilion. A comparison of the King James to the Geneva illustrates the ease
with which the two renderings of σκηνή can be interchanged. Geneva reads.
'For in the time of trouble he shall hide me in his *Tabernacle*: in the secret place
of his *pavilion* shall he hide me.' The King James simply reverses the order: 'For
in the time of trouble he shall hide me in his *pavilion*: in the secret of his *Tabernacle* shall he hide me.' To these translators the one word must have seemed as
appropriate in a religious context as the other, and it probably did to Spenser.
There is, of course, the question why, if he was alluding to the verses in
Hebrews, he violated the translators' consensus there; and there may be more
than one answer: he may have been thinking in Greek rather than in English (a
probability if he came to the verses through John of Damascus) and therefore
not been affected by the English precedent; or metrical considerations could
have dictated a trisyllabic alternative to *tabernacle*; or he may have decided that
a personification which owes something of its character to Chaucer and the
Chartrians would be more at home in a structure associated with medieval
chivalry than in a more exclusively religious edifice. He may indeed have reasoned that since *pavilion* had the greater secular currency it would serve better
than *tabernacle* to mediate between *natura*'s more traditional associations and
his patristic reinterpretation of the figure.

In any event, Spenser could scarcely have been more specific about the character of his pavilion's construction. Not only does he eliminate the skill of craftsmen: he tells us that 'th 'earth her self of her owne motion, / Out of her fruitfull bosome made to growe / Most dainty trees' (VII, vii, 8) to form this bower. Do these lines tell us that this is a tabernacle 'which the Lord pitched'? Earth's *own* motion sounds more naturalistic than theological and may be indebted to *natura creatrix*, but in an allegory in which Nature is transfigured into 'the highest him,' the difference between earth's motion and God's matters less than it would in the usual Western context. Furthermore the Transfiguration-tabernacle typology affords a precedent for a σκηνή formed of trees. Jean Danielou (*The Bible and the Liturgy*, 333–47) shows that the Transfiguration corresponds in early Christian thought to the Jewish feast of Tabernacles, which was at once agricultural and, like the Transfiguration (and the Mutabilitie Cantos), eschatological. Israel dwelt for eight days in tabernacles constructed of branches in order both to celebrate the harvest and to signify expectation of the Messianic age (hence the significance of the eight days); as their fathers during the Exodus lived in tents before entering the promised land, the children resided in leafy huts to indicate their anticipation of the Kingdom. (Peter, a good Jew, should therefore have recognized that building a tabernacle was an eschatological act; that is probably why John of Damascus says that when Peter spoke 'not knowing what he said' [Luke 9:33], he spoke in fact 'by the inspiration of the Spirit foretelling the things to come' [22].) John of Damascus does not mention the Jewish festival or the vegetation motif, but at least one Greek Father does. Danielou quotes Methodius' saying that '"the prescriptions of the levitical law concerning the Feast of Tabernacles foreshadow the resurrection of the body"'; and Danielou interprets Methodius to be saying as well that Christ came 'to inaugurate the true feast of Tabernacles prefigured in the Jewish liturgy. And the beginning of this *Scenopegia* [pitching of tents] is the Incarnation itself' (345, note 27) – which is to say Christ's body, the 'Tabernacle, not made with hands.'

Whether Spenser could have read Methodius is uncertain (I have found no Renaissance editions), and this interpretation of Jewish Tabernacles is not commonly a part of Transfiguration exegesis. Nevertheless, a representation of Nature which associates her with Christ on Tabor, places her in a pavilion of branches, and anticipates the perfection of the eighth day (and canto) is sufficiently reminiscent of the typology to suggest the possibility of influence. Even without recourse to any single source of interpretation, we have enough reasons for associating a tabernacle or pavilion with the Transfiguration to suggest that the simile of stanza seven dictated the imagery of eight.

Notes

ABBREVIATIONS

Journals

ELH	*Journal of English Literary History*
ELR	*English Literary Renaissance*
MLN	*Modern Language Notes*
MLS	*Modern Language Studies*
MP	*Modern Philology*
N&Q	*Notes and Queries*
PMLA	*Publications of the Modern Language Association of America*
PQ	*Philological Quarterly*
RES	*Review of English Studies*
SEL	*Studies in English Literature, 1500–1900*
SP	*Studies in Philology*
TLS	*Times Literary Supplement*

Books

LF	*A Library of Fathers of the Holy Catholic Church Anterior to the Division of the East and West,* trans. by members of the English Church. (Oxford: James Parker; London: Rivingtons 1838-seq)
STC	*A Short-Title Catalogue of Books Printed in England, Scotland, & Ireland and of English Books Printed Abroad, 1475–1640,* compiled by A.W. Pollard and G.R. Redgrave, rev. W.A. Jackson, F.S. Ferguson, and Katharine F. Pantzer, 2nd ed., 3 vols (London: The Bibliographical Society and Oxford University Press 1976–1991)

Introduction

1 F.M. Padelford, 'Spenser and the Puritan Propaganda,' *MP*, 11 (1913–14), 85–106; 'Spenser and the Theology of Calvin,' *MP*, 12 (1914–15), 1–18; 'Spenser and the Spirit of Puritanism,' *MP*, 14 (1916–17), 31–44

2 Anthea Hume, *Edmund Spenser: Protestant Poet* (Cambridge: Cambridge University Press 1984); John N. King, *Spenser's Poetry and the Reformation Tradition* (Princeton: Princeton University Press 1990), chapters 2 and 3, 47–147, and King, *Tudor Royal Iconography: Literature and Art in an Age of Religious Crisis* (Princeton: Princeton University Press 1989)

3 Hume, 98

4 I refer to an unpublished doctoral dissertation by Thomas Philip Nelan, SJ, New York University, 1943. The N.Y. U. Press published a radically abridged version (only 21 of an original 456 pages) in 1946, under the title *Catholic Doctrines in Spenser's Poetry.* Nelan's work has been almost entirely, and unjustly, ignored by Spenser scholars.

5 For a full and perceptive discussion of this Calvinist-Catholic confrontation at the beginning of canto ten, see James Schiavone, 'Predestination and Free Will: The Crux of Canto Ten,' *Spenser Studies*, X (1992), 175–95. All quotations from *The Faerie Queene* are from A.C. Hamilton's edition (London and New York: Longman 1977), hereafter cited as 'Hamilton (1977).'

6 An exception is Patrick Grant in *The Transformation of Sin: Studies in Donne, Herbert, Vaughan and Traherne* (Montreal: McGill-Queen's University Press & Amherst: University of Massachusetts Press 1974).

7 S.F. Johnson, 'Spenser's "Shepherd's Calendar,"' *TLS* (7 September 1951), 565. C.A. Patrides, 'Renaissance Thought on the Celestial Hierarchy: the Decline of a Tradition,' *Journal of the History of Ideas*, 20 (1959), 155–66

8 That Spenser was acquainted with some of the great humanist presses and their publications seems evident from names in Book Six of *The Faerie Queene* – Calepine, Mirabella, and Aldus. See Humphrey Tonkin, *Spenser's Courteous Pastoral: Book VI of the 'Faerie Queene'* (Oxford: Clarendon Press 1972), 66.

9 Nine of those are printings of Erasmus' 1526 edition by Froben (1528, 1534, 1545, 1548, 1560, 1563, 1567, 1571). There were also translations by Gallasius (Paris 1570) and Feuardent (Paris 1575 & Cologne 1596). For a partial account of these see Irénée de Lyon, *Contra les Hérésies*, livre IV, tone II, ed. Adelin Rousseau, *Sources Chrétiennes*, 100 (Paris: du Cerf 1965), 34–8.

10 There were no Greek editions of Athanasius until 1601, but translations go back to 1482. Petrus Nannius' version was published by Froben in 1556 and seems to have been the standard text until the Benedictine edition of 1698;

Nannius appeared in 1564, 1572, and 1581. For details of these editions, see introductory material in *Sur L'Incarnatione du Verbe* in *Sources Chrétiennes*, 199 (Paris: du Cerf 1973), 163–5. See also volume 4 (Athanasius) of *A Select Library of Nicene and Post-Nicene Fathers*, ed. Philip Schaff & Henry Wace (Grand Rapids: Eerdmans 1953), xi. (This series is subsequently cited as 'Schaff & Wace' with volume number.)

11 The translators of the Basel editions were L. Sifanus and J. Lewenklaius; those of the Cologne, J. Norimantanus, G. Trapezuntius, and J. Oecolampadius. P.F. Zinus' translation of the *Hexaemeron* was published in Venice (Aldus) in 1553.

12 ΓΡΗΓΟΡΙΟΥ ΤΟΥ ΝΑΖΙΑΝΖΗΝΟΥ ... ΑΠΑΝΤΑ, τὰ μέχρι νῦν μὲν εὑρισκόμενα ... Basel 1550. Billius' 1569 edition was from Ioannes Benenatus in Paris and his 1583 edition with *Scholia* from Paris *apud Nicolaum Chesneau*.

13 Sancti Maximi, *Centvriae quatuour de charitate* ... Hagenau: Iohannes Secerius, 1531 & B. Maximi Monachi *Capitum Theologicorum Centuriae Quinque*, Parisiis, Apud Guil. Morelium, 1560

14 See chapter 4, 80–1 and bibliography. Also of importance is a Latin translation of the Damascene's most influential work, *De Fide Orthodoxa* by Jacobus Fabrus Stapulensus (Jacques Lefèvre d'Etaples), which was published in Paris by Henri Estienne in 1507. This translation appeared separately and in collections several times before it was replaced by Billius' version, most notably in a second edition, with commentary, by Iodocus Clichtoneus in 1512 and in a two-text version, also edited by Clichtoneus, in 1548; for the latter, see bibliography. (Billius includes Clichtoneus' commentary with his new translation in 1577.) For a history of the texts see Irena Backus, 'John of Damascus, *De Fide Orthodoxa*: Translations by Burgundio (1153/54), Grosseteste (1235/40) and Lefèvre d'Etaples (1507),' *Journal of the Warburg and Courthauld Institutes*, 49 (1986), 211–17.

15 See bibliography. Erasmus' Latin Chrysostom was superseded by Sir Henry Savile's Greek edition, published by John Norton at Eton in 1612 (*STC* 14629, 146295, 14629 a, b, c). This is the first major patristic edition in England and is of interest not only for that reason (and because it remains the standard Greek text of Chrysostom) but because some of the translators of the King James Bible (1611) were involved in its production. For a full bibliography of Chrysostom editions, see Dom Johannes Chrysostomus Bauer, *S. Jean Chrysostome et ses oeuvres dans l'histoire littéraire* (Louvain: Bureaux du recueil 1907).

16 See G.J. Cuming, 'Eastern Liturgies and Anglican Divines 1510–1662' in *The Orthodox Churches and the West*, ed. Derek Baker (Oxford: Basil Blackwell 1976), 231.

17 The listing of sixteenth-century patristic editions in this paragraph obvi-

ously makes no pretense of being systematic; its intention is not to serve as a bibliographical reference but simply to illustrate the ready availability in print of some of the most prominent patristic and liturgical texts. In the chapters that follow I shall go into more detail about some of these editions and introduce others. I have relied almost entirely on editions of the Fathers which Spenser, by reason of date, could have read; except in a few instances in which I was unable to have access to one of the sixteenth-century books, all my quotations are from those editions. A full and accurate bibliography of Renaissance patristic editions is much needed. For lack of one no one can be certain he has seen all the books which are pertinent to a study of this kind; I am certain I have not. I believe, however, that I have examined the most important editions of the most influential Fathers, and those Spenser is most likely to have seen – most of these are in the Cambridge University and the Pembroke College libraries. In identifying and locating these books I have relied upon such sources as the *National Union Catalogue*, the *Catalogue of the British Library*, Pollard and Redgrave's *Short-Title Catalogue*, H.M. Adams, *Catalogue of Books Printed on the Continent of Europe, 1501–1600, in Cambridge Libraries*, 2 vols (London: Cambridge University Press 1967), and Emile Legrand, *Bibliographie Hellénique des xve et xvie siècles*, 4 vols (Paris: G.P. Maisonneuve & Larose 1962). Legrand is especially helpful in identifying editions of Byzantine liturgical books, not so carefully listed elsewhere. Migne's prefatory matter is frequently helpful, and Migne sometimes uses a sixteenth-century text. Modern scholarly editions like those in the *Sources Chrétiennes* series frequently include a history of the printed text. For a bibliography of Renaissance patristic editions and editions of liturgies cited in this study, see 253–6

18 On English publication of the Fathers see William P. Haugaard, 'Renaissance Patristic Scholarship and Theology in Sixteenth-Century England,' *Sixteenth Century Journal*, 10 (1979), 37–60. Haugaard lists 84 English editions of patristic works, 74 of them after 1536. Augustine accounts for 36 of these, so for the purpose of the thesis of this book, which refers Spenser to the Eastern and pre-Augustinian Fathers and to doctrines of theirs which differ from Augustine's, we may say that England produced 48 patristic editions in the sixteenth-century. See also S.L. Greenslade, *The English Reformers and the Fathers of the Church* (Oxford: Clarendon Press 1960).

19 Greenslade, 5, 6

20 See *The First Authorized English Bible and the Cranmer Preface*, ed. Harold R. Willoughby (Chicago: University of Chicago Press 1942). Cranmer's ownership signature appears on the title page of a copy of Wolfgang Musculus' translation of St John Chrysostom's *In Omnes Pauli Apostoli Epistolas* (Basel

1536) in the library of St John's College, Cambridge. See bibliography. Antonia McLean remarks upon the number of editions of works by the Greek Fathers which were in Cranmer's library, including Athanasius, Chrysostom, Basil, Gregory of Nyssa, Gregory of Nazianzus, John of Damascus, and Dionysius the Areopagite. See her *Humanism and the Rise of Science in Tudor England* (New York: Neale Watson Academic Publications 1972), 95–6. McLean's source is *The Lumley Library: the Catalogue of 1609*, ed. Sears Jayne & Francis R. Johnson (London: British Museum 1956). An examination of the *Catalogue* indicates that Cyril of Jerusalem should be added to the list.

21 *An Exposition Vpon the Epistle of S. Paule the Apostle to the Ephesians*: by S. Iohn Chrysostome, Archbishop of Constantinople, Truely and faithfully translated out of Greeke ... At London: Printed by Henry Binneman and Ralph Newberie, 24 December, 1581; from 'To the Reader,' fol iii^r. See bibliography.

22 See E.S. Leedham-Green, *Books in Cambridge Inventories: Book-lists From Vice-Chancellor's Court Probate Inventories in the Tudor and Stuart Periods*, 2 vols (Cambridge: Cambridge University Press 1986). The 'Catalogue of Books' is in Volume II.

23 Leedham-Green I, 311–12

24 That is probable to the extent of that edition's popularity. There were other five-volume Chrysostoms (all translations) by 1569, so one can only guess. See Leedham-Green, II, 204 and Bauer, *Chrysostome et ses oeuvres*, 152–92.

25 Bishop Matthew Wren's 1617 list of books in the Pembroke library contains the following entry: 'Chrysostomus lat. in 5 vol. (accessit A°1536).'

26 I base this assertion on my own examination of Pembroke's sixteenth-century patristic holdings and on consultation with Cambridge librarians and with Miss Leedham-Green.

27 Lisa Jardine tells us that in sixteenth-century Cambridge 'members of a single college mixed frequently for instruction. It was presumably in the course of such lectures and debates at Pembroke Hall that Spenser became acquainted with [Gabriel] Harvey ...' (*The Spenser Encyclopedia*, ed. A.C. Hamilton, et al. [Toronto: University of Toronto Press 1990], 131). The same academic intimacy could presumably have fostered or ripened an acquaintance with Andrewes. The only speculation on the matter which I know is by Gustavus Paine, who is curious about the possible influence of Spenser on Andrewes: 'One of the friends with whom [Andrewes] walked and talked was Edmund Spenser. Did Spenser affect at all the writing style of Andrewes, and through him that of the King James Bible?' Gustavus S. Paine, *The Men Behind the King James Version* (Grand Rapids, Mich.: Baker Book House 1977; originally published by Thomas Y. Crowell as *The Learned*

Men, 1959), 16–17. I find it surprising that there is no entry for Andrewes in
The Spenser Encyclopedia.

28 Patrick Collinson, *Archbishop Grindal, 1519–1583: The Struggle for a Reformed
Church* (London: Jonathan Cape 1979), 36. Thanks to the Assistant Librarian
of Queen's College I have examined a list of 'the Grindal Bequest, 1583.'
The Athanasius was the Nannius translation of 1556; the Basil was Erasmus' edition of the *Opera* from Froben in 1551; the Ambrose was an *Opera,*
'5 vols in 2,' from Basel in 1538; and the Gregory Nazianzus was the Lewenklaius translation from Basel in 1550.

29 *The Remains of Edmund Grindal, D.D.,* ed. William Nicholson, for The Parker
Society (Cambridge: Cambridge University Press 1843), 291

30 See bibliography. In a copy of this edition now in the University Library,
Cambridge, Cecil inscribed: *Guilelmus Cecilius, uxori suae Mildredá Cecelia,*
1553. Grindal himself owned a copy of this edition, which he gave to Pembroke. The library's register of donations gives neither date nor place of
publication, but it does list the contents, which correspond in all respects to
those of the 1529 edition (except that it lists the contents of the second volume before the first). Unfortunately this book is no longer at Pembroke, but
it may have been when Spenser was; one cannot tell whether it was a
bequest or an earlier gift.

   The 1596 edition, from Heidelberg, is a revision of the 1529 from Verona:
'*Expositio in divi Pauli epistolas.* – Graeca veronensis editio [1529] locis quam
plurimis mutila, integritati restituta ope Mss. illustr. bibliothecae Palatinae
et Augustanae – Divi Joannis Apocalypsis cum commentario Andreae Cae-
sariensis latine reddito Theodori Peltani opera. – Apud Hieronymum Com-
melinum ...' I quote from Bauer, *Chrysostome et ses oeuvres,* item 99, 102.

31 Both Whitgift and Young became Masters of Pembroke in 1567; Whitgift
held the position only from April to July, when Young succeeded him. We
know lamentably little about John Young's intellectual interests, and one
cannot claim with any certainty that he was a student of the Fathers. We
cannot, however, dismiss the possibility or the corresponding one that
while Spenser served as Young's secretary he was exposed to patristic
scholarship and had access to patristic editions. Young's association with
Grindal may have entailed common scholarly pursuits; Young was a friend
of and ultimately wed the widow of Thomas Watts, whose library,
bequeathed to Pembroke, contained several editions of the Fathers: Young's
only published sermon, 'preached before the queenes maiestie' in 1575
(*STC* 26110) quotes from Jerome, Lactantius, Justin Martyr, and Clement of
Alexandria, though one could scarcely claim the homily to be informed in
any profound way by patristic ideas. Also Spenser's association with
Young, as Alexander Judson suggests, may have afforded the poet access to

Grindal. See entry for Young in the *DNB* as well as Judson's *A Biographical Sketch of John Young, Bishop of Rochester, with Emphasis on His Relations with Edmund Spenser* in *Indiana University Studies*, no 103, vol 21 (1934–5).

32 See above, note 21.

33 London (1581), 309

34 Hamilton (1977), 17

35 Ibid., 97

36 London (1581), 309, 317; Verona (1529), I, fols 198^r & 199^v

37 Why doubt about Spenser's knowing Greek persists is puzzling in view of his having been educated in two schools where Greek was part of the curriculum. Judson records that in a public examination at Merchant Taylors in 1572 students were examined in Homer as well as Horace and Cicero; there is plentiful evidence for Greek studies at sixteenth-century Cambridge; Lisa Jardine tells us that the 1560 statutes of Trinity College provided for two lectureships in Greek and Latin literature and one in Greek grammar; and at Corpus in the 1570's 'noon Greek studies consisted of the construing of a text (such as some Homer or Demosthenes), followed by grammar instruction.' Pembroke's Greek lecturer was Gabriel Harvey. See Lisa Jardine's 'Cambridge' in *The Spenser Encyclopedia*, 130–1, and Alexander C. Judson, *The Life of Edmund Spenser* (Baltimore: Johns Hopkins 1945), 14.

38 Henri Estienne, *Thesaurus Graecae Linguae* (1572), vol IV, col 497

39 London (1581), 317. For a full discussion see my '"Pourd out in Loosnesse,"' *Spenser Studies* III (1982), 73-85.

40 C.A. Patrides, *Premises and Motifs in Renaissance Thought and Literature* (Princeton: Princeton University Press 1982), 32

41 A. C. Hamilton, *The Structure of Allegory in 'The Faerie Queene'* (Oxford: Clarendon Press 1961), 6

42 Ibid., 12; italics added.

43 S.K. Heninger, Jr, *Sidney and Spenser: the Poet as Maker* (University Park and London: Pennsylvania State University Press 1989), 394

44 Sean Kane, *Spenser's Moral Allegory* (Toronto: University of Toronto Press 1989), xi

45 Elizabeth Bieman, *Plato Baptized: Towards the Interpretation of Spenser's Mimetic Fictions* (Toronto: University of Toronto Press 1988), 8

46 Ibid., 12

47 Ibid., 9

48 Ibid., 12

49 Ibid., 206

50 Ibid., 207

51 Hamilton (1977), 122

52 Ibid., 483
53 Matthew 26:7; Mark 14:3; Luke 7:37–38; John 11:2 and 12:3. In Luke's and John's versions, the woman anoints Christ's feet rather than his head.

Chapter One

1 Rosemond Tuve, *Allegorical Imagery: Some Mediaeval Books and Their Posterity* (Princeton: Princeton University Press 1966), 110
2 Virgil Whitaker presents the fullest discussion of the problem in 'The Theological Structure of *The Faerie Queene*, Book I,' *ELH*, 19 (1952), 151–64; reprinted in *Essential Articles for the Study of Edmund Spenser*, ed. A.C. Hamilton (Hamden, Conn.: Archon Books 1972), 101–12.
3 James Nohrnberg, *The Analogy of 'The Faerie Queene'* (Princeton: Princeton University Press 1976), 170; John Erskine Hankins, *Source and Meaning in Spenser's Allegory: a Study of 'The Faerie Queene'* (Oxford: Clarendon Press 1971), 118–19. There is an extensive literature on both the Well and the Tree (or the Balm). Work before 1969 is summarized in a long footnote by D. Douglas Waters in 'Spenser's "Well of Life" and "Tree of Life" Once More,' *MP*, 67 (1969), 67. (Waters accepts the conventional reading of the Tree as the eucharist but argues that the Well represents the Word rather than baptism.) Since Waters, the only critics besides Hankins and Nohrnberg who have questioned the usual identification of the Balm with holy communion are Michael O'Connell in *Mirror and Veil: the Historical Dimension of Spenser's 'Faerie Queene'* (Chapel Hill: University of North Carolina Press 1977), who takes a position close to Rosemond Tuve's – that neither Well nor Balm is exclusively sacramental but that both are 'symbols for the spiritual events of which the sacraments are themselves symbols' (66) and Anthea Hume, whose interpretation resembles Waters': the Well is 'Christ's doctrine,' and the Tree, 'I think, Christ himself' (104–5). Here is one of the instances to which I alluded in the Introduction to this book in which Professor Hume's effort to make Spenser a consistent Protestant produces a reading which strains against the more obvious meaning of Spenser's language.
4 *Institutes of the Christian Religion*, trans. John Allen (Philadelphia: Presbyterian Board of Education 1936), II, 598; *The Book of Common Prayer, 1559: The Elizabethan Prayer Book*, ed. John E. Booty (Charlottesville: University Press of Virginia 1976), 269
5 *Book of Common Prayer* (1559), 275
6 Basel (1530), II, 80–3. I quote the following passages from the English translation by P. Harkins in *Baptism: Ancient Liturgies and Patristic Texts*, ed. André Hamman (Staten Island, N.Y.: Alba House 1967), 165–72.

7 *Ad Neophytos*, 2: Hamman, 167; Basel (1530), II, 80

8 *Ad Neophytos*, 2: Hamman, 168; Basel (1530), II, 81

9 *Ad Neophytos*, 2: Hamman, 167; Basel (1530), II, 80–1

10 Dionysius' most famous contribution to medieval theology was, as everyone knows, his ordering of the angels in the *Celestial Hierarchy*. But his other
works were also known. Aquinas quotes from the *Ecclesiastical Hierarchy* in
the articles of the *Summa* on baptism (and elsewhere). See *ST*, III, 72, 4, reply
to obj. 1 (all references to the *Summa* are to the translation by 'Fathers of the
English Dominican Province,' 3 vols [New York: Benziger Brothers 1947];
for this passage see II, 2427). For an indication of the variety of Renaissance
editions see Adams, nos 520–33. I quote from an accurate English translation by Thomas L. Campbell, *The Ecclesiastical Hierarchy* (Lanham, Md.:
University Press of America 1981). I have compared Campbell's translation
with a sixteenth-century Greek version in a two-text edition, *Ad Timotheum
de ecclesiastica hierarchia* (Basel 1539) and with a Latin translation (Cologne
1556). For details of these editions, see bibliography.

11 *Ecclesiastical Hierarchy*, II, iii, 6: Campbell, 31; Basel (1539), 17–18; Cologne
(1556), 214–15

12 There were 6 editions of the *Catecheses* between 1560 and 1564, 5 of them in
the latter year. The first, a two-text version by Joannes Grodecius (Vienna
1560) is no longer extant. *S. Cyrilli Hier. Catecheses ad Illuminandos et Mystagogicae, Interpretatus est Joannes Grodecius* was published at Rome in 1564.
The same year that translation also appeared at Cologne, Antwerp, and
Paris. In the same year, from Paris, came a Greek edition, *apud Guil. Morelium* (see Schaff & Wace, VII, liv–vi). The English in the following passages is
a translation from the Greek of this 1564 Paris edition in comparison with
the Latin of the Cologne edition. Passages from the *Procatechesis* are entirely
from the Latin; I have been unable to find a Greek version. For full citations
see bibliography. For a complete English version see the translation by R.W.
Church in *LF* (1872), with a preface by John Henry Newman. The Church
translation is available in *St. Cyril of Jerusalem's Lectures on the Christian Sacraments*, ed. F.L. Cross (Crestwood, N.Y.: St. Vladimir's Seminary Press
1977). (Modern scholars debate whether Cyril is in fact author of the *Catecheses*, but that question has no bearing on their possible influence upon
Spenser.)

13 *Catecheses*, III, iv: Paris (1564), 204; Cologne(1564), 194

14 Ibid., III, iv: Paris (1564), 204; Cologne (1564), 194

15 *Procatechesis*, XVI: Cologne (1564), 6

16 *Exhortatio ad Baptismum*, I. Basil the Great wrote two baptismal homilies,
this being one of them, as well as a treatise, *De Baptismate*, in two books.
These works bear various titles in the different editions available to

Spenser: Omnia D. Basilii Magni ... Quae extant *Opera*. A Iano Cornario ... & Adamo Fumano latinitate donata ... Venetiis ad signum spei, 1548, fols 153–7, 164–5, 286–306; *Opera* D. Basilii Magni ... *Omnia* ... per Wolfgangum Musculum ... castigate ... Basileae, per Ioan. Oporinum, et Haeredes Ioannis, Heruagii, 1565, I, 443–50, 450–53; 463–66, 466–67, 468–84; *En Amice Lector*, Thesaurum damus inaestimabilem D. Basilium ... et Erasmi Roterodami praefationem ... Basileae ex officina Frobeniana, An. XXXII, 336–44, 359–62; Divi Basilii Magni *Opera Graeca* quae ad nos extant omnia, Froben, Basileae, 1551, 581–607. I quote the English translation of T. Halton in Hamman, 77, comparing it with the Greek of Basel (1551), 188, and with Musculus' Latin, Basel (1565), I, 444. For these editions see bibliography.

17 *In Sanctum Baptisma, oratio panegyrica, XI*. This is one of the most famous patristic homilies on baptism, widely cited by the other Fathers. It was preached at Constantinople in AD 381 – not at Easter but at the feast of Epiphany, the observance of Christ's baptism in Eastern liturgy and therefore another customary occasion for baptism in the ancient Church. I quote from the anonymous translation in Hamman (94), comparing it with the Greek from the Basel edition of 1550 (226) and the Latin of Billius (Paris 1569), 431. For details of these editions see Introduction, note 12, and bibliography.

18 *In Sanctum Baptisma, XI*: Hamman, 94; Basil (1550), 226; Paris (1569), 430

19 Tuve, *Allegorical Imagery*, 110

20 There were 67 editions of the Sarum Missal between 1487 and 1557, and the accompanying Manual, containing the full text of the Easter vigil and baptismal rites, was published 28 times between 1498 and 1555 (*STC*, Missals, nos 16164–16219; Manuals, nos 16138–16156). I have used a 1526 Parisian edition of the Manual (see bibliography), *STC* 16147, with a handsome woodcut of Saint George on its title page. The *ordo* is on fols xxix^r–xxxi^r.

21 *Ecclesiatical Hierarchy*, II, iii, 5: Campbell, 30; Basil (1539), 17; Cologne (1556), 214

22 *De Fide Orthodoxa*, IV, ix. For sixteenth-century editions see Introduction, note 14, and Adams, nos 264–79. I quote from the English translation by S.D.F. Salmond in Schaff & Wace, IX, 78, which I have compared with the Greek and Latin of the two-text edition of 1548 as well as with the later Latin version of Billius (1577): Basel (1548), 297; Paris (1577), fol 302^v. (See bibliography.) In both 1548 and 1577 the passage in question is numbered IV, x, rather than IV, ix.

23 *De Baptismate*, I, ii. I quote the English translation by Sister M. Monica Wagner in Saint Basil, *Ascetical Works* (New York: Fathers of the Church 1950), 383. For passages quoted see Basel (1551), 593 and Basel (1565), 465.

24 *De Baptismo Liber*, V. I translate from a Parisian *Opera* of 1545, fol 271^v. For

information on this edition, see bibliography. This edition contains no chapter divisions, which I supply from the two-text version of *Tertullian's Homily on Baptism*, trans. & ed. Ernest Evans (London: SPCK 1964). There were 22 copies of various editions of Tertullian among the possessions of Cambridge scholars who died between 1537 and 1598 (Leedham-Green, II, 740–1), but editions before 1545 did not contain *De Baptismo Liber*. For further information on Renaissance editions, see Evans's Introduction, xxxvi.

25 G.W. Bromiley, *Baptism and the Anglican Reformers* (London: Lutterworth Press 1953), 181

26 In the *Pentecostarion*, the Greek liturgical sequence from Easter to Pentecost, available to a sixteenth-century reader in 6 Western editions (1525, 1544, 1552, 1567, 1579, 1586 – see Legrand and chapter 2, note 11, below), the third, fourth, and fifth Sundays after Easter are devoted to baptismal typology – another testimony to the close link in patristic thought between baptism and the paschal season. The Gospel lesson for the third Sunday is the account of Christ's healing the paralytic at the pool of Bethsaida (John 5:1–15); for the fourth Sunday, Christ's encounter with the Samaritan woman at Jacob's well, another type of the font (John 4:5–42); and for the fifth, the healing of the blind man in Siloam, to which Spenser obviously alludes (John 9:1–38).

27 *De Sacramentis*, III, xi. (This is another of the mystagogia.) There were numerous sixteenth-century editions of Ambrose, and many seem to have found their way to Cambridge (see Adams 934–54 and Leedham-Green, II, 22–3). I have used an *Omnia Opera* edited by Erasmus and published by Froben in 1555 (see bibliography).

28 Ambrose in *De Sacramentis*, II, vii (in the 1555 edition, vol IV, 432); Gregory of Nyssa, *De Sancto Baptismate*, in the Lewenklaius edition of 1571, 261 (see bibliography). *De Sancto Baptismate* is an Epiphany rather than an Easter homily but another *locus classicus* for patristic baptismal theory. It was not available, so far as I have been able to determine, in Greek. A copy of the Lewenklaius translation is now in the Pembroke collection and is one of the patristic editions which stands a good chance of having been in the collection in Spenser's day.

29 *The Catechism of the Council of Trent* II, ii, 43; trans. J. Donovan (New York: Catholic Publications Society 1829), 163

30 See rite for blessing the font at the Holy Saturday Easter Vigil (*benedictio fonti*) in the Sarum Manual, Paris (1526), fol. xxxiiii[r&v].

31 Ibid., fol xxxv[r&v]

32 *Exhoratio ad Baptismum*, II: Hamman, 78; Basel (1551), 188; Basel (1565), I, 445

33 *Catechesis*, I, i & *Procatechesis*, XVI: Paris (1564), 185; Cologne (1564), 187, 6

34 *Adversus eos qui differunt baptismum, oratio* (J.-P. Migne *Patrologiae cursus completus ... series Graeca* (Paris 1857–1912) 162 vols, 46, 417C–D. Hereafter cited as *PG.*). I have not been able to find this homily in a sixteenth-century edition but quote from it nonetheless because it states so clearly a pattern of symbolism which Spenser could have discovered elsewhere. The English translation is from G.M. Lukken, *Original Sin in the Roman Liturgy* (Leiden: E.J. Brill 1973), 92.

35 *Catechesis*, I, ix: Paris (1564), 192; Cologne (1564), 189–90

36 Hamilton (1977), 153 (gloss on I, xi, 48)

37 Frank Kermode, '"The Faerie Queene," I and V,' in *Shakespeare, Spenser, Donne: Renaissance Essays* (New York: Viking 1971), 43

38 *Books I and II of The Faerie Queene, The Mutability Cantos and Selections from The Minor Poetry*, ed. Robert Kellogg and Oliver Steele (New York: Odyssey Press 1965), 47

39 Anders Nygren in *Agape and Eros*, trans. Philip S. Watson (Philadelphia: Westminster Press 1953), quotes passages from Luther which seem to teach *theosis*: 'A Christian is a "divine, heavenly man"'; 'He who abides in love is no longer "a mere man, but a god ... for God Himself is in him and does such things as no man nor creature can do."' But Nygren adds that Luther's saying such things has 'nothing to do with mystical "deification." It is his way of emphasizing as strongly as possible the fact that the real subject of Christian love is not man, but God Himself' (734). By 'mystical "deification"' Nygren refers to the conception of the Greek Fathers, with which I am concerned here and which he discusses very lucidly in his chapters on Irenaeus and Dionysius the Areopagite (411 ff and 584 ff). The difference is that the Fathers say man, by union with Christ, is literally deified; Luther is saying that man is deified *so to speak* when God's love flows through him – Luther's tube metaphor. Nygren is also quite good in his demonstration that Florentine Neoplatonist talk of human divinity is something entirely different from the Fathers' conception of *theosis*, for it refers to man's original constitution rather than to his reconstitution by grace (672 ff). It is more nearly Pelagian than Christian. Jaroslav Pelikan (in *Imago Dei: The Byzantine Apologia for Icons*, The A. W. Mellon Lectures in the Fine Arts, 1987 ... Bollingen Series XXXV, 36 [Princeton: Princeton University Press 1990]) finds a very clear statement of *theosis* in *The Consolation of Philosophy*, III, pr. x, 23–5 (141). Pelikan treats the patristic conception of *theosis* in other parts of this study in reference to the Byzantine rationale for iconography. For his more strictly theological discussion of the matter see *The Christian Tradition: A History of the Development of Doctrine I: The Emergence of the Catholic Tradition (100–600)* (Chicago: University of Chicago Press 1971), 141–55. The fullest discussion of deification specifically in Greek patrology is that of M. Lot-Borodine, *La déification de l'homme selon la doctrine des Pères grecs* (Paris: du

Cerf 1970). See also J.N.D. Kelly, *Early Christian Doctrines* (London: Adam & Black 1968), 375-400, and Vladimir Lossky, *The Vision of God*, trans. Asheleigh Moorhouse (Leighton Buzzard, England: The Faith Press 1973).

40 Pelikan, *Imago Dei*, 96

41 αὐτὸς γὰρ ἐνηνθρώπησεν, ἵνα ἡμεῖς νῦν μὲν θεοποιηθῶμεν (*De Incarnatione Verbi*, LIV). Spenser presumably could not have seen Athanasius' Greek, and Petrus Nannius' 1556 translation (see Introduction, 5 & note 10) takes a distinct liberty with the original which mutes its force: *Is enim ideo homo factus est, vt nos dii efficeremur*, in a 1581 Parisian edition, *apud Michaelem Sonnivm* (see bibliography), vol I, 48. To be made 'gods' is surprising enough from a modern perspective and presumably from a sixteenth-century one, but not quite so surprising as simply to be 'made God.' The most literal way possible to render the Greek (without respect for normal English usage) would be: 'For He [Christ] was humanified in order that we might be deified.' *Gods* can be inferred from the plural subject (ἡμεῖς), but Athanasius almost certainly speaks collectively. In the Greek Christian tradition θεοποιέω signifies the assimilation of man (humanity) to God through the Incarnation, as my subsequent discussion demonstrates. That is certainly Athanasius' meaning. Had Spenser had access to only this one statement of the doctrine of *theosis* and only in Nannius' translation, we could not be confident of his grasping that meaning. But, as I show, the range of reference available to him was much wider.

42 *Contra Arianos orationes quatuor*, II, xxi, 59; I quote from the translation by John Henry Newman as edited by Archibald Robertson in Schaff & Wace, IV, 380 (italics added). For the sixteenth-century Latin version see Paris (1581), vol I, 138. There *oratio secunda* is numbered as *sermo tertius*.

43 *Contra Arianos*, II, xxi, 69: Schaff & Wace, IV, 386; Paris (1581), I, 142

44 *Contra Arianos*, II, xxi, 69: Schaff & Wace, IV, 386; Paris (1581), I, 143

45 *The Homilies of S. John Chrysostom ... on the Gospel of St. Matthew* (II, iii), trans. George Prevost in *LF* (1843), XI, 20. For sixteenth-century Latin version see Basel (1530), III, 12–13.

46 *De Fide Orthodoxa*, III, xii: Schaff & Wace, IX, 56-7; Basel (1548), 222; Paris (1577), fol 264^r

47 *Contra Haereses*, IV, xx, 2, 5. I quote from *Five Books of S. Irenaeus Against Heresies*, trans. John Keble in *LF* (1872), XLII, 365, 367. Spenser would have been most likely to read *Contra Haereses* in Erasmus' frequently reprinted version (there were no sixteenth-century Greek editions). See Introduction, 4 and note 9. For Erasmus' Latin of the passages quoted see Paris (1545), 359–61; for details of that edition see bibliography.

48 *De Baptismate*, I, ii: New York (1950), 358; Basel (1551), 586; Basel (1565), I, 456

49 *In Epistolam ad Galatas*, III, 27: Verona (1529), II, fol 97^r. The only complete translation (Latin) of Chrysostom's Pauline homilies was that of Muscu-

lus published at Basel in 1536 (see bibliography). For this passage see II,
544.

50 Quoted by Hugh M. Riley in *Christian Initiation: a Comparative Study of the
Interpretation of the Baptismal Liturgy in the Mystagogical Writings of Cyril of
Jerusalem, John Chrysostom, Theodore of Mopsuestia, and Ambrose of Milan*, The
Catholic University of America Studies in Christian Antiquity, ed. Johannes
Quasten (Washington: The Catholic University of America Press 1974), 423

51 See above, 29.

52 *De Baptismo Liber*, VII: Evans, 17; Paris (1545), fol 271^v.

53 *Procatechesis*, VI: Cologne (1564), 3. Here and subsequently I quote the
Psalms from 'The Psalter or Psalms of David after the translation of the great
Byble, Poynted as it shall be sayde or sung in churches, 1566,' attached to
an edition of the Book of Common Prayer by Jugge & Cawood, 1566; STC
16297.5.

54 *Catechesis*, III, ii: Paris (1564), 203; Cologne (1564), 194

55 *Contra Arianos*, I, xii, 46, 47; Schaff & Wace, IV, 333; Paris (1581), I, 103. (In the
1581 edition this is *oratio secunda*.)

56 *Catechesis*, III, vi: Paris (1564), 205; Cologne (1564), 195

57 *De Sacramentis*, VI, ii; I quote from the translation by Roy J. Deferrari in Saint
Ambrose, *Theological and Dogmatic Works* (Washington: Catholic University
of America Press 1963), 321. For sixteenth-century Latin version see Basel
(1555), IV, 444.

58 *Of the Laws of Ecclesiastical Polity*, V, lxvi, 6. In Everyman's Library edition
(London: J. M. Dent 1907), II, 314

59 New York (1947), II, 2427–2428. Both Aquinas and Hooker are talking about
the use of chrism in confirmation, but that does not bear directly on the
theological issue since confirmation is simply the original rite of post-baptismal unction detached from baptism, as Aquinas surely knew and as
Hooker explains (V, lxvi, 5–6).

60 So far as I know the only case that has ever been made for the Balm as
Chrism is in Father Thomas Nelan's unpublished and largely ignored dissertation (see Introduction, note 4). The only subsequent reference I know
to Nelan's treatment of the Balm is by Whitaker (1950) in a footnote, 221,
note 136.

61 *Ecclesiastial Hierarchy*, II, iii, 8: Campbell, 32; Basel (1539), 19; Cologne (1556),
215

62 Carol V. Kaske, 'The Dragon's Spark and Sting and the Structure of Red
Cross's Dragon-fight: *The Faerie Queene*, I, xi–xii,' *SP*, 66 (1969), 638

63 Kaske (1969), 637

64 In patristic thought and in the Eastern Church there seems to be no clear
distinction between baptismal unction and healing unction. Both are sacra-

ments and for all practical purposes the same sacrament; chrismation, by deifying, regenerates and heals, and the healing which unction bestows upon the sick is of soul as well as body and thus signifies the deification effected by chrismation. To be deified in Christ is, by definition, to be healed of all mortal infirmities, and the only true healing of all mortal infirmities is deification in Christ.

65 That traditional identification was debated in the sixteenth century. John Fisher's 'defense of the common position of the Latin Church, entitled *The Single Magdalene (De unica Magdalena)* and published in Paris under date of February 22, 1519, unwittingly constituted his training ground in the use of Scripture and tradition for far more fundamental controversy with Luther, Oecolampadius, and Henry VIII's partisans for the divorce.' Edward Surtz, SJ, *The Works and Days of John Fisher* (Cambridge, Mass.: Harvard University Press 1967), 5

Chapter Two

1 I, 379. See also F.M. Padelford and Matthew O'Connor, 'Spenser's Use of the St. George Legend,' *SP*, 23 (1926), 142–56.

2 William Nelson, *The Poetry of Edmund Spenser: A Study* (New York: Columbia University Press 1963), 150

3 'A Gallant Familiar Letter,' *Spenser: Poetical Works*, ed. J.C. Smith and E. de Selincourt (London: Oxford University Press 1969), 628. See David R. Shore's recent argument that 'Hobgoblin' is Harvey's reference to himself, rendering 'slightly less sure our understanding of the genesis of *The Faerie Queene*': 'Spenser, Gabriel Harvey, and "Hobgoblin Runne Away with the Garland from *Apollo.*"' *Cahiers Elisabéthains*, 31 (1987), 59–61.

4 *Institutes*, III, xx, 27; II, 134. Thomas Norton's sixteenth-century translation (London, 1561) renders *larvae*, rather oddly, as *visors*. The meaning is evidently the OED's number 3: 'An outward appearance or show under which something different is hid; a mask or disguise.' It would seem to follow that George and Hippolytus are masks or disguises for demons, bogeys.

5 Nelson (1963), 150

6 See Patrick Grant, *Images and Ideas in Literature of the English Renaissance* (Amherst, Mass.: University of Massachusetts Press 1979), 42–3

7 *Iam vero Georgium etiam Herculem inuenerunt, quemadmodum et Hippolytum alterum. Huius equum phaleris ac bullis religiosissime adornatum tantum non adorant ac subinde nouo quopiam munusculo demerentur; per huius aeream galeam deierare plane regium habetur.* See *Moriae Encomivm*, ed. Clarence H. Miller in *Opera Omnia Desiderii Erasmi Roterodami* (Amsterdam-Oxford: North-Holland Publishing Co. 1979), Series IV, vol III, 122. I quote Clarence

228 Notes to pages 43–8

Miller's English translation, *The Praise of Folly* (New Haven: Yale University Press 1979), 63-4. According to Professor Miller, the omission of this attack on England's patron in Thomas Chaloner's 1549 English translation was deliberate.

8 Padelford and O'Connor, 'Spenser's Use of the St. George Legend,' 142, 153. For the source of their quotation from Lydgate see 'The Legend of St. George,' 1.20, in *The Minor Poems of John Lydgate*, ed. Henry Noble Mac-Cracken for the *Early English Text Society*, extra series, 107 (London: Kegan Paul, Trench, Trübner 1911), 146.

9 Grace Warren Landrum, 'St. George *Redivivus*,' *PQ*, 29 (1950), 382

10 For Lydgate see note 8. For de Voragine, Mantuan, and Barclay see *The Life of St. George* by Alexander Barclay, ed. William Nelson for EETS, original series, 230 (London: Geoffrey Cumberlege, Oxford University Press 1955). Barclay includes the pertinent passages from Mantuan in his margins. Nelson adds, in an appendix, de Voragine's version from *The Golden Legend* in Wynkyn de Worde's edition, 112–18. See also *Variorum*, I, 379–90.

11 Legrand lists 4 editions of the April *Menaion* before 1589, 6 of the *Pentecostarion*, and 9 of the *Octoechos*. I have translated from a 1569 edition of the *Menaion* and a 1544 edition of the *Pentecostarion* (see bibliography). Though Byzantine liturgical books were widely printed and evidently widely circulated in the sixteenth century, they are now much less easy to find than patristic editions of the same period. Consequently, I have not been able to examine an *Octoechos* which Spenser might have seen. That lack, however, is of no great moment for an examination of the Saint George liturgy, for the parts of the *Octoechos* appointed to be sung in the paschal liturgies are considered part of the *Pentecostarion* and are included in it. Since neither the 1569 *Menaion* nor the 1544 *Pentecostarion* have sequential pagination and since neither is likely to be accessible to a reader of this book, I refer in notes to twentieth-century texts (MHNAION TOY AΠΡΙΛΙΟΥ [AΘHNAI: ΦΩC 1972] and ΠΕΝΤΗΚΟΣΤΑΡΙΟΝ [AΘHNAI: ΦΩC nd]). Except in punctuation, capitalization, and very occasionally in accentuation, I have found no discrepancies between the older and more recent editions. There *are* some discrepancies in rubrics between Renaissance and modern editions; therefore, my summary of how Easter hymns are combined with those for Saint George is based on the 1569 *Menaion*. Once again, the lack of pagination makes citation of individual rubrics impossible.

12 Athens (1972), 169

13 Ibid. (1972), 168

14 Ibid. (1972), 164

15 Ibid. (1972), 177

16 Ibid. (1972), 165

17 *Pentecostarion*; Athens (nd), 3

18 The *which* clause is intentionally restrictive; the entire paschal canon is not repeated at matins (except on Sundays) in the Easter season, only the so-called *katavasia*, which announce the theme of each ode.

19 Athens (nd) 3

20 Ibid., 5; this hymn is what is called in the Byzantine rite an *Exapostalarion*; this one is appointed for Easter matins and is repeated at matins throughout the season.

21 Athens (nd), 13–14; 111

22 Ibid., 14; this verse is sung only on Easter Tuesday, not again on the fourth Sunday.

23 Athens (nd), 5

24 Ibid., 2

25 Ibid., 1, 5

26 Ibid., 2

27 Ibid., 2

28 Ibid., 5; These two passages come from a matins and vespers sequence built upon 'Let God arise and let his enemies be scattered,' which contains the vanishing smoke and the gate of Paradise.

29 Ibid., 5

30 I have found the paschal canon in 4 sixteenth-century editions of the Damascene's work (there may be other instances). Two of these we have already considered – the 1548 edition of Jacobus Fabrus Stapulensus' version of *De Fide Orthodoxa* (translation of the canon by Aldus Manutius Romanus) and Billius' 1577 edition of the *Opera*. Manutius' translation also appeared in an *Opera* published in Cologne in 1546 and in one from Basel in 1575 (the Pembroke copy of the latter is one of Lancelot Andrewes's gifts).

31 We should not, however, forget that there were only two more sixteenth-century editions of the *Pentecostarion* than of the April *Menaion* (see note 11).

32 Athens (1972), 167; italics added.

33 Ibid., 169

34 Ibid., 165. In addition to these passages in the liturgy proper, the following verses from Wisdom are printed in the April *Menaion* as part of the 'prophecies' for vespers: 'He shall put on righteousness as a breastplate, and true judgment instead of an helmet. He shall take holiness for an invincible shield' (V, 18–19).

35 Ibid., 169

36 Ibid., 179

37 Ibid., 170

38 Kaske, 'The Dragon's Spark and Sting' (1969)

39 For what the Fathers meant by τροπαιοφόρος see entries for τρόπαιον and τροπαιοφόρος in G.W.H. Lampe, *A Patristic Greek Lexicon* (Oxford: Clarendon Press 1961).

40 Athens (1972), 165

41 Ibid., 166

42 Ibid., 165

43 Padelford and O'Connor, 'Spenser's Use of the St. George Legend,' 156.

44 Grant, *Images and Ideas* (1979), 44

45 Kellogg and Steele, *Books I and II of 'The Faerie Queene,'* 12–13

46 Hamilton (1977) glosses lines 3–4 of I, xii, 6 as 'Christ's entry into Jerusalem' and refers also to I, xii, 13, where the citizens of Eden strow their garments in the streets for Red Crosse (156).

47 The Byzantine Palm Sunday liturgy, preceding that of Easter, is not found in the *Pentecostarion* but in the Lenten liturgical book, the *Triodion*, of which, according to Legrand, there were eleven editions between 1522 and 1589. Since I have been unable to find any of these, I translate here (and in later chapters) from a 1614 edition, another of the gifts of Lancelot Andrewes to the Pembroke library (it is bound together with a 1602 *Pentecostarion*). For full citation, see bibliography. The contemporary edition here cited is ΤΡΙΩΔΙΟΝ ΚΑΤΑΝΥΚΤΙΚΟΝ ... ΑΚΟΛΟΥΘΙΑΝ ΤΗΣ ΑΓΙΑΣ ΚΑΙ ΜΕΓΑΛΗΣ ΤΕΣΣΑΡΑΚΟΣΤΗΣ (ΑΘΗΝΑΙ: ΦΩΣ 1987). This passage, Athens (1987), 387

48 Athens (1987), 384

49 Ibid., 383

50 Hamilton (1977), 149, makes this connection, quoting the description of the magic well from *the Golden Legend*.

51 By 'relative silence' I mean that although most commentators acknowledge this symbolism, none of them seems much bothered by the lack of precedent for it in the sources they cite for Spenser's knowledge of Saint George. Those who address the matter directly have not been very convincing in their explanations. Josephine Waters Bennett thinks 'the identification of St. George with Christ, the dragon-slayer of the Apocalypse, was probably not original with Spenser' (*The Evolution of 'The Faerie Queene'* [Chicago: University of Chicago Press 1942], 110), but her subsequent effort to draw the idea from the Western, medieval legend is not persuasive. Although James Nohrnberg lists 'four prototypes for the Redcrosse of the last adventure' (*The Analogy of 'The Faerie Queene,'* 186 ff), none of them seems so likely a source as the liturgy.

52 For Nohrnberg, see preceding note; for Grant, *Images and Ideas* (1979), 43–6.

53 Grant (1979), 44

54 Quoted in Elkin Calhoun Wilson, *England's Eliza* (Cambridge, Mass.: Har-

vard University Press 1939), 186; *Variorum*, I, 390, quotes a slightly different version of Vennar's poem.
55 Athens (1972), 175–6
56 Grant (1979), 43–4
57 Nohrnberg, *The Analogy of 'The Faerie Queene,'* 196

Chapter Three

1 *Ecclesiastical Hierarchy*, III, i, 1: Campbell, 33; Basel (1539), 19–20; Cologne (1556), 238
2 *De Mysteriis*, VIII, 43: Deferrari, 20; Basel (1555), IV, 426
3 Jean Danielou, *The Bible and the Liturgy* (Ann Arbor, Mich.: Servant Books 1956), 140
4 *Variorum*, I, 309
5 Bennett, *The Evolution of the 'Faerie Queene'* (1942), 113; see also Bennett in *Explicator*, I, no 8 (June 1943), no 62. James McAuley argues vigorously against the thesis that Spenser intended a Roman marriage rite but, for reasons which seem insufficient, rejects as well a Christian interpretation: 'The Form of Una's marriage Ceremony in "The Fairie Queene,"' *N. & Q.* ns 21:11 (November 1974), 410–11.
6 *Procatechesis*, VI: Cologne (1564), 3
7 *Catechesis*, IV, ii: Paris (1564), 208; Cologne (1564), 196
8 *Procatechesis*, I: Cologne (1564), 1
9 See Bennett, 115, and *Variorum*, 'The Minor Poems,' II, 270
10 *De Sacramentis*, V, ii, 5–6: Deferrari, 311; Basel (1555), IV, 441
11 *In Canticum Canticorum*, I, i & iii; I translate from a two-volume *opera* (Latin), published in Cologne in 1573. For full citation see bibliography; for these passages see I, 300, 330.
12 *In Canticum Canticorum*, X: Basel (1571), 400
13 *De Mysteriis*, IX, 58: Deferrari, 27; Basel (1555), IV, 428; *De Sacramentis* V, ii, 7–8 and V, iii, 17; Deferrari, 311, 314; Basel (1555), IV, 441–442
14 *Sarum Manual*, Paris (1526), fol xxii[r]
15 Ibid., fol. xxii[v]
16 Here the *Manual* goes into a great many ceremonial details missing in Spenser's allegory – lighting a taper, placing it on a spear, and carrying it in procession. Either Spenser simplified for his purposes or relied in this instance on the succinct rubric of the Missal, which I quote here. I have translated from a 1514 edition of the Missal (see bibliography), fol lxxii[v].
17 *Missal*, fol lxxii[v]
18 *Manual*, fol xxviii[r]
19 Ibid., fol xxvi[v]

20 *Missal*, fol cxxiv^r
21 See Introduction, note 9
22 *Missal*, fol cxxiv^r
23 Booty, *Book of Common Prayer (1559)*, 259–60
24 *Catechesis*, V, iii: Paris (1564), 214–15; Cologne (1564), 198
25 Thomas Cain, *Praise in 'The Faerie Queene'* (Lincoln, Nebraska: University of Nebraska Press 1978), 78
26 *Ecclesiastical Hierarchy*, II, iii, 8: Basel (1539), 19; Cologne (1556), 215; Campbell here translates too freely: 'white as light' (32)
27 *Manual*, fol xxxvi^v
28 fol xxxvii^r
29 *Procatechesis*, III: Cologne (1564), 2
30 *Catechesis*, IV, viii: Paris (1564), 210–11; Cologne (1564), 197
31 Athens (1972), 169
32 Heninger, *Sidney and Spenser*, 330

Chapter Four

1 Irenaeus, *Contra Haereses*, IV, xx, 2, 5. See Chapter 1, note 47.
2 John of Damascus, Homily on the Transfiguration of Our Lord Jesus Christ, XII. I quote all passages from this homily in my own translation in the *Greek Orthodox Theological Review*, 32 (1987), 1–29. For this passage, see 22. Spenser could have read the homily in Billius' edition of the Damascene *Opera* (for which see Introduction, page 5 [note 14], the bibliography, and subsequent discussion in this chapter, 80-1). The passage here quoted is on fol 363^r. My translation is from Billius' Greek, which Migne (*PG*, 96, 545–76) reproduces with a few alterations and numerous errors. The only other English translation I know of is by J.A. McGuckin in *The Transfiguration of Christ in Scripture and Tradition*: Studies in the Bible and Early Christianity, vol 9 (Lewiston, N.Y.: Edwin Mellen Press 1986), 202–5. McGuckin's version is less literal than mine.
3 For a full discussion see R.W. Pfaff, *New Liturgical Feasts in Later Medieval England* (Oxford: Clarendon Press 1970), 13, 29–30. See also Arthur Michael Ramsey, *The Glory of God and the Transfiguration of Christ* (London: Longmans 1949), 128–29.
4 I base this statement on an examination of the lectionary of epistle and gospel readings in the 1559 Prayer Book.
5 I quote from the liturgy for the feast of the Transfiguration on 6 August, in the August *Menaion*. This was available in editions of 1549, 1558, 1568, 1569, 1591, and 1592 (see Legrand). The 1591 edition from which I quote is the only one of these I have been able to see; it is still conceivably early enough

to have contributed to the Mutabilitie Cantos, but in any event there is little likelihood that its text varies from that of the earlier editions. For full citation see bibliography. The modern edition to which I make page references is MHNAION TOY AYΓOYΣTOY (AΘHNAI: ΦΩC 1976) – these passages, 70, 78.

6 Vladimir Lossky, *The Mystical Theology of the Eastern Church* (New York: St. Vladimir's Seminary Press 1976), 101. I am indebted for this reference and for a good discussion of the issue to Eric D. Perl, 'St. Gregory Palamas and the Metaphysics of Creation,' *Dionysius*, 14 (1990), 105–30. For a discussion of Palamas' thought and how it developed as a response to westernizing tendencies in Byzantine theology, see John Meyendorff, *A Study of Gregory Palamas*, trans. George Lawrence (Leighton Buzzard, England: The Faith Press 1964), especially I, iii: 'Barlaam and the Councils of 1341,' 42–62. For a discussion of the confrontation between Palamism and Thomism at the Council of Florence (1438–45) see Meyendorff's *Byzantine Theology: Historical Trends and Doctrinal Themes* (New York: Fordham University Press 1974), chap. 8, 'Encounter with the West,' 91–114.

7 A good summary of the scholarship is to be found in S.P. Zitner's Introduction to his edition of *The Mutabilitie Cantos* (London: Thomas Nelson 1968), 48–50. Zitner argues for Chartrian rather than Florentine influence, as does Robert Ellrodt in *Neoplatonism in the Poetry of Spenser* (Geneva: Librairie E. Droz 1960), 63 ff. Hamilton's glosses (1977) and Elizabeth Heale's rehearsal of conventional interpretations (*The Faerie Queene: A Reader's Guide* [Cambridge: Cambridge University Press 1987], 170–7) suggest that the last twenty years of scholarship have broken no new ground. Nohrnberg, eclectic as usual in his ascriptions of influence, is nevertheless explicit in his rejection of a Christian interpretation: 'the highest him, that is behight / Father of Gods and men by equall might' does not, he says, refer 'to the Christian God, for the case is actually tried before Nature herself. Rather closer is the Timaeic demiurge ...' (740). G.F. Waller in 'Transition in Renaissance Ideas of Time and the Place of Giordano Bruno,' *Neophilologus*, 55 (1971), 3–15, makes a case for Bruno's influence which in my judgment was effactually refuted thirty-four years earlier by Angelo M. Pellegrini in 'Bruno, Sidney, and Spenser,' *SP*, 40 (1943), 128–44. See also Frank Kermode's notes on the Mutabilitie Cantos in *Spenser: Selections from the Minor Poems and 'The Faerie Queene'* (London: Oxford University Press 1965), 225–230.

8 If when C.S. Lewis says that Dame Nature is 'really an image of God himself,' he intends the *imago dei*, he has caught in a phrase the theology I am ascribing to Spenser. See *Spenser's Images of Life*, ed. Alastair Fowler (Cambridge: Cambridge University Press 1967), 15.

9 See above, note 2.

10 John Erskine Hankins, *Source and Meaning in Spenser's Allegory,* 296–7. For Erigena see *Periphyseon (The Division of Nature),* trans. I.P. Sheldon-Williams, rev. John J. O'Meara (Washington: Dumbarton Oaks 1987), 29, 40.

11 'The Cosmic Christ' in *Jesus Through the Centuries: His Place in the History of Culture* (New Haven: Yale University Press 1985), 68–9 (transliterated Greek in original).

12 The *Menaion* for January was published in 1533, 1552, 1558, 1569, 1582, and 1595. I quote from the last of these, which is the only one I have been able to see. For full citation, see bibliography. The contemporary edition on which I have relied for page references is MHNAION TOY IANOYAPIOY (AΘHNAI: ΦΩC 1960). For this passage see 146–7.

13 Athens (1960), 134–5

14 *Triodion*: Athens (1987), 481–2; italics added.

15 Ibid., 487–98

16 *De Incarnatione Verbi*, VIII: Paris (1581), I, 27

17 *De Incarnatione Verbi*, XLV; Paris (1581), I, 44; italics added.

18 *Contra Arianos*, II, xxi, 63: Schaff & Wace, IV, 383; Paris (1581), I, 140; italics added.

19 Athens (1976), 66

20 Homily, XVIII: Weatherby (1987), 23 (italics added); Paris (1577), fol 365^v

21 Homily, XVI; Weatherby (1987), 21; Paris (1577), fol 364^r

22 Athens (1976), 70

23 *Homilies on Matthew*, LVI, vii: Prevost, II, 766; Basel (1530), III, 324–5; in the 1530 edition, this homily is numbered 58.

24 Homily, XIII: Weatherby (1987), 17–18; Paris (1577), fol 363^r

25 J. Pelikan, *Imago Dei*, 150

26 Mark 9:1 – 'There be some of them that stand here, which shall not taste of death, till they have seen the kingdom of God come with power.' Luke 9:27 – 'There be some standing here, which shall not taste of death, till they see the kingdom of God.'

27 See above, note 23.

28 *Contra Haereses*, IV, xx, 2, 5; LF (1872), XLII, 365; Paris (1545), 359

29 V. Lossky, *The Vision of God*, 35

30 *The Divine Names*, I, iv. I quote the translation by C.E. Rolt (London: Macmillan 1940), 58; the bracketed *in* corrects a typographical error. Spenser had access to a Latin translation published in Cologne, 1556; this passage appears on 383. The Greek text was available to a sixteenth-century reader in a Parisian edition of 1562 (see bibliography); the passage here quoted is

on 246 of volume one. A copy of this book in the Pembroke library was very likely part of the sixteenth-century collection.

31 I quote a 1963 translation of Basil's *Exegetic Homilies* by Sister Agnes Clare Way (Washington: Catholic University of America Press 1963), 285–6 (italics added); Basel (1551), 105; Basel (1565), I, 274.

32 See note 30.

33 Spenser had access in sixteenth-century editions to the major hexaemeral treatises. Of these, Basil's is probably the most important, and Spenser could have read it in Greek (in Basel, 1551) and in Latin (in Basel, 1565). Both of these editions include all 11 homilies, not separating 10 and 11 ('On the Origin of Man') as modern editions do. Gregory of Nyssa's *Hexaemeron*, in P. F. Zinus' translation, was published in Venice in 1553 (see bibliography). Spenser could have read Gregory's *De Hominis Opificio*, intended as a supplement to his brother Basil's *Hexaemeron*, in both Greek and Latin in a two-text edition from Basel in 1567 (see bibliography). The translation is also included in Basel, 1571. Ambrose's *Hexaemeron*, derivative from Basil's, appears in Basel, 1555.

34 *De Civitate Dei*, XXII, 30; I quote from the translation of Henry Bettenson (Hammondsworth, England: Penguin, 1972), 1091. For a full explication of patristic conceptions of the eighth day, see Danielou, *The Bible and The Liturgy*, 262–75.

35 Athens (1987), 487

36 Alastair Fowler, *Spenser and the Numbers of Time* (London: Routledge & Kegan Paul 1964), 58

37 *Homily*, VIII: Weatherby (1987), 12; Paris (1577), fols 361^r–361^v

38 Athens (1976), 67

39 Ibid., 67

40 *De Mysteriis*, VII, 34: Deferrari, 17; Basel (1555), IV, 425

41 *In Canticum Canticorum*, XI: Basel (1571), 405

42 Robin Headlam Wells, *Spenser's 'Faerie Queene' and the Cult of Elizabeth* (London: Croom Helm 1983), 14ff; King, *Tudor Royal Iconography* (1989), 199–200, and King, *Spenser's Poetry and the Reformation Tradition* (1990), chapter 2, 'Spenserian Iconoclasm,' and chapter 3, 'Spenser's Royal Icons'

43 For the history of *natura* see George D. Economou, *The Goddess Natura in Medieval Literature* (Cambridge, Mass.: Harvard University Press 1972) and Ernst Robert Curtius, *European Literature and the Latin Middle Ages*, trans. Willard R. Trask (Princeton: Princeton University Press 1953), 112, 113–17, 121–2. The literature on the subject of *natura* is, to say the least, vast.

44 Josephine Waters Bennett, 'Spenser's Venus and the Goddess Nature of the *Cantos of Mutabilitie*,' *SP*, 30 (1933), 160–92. This is summarized in *Vari-*

orum, VI, 410–16 and has become one of the standard glosses on Dame
Nature.

Chapter Five

1 *De Civ. Dei*, XIV, 7 (Penguin 1972), 557
2 New York (1947), I, 697
3 *De Civ. Dei*, IX, 4; here I do not quote Augustine directly but Aquinas's para-
   phrase in *ST*, I–II, 24, 2, (New York 1947, I, 697). It would be more accurate to
   say that while both reject the common acceptation of the 'Stoic' teaching,
   both seek to reconcile it with the Platonic and Aristotelian and to prove that
   the Stoics really did also believe that one's passions are good if his loves are
   good.
4 New York (1947), I, 698
5 'An Ascetical Discourse' (*Sermo Asceticus*): *Ascetical Works*, New York
   (1950), 207; Basel (1551), 380; Basel (1565), II, 245. Raleigh's quotation of this
   passage in his *History* is testimony to Basil's currency as an authority (*Hist.*
   1, 2, 2). I am indebted to Kane (37) for this reference.
6 New York (1950), 207; Basel (1551), 380; Basel (1565), II, 245
7 New York (1947), II, 1772
8 II, 1769
9 II, 1767
10 New York (1950), 207–9; Basel (1551), 380; Basel (1565), II, 245–6
11 New York (1947), I, 484
12 Nohrnberg, *The Analogy of 'The Faerie Queene,'* 285
13 Most readily in Nannius' translation (Basel: Froben 1556) and subsequently
    in editions of 1564, 1572, and 1581. That the authenticity of Athanasius' *Vita
    Antonii* has been questioned by modern scholars has no bearing upon an
    argument for its sixteenth-century influence.
14 *Vita Antonii*, XIV: Paris (1581), V, 638
15 Ibid., XX: Paris (1581), V, 639–40
16 *Capitum Theologicorum Centuriae Quinque*, III, 49, 52, 56; Paris (1560), 141,
    144, 147. I quote the English translation by G.E.H. Palmer, Philip Sherrard,
    and Kallistos Ware in *The Philokalia: The Complete Text* (London: Faber &
    Faber 1981), II, 221, 222, and 224.
17 *Homilies on I Corinthians*, XXXIII, 4; LF (1839), II, 462, 463 (first italics in
    original, second added); Verona (1529), I, fol 212ʳ; Basel (1536), II, 416–17.
    In Chrysostom's commentary on Ephesians 6, in his discussion of 'the
    armour of a Christian man,' we encounter a comparable insistence upon
    complete mortification. Saint Paul's 'Hauing subdued all things' (in Bin-

neman & Newberie's translation, 1581) means '(hauing subdued) both our passions, & our absurd lusts, & all things that are troublesome unto us. He [Saint Paul] said not barelie, hauing wrought upon these things, but hauing so wrought, that you destroy them' (308; italics added).

18 *De Virginitate Liber*, XII; I quote from the English translation by William Moore and Henry Austin Wilson in Schaff & Wace, V, 357; *De Virginitate Liber* would have been accessible to Spenser in the original Greek and in a Latin version by Livineius Gandensus in a two-text edition from Antwerp in 1574 (see bibliography). For this passage see 100, 101. Chrysostom's *De Virginitate* was published in a companion volume (two-text, tr. Gandensus) in 1575 (see below, note 22).

19 *De Hominis Opificio*, XVII, iii, iv; Schaff & Wace, V, 407; *De Hominis Opificio* would have been accessible to Spenser in the original Greek and in the Latin translation of Lewenklaius in a two-text edition of 1567 (see bibliography). For these passages see 182–3, 184–5. Lewenklaius' translation (but without the Greek text) also appeared in the 1571 *Opera Omnia* by Sifanus and Lewenklaius (see bibliography).

20 *De Virginitate Liber*, XIII: Schaff & Wace, V, 360; Antwerp (1574), 120, 121

21 Binneman & Newberie (1581), 258–9

22 *De Virginitate*, X, iii; I translate the Greek from a two-text edition (Latin translation by Livineius Gandensus) from Antwerp in 1575 (see bibliography); for this passage see 15. For a recent (freely translated) English version, see John Chrysostom, *On Virginity, Against Remarriage*, trans. Sally Rieger Shore, *Studies in Women and Religion*, vol IX (New York and Toronto: Edwin Mellen 1983), 14.

23 *De Virginitate*, XIV, iii: Antwerp (1575), 22; Shore (1983), 21

24 *De Vita Moysis*, II, 93; *PG*, 44, 353A; Basel (1571), 505

25 Ibid., II, 276, 277: *PG*, 44, 416 A–B; Basel (1571), 522–3

26 The liturgical books containing the Sunday matins and vespers hymns are the *Octoechos* and the *Paracletice*; lacking access to any of the 9 sixteenth-century editions of the former (see chapter two, note 11) or 6 of the latter, I translate from a modern edition of the *Paracletice*: ΠΑΡΑΚΛΗΤΙΚΗ, ΠΕΡΙΕΧΟΥΣΑ ΑΠΑΣΑΝ ΤΗΝ ΑΝΗΚΟΥΣΑΝ ΑΥΤΗ, ΑΚΟΛΟΥΘΙΑΝ ... ΕΚΔΟΣΕΙΣ, ΑΘΗΝΑΙ: ΦΩC, 1979, 304.

27 Athens (1979), 359; the following hymn identifies dispassion with deification: 'Of old Adam, overcome by strategem, falls and shatters himself, beguiled by the hope of *theosis*; but he arises, deified by the union of the Word and by the Passion and carries off passionlessness as a prize; he is glorified as the Son, sitting upon the throne together with the Father and the Spirit,' Athens (1979), 12. *Sitting together with* (συνεδρεύων) is nicely

ambiguous, modifying either the Son or Adam or (the probable intention) both; by deification through the Incarnation and the Passion, Adam has become Christ.

28 *Triodion*: Athens (1987), 107
29 See below, 106–7
30 Athens (1979), 411
31 Ibid., 433
32 *Vita Antonii*, VII, V: Paris (1581), V, 636, 635
33 *Capitum Theologicorum*, III, 46, 47; *Philokalia* (1981), II, 221; Paris (1560), 140
34 See Lampe's citations for συνεργία, συνεργέω, and συνεργός.
35 I translate the following quotations from a Greek edition of 1550, which was followed in 1551 by a Latin translation by Gentianus Hervetus, both from the publishing house of Laurentius Torrentinus in Florence (see bibliography). Hervetius' translation was republished at Basel in 1556, at both Basel and Paris in 1566, and again at Paris in 1572 and 1590. There was another Greek edition from Heidelberg in 1592.
36 *Stromateis*, VII, iii, 16: Florence (1550), 302; Florence (1551), 235
37 Ibid., VII, xi, 65: Florence (1550), 314; Florence (1551), 250
38 Ibid., VII, xiv, 84: Florence (1550), 320; Florence (1551), 257
39 Ibid., VII, xiv, 86: Florence (1550), 321; Florence (1551), 258
40 Ibid., VII, xvi, 95: Florence (1550), 324; Florence (1551), 261. Clement's use of ἀπάθεια and the derivation of his ethical conceptions from classical philosophy is the subject of a considerable literature. He is frequently called a Stoic. Salvatore R.C. Lilla, in *Clement of Alexandria: a Study in Christian Platonism and Gnosticism* (London: Oxford University Press 1971), makes a convincing case for Clement's debt to Philo and Middle Platonism, and for parallels between his positions and those of Neoplatonism, especially with respect to the close link between ἀπάθεια and deification, ὁμοίωσις θεῷ. Lilla also points out that Clement allows for the 'ethics of μετριοπάθεια' (p. 103), which is to say of control or moderation rather than extinction of the passions – an ethical posture much closer to the Augustinian and Thomistic – but this 'does not represent for Clement the ideal of perfection,' (p. 103) that ideal being, of course, complete dispassion. Although Lilla's thesis is the Middle Platonic provenance of Clement's ethics, he freely grants that Clement's Christianity sets him apart from his antecedents in a radical way. For the pagan philosophers, the achievement of ἀπάθεια and of likeness to divinity is the work of human reason; for Clement it is the work of divine grace; 'For Clement, it is Christ, the Logos, who has the task of healing the passions of man ...' (p. 113).

41 Ibid., III, iv, 25: Florence (1550), 173; Florence (1551), 90. Philip is not named in either Gospel account.

42 Ibid., VII, xii, 72: Florence (1550), 316; Florence (1551), 253

43 Ibid., VII, xi, 64: Florence (1550), 314; Florence (1551), 250

44 Ibid., VII, iii, 13: Florence (1550), 302; Florence (1551), 234. Lilla (*Clement of Alexandria*) comments on this paradox: 'Although Clement ... seems to consider the virtue of the ... γνωστικός as a divine gift ... on the other hand he lays strong emphasis on the importance of human efforts without which it would be impossible to attain virtue ... Clement's real thought must have been that virtue is the product of the combined activity of God and man: he seems therefore to be in favour of what is called "synergism"' (p. 66). (See above, p. 105.)

45 *Tusculanae Disputationes*, III, viii, 16. For a succinct discussion of the relation of *temperance* (*temperantia*) to σωφροσύνη see note in the *OED* at the end of the entry for *temperance*.

46 *Ethica Nicomachea*, VII, ix, 1152a; I quote the translation by W. D. Ross in *The Basic Works of Aristotle*, ed. Richard McKeon (New York: Random House 1941), 1051.

47 New York (1947), II, 1827

48 Ibid., II, 1827, 1830

49 Padelford, 'The Virtue of Temperance in the *Faerie Queene*,' *SP*, 18 (1921), 334–46 (*Variorum* II, 420–2). See also Charles G. Osgood, 'Comments on the Moral Allegory of *The Faerie Queene*,' *MLN*, 46 (1931), 502–7 (*Variorum* II, 422–3); Osgood builds upon Padelford's discussion, making interesting distinctions between temperance and continence. For a recent and contrary reading which places heavy emphasis on temperance as moderation and relies upon Aristotle and Aquinas, see Gerald Morgan, 'The Idea of Temperance in the Second Book of *The Faerie Queene*,' *RES*, 37 (1986), 11–39.

50 Hamilton (1977), 294; Harry Berger, Jr, *The Allegorical Temper: Vision and Reality in Book II of Spenser's 'Faerie Queene'* (New Haven: Yale University Press 1957), 66; Estienne (Geneva, 1572), II, col 134C.

51 Viola Hulbert, 'A Possible Christian Source for Spenser's Temperance,' *SP*, 28 (1931), 184–210; passages quoted are from 184–5, 188. That subsequent scholars have not pursued Professor Hulbert's suggestions with any measure of seriousness is almost certainly owing to the enormous influence of Rosemond Tuve on Spenser studies. Miss Tuve (1966) dismissed distinctions between temperance and continence as merely 'space taking.' 'Long, long before Spenser's time, in materials remaining current, Continence had been accepted as one of the forms of Temperance'; she refers to Cicero, Macrobius, and Seneca (66) and might well have included Aquinas. She does

not therefore believe that Spenser would have distinguished the two in Aristotelian fashion. In discouraging such an approach to Book Two, Miss Tuve relies more heavily upon the philosophical tradition and the vocabulary of the virtues than upon the evidence of the poem itself. She does not therefore consider the possibility, introduced by names like *Acrasia* and *Acrates*, that Spenser may have, for whatever reason, revived a distinction which 'long, long before' had blurred.

52 *The Book of the Courtier,* trans. Sir Thomas Hoby (1561) (London: Everyman 1928), 271

53 *Long Rules,* Q. 16, r: *Ascetical Works,* New York (1950), 268; Basel (1551), 453; Basel (1565), II, 267

54 Ibid., Q. 17, r: New York (1950), 272; Basel (1551), 454; Basel (1565), II, 268

55 Ibid., Q. 16, r: New York (1950), 269–70; Basel (1551), 453–4; Basel (1565), II, 267

56 See *Lexicon Athanasianum,* Guido Müller, SJ (Berlin: Walter de Gruyter 1952), cols. 368, 1406. For whatever word counts are worth, Lampe's patristic citations for ἐγκράτεια and related forms run to two-and-a-half columns, for σωφροσύνη and related forms to a bit more than half a column.

57 As for instance, when the 'spirit of fornication' boasts of having seduced those who sought to be continent (σωφρονεῖν), when Athanasius pairs σωφροσύνη with παρθενίας (virginity), and when Anthony bids his disciples to renounce all pleasures and love σωφροσύνη. (*Vita Antonii,* VI, LXXIX, LXXXVII). In the first instance σωφρονεῖν is paired with the single instance (mentioned above) of a form of ἐγκράτεια – ἐγκρατευομένους – leaving little doubt as to how Athanasius intended being temperate to be conceived.

58 *Encratic* does not appear in the OED but will be helpful in this discussion. Webster's International (2nd ed.) lists it as 'rare.' I do not use it to refer to Encratitism, a heresy, for which there seems to be no adjective.

59 *Stromateis,* III, xii, 86: Florence (1550), 186; Florence (1551), 104

60 Ibid., III, i, 4: Florence (1550), 169; Florence (1551), 85

61 Ibid., II, xviii, 80: Florence (1550), 154; Florence (1551), 67

62 Helen North, *Sophrosyne: Self-Knowledge and Self-Restraint in Greek Literature* (Ithaca: Cornell University Press 1966), 348

63 *Stromateis,* II, xviii, 81: Florence (1550), 154; Florence (1551), 67

64 Ibid., III, vii, 57: Florence (1550), 180; Florence (1551), 97–8

65 North, 321

66 Ibid., 331–2; North cites *Stromateis,* III, x, 51

67 Ibid., 329–30

68 Ibid., 330; North attributes this to the *Protrepticus* but gives no citation. I have not found the passage to which she refers.

69 Athens (1987), 44

70 Ibid., 176

Chapter Six

1 Carol V. Kaske, 'The Bacchus Who Wouldn't Wash: *Faerie Queene* II. i–iii,' *Renaissance Quarterly,* 29 (1976), 202; Lauren Silberman, 'The Faerie Queene, Book II and the Limitations of Temperance,' *MLS,* 17 (1987), 9

2 Hamilton (1977), 163

3 'The Development of Guyon's Christian Temperance,' *ELR,* 7 (1977), 52

4 *The Axiochus of Plato,* trans. Edmund Spenser, ed. Frederick Morgan Padelford (Baltimore: Johns Hopkins 1934), 58

5 Harold L. Weatherby, '*Axiochus* and the Bower of Bliss: Some Fresh Light on Sources and Authorship,' *Spenser Studies,* 6 (1986), 95–113

6 For this usage see chapter five, note 58.

7 Berger, *The Allegorical Temper* (1957), 152

8 New York (1947), I, 840

9 For Berger see especially chapter two of *The Allegorical Temper,* 'Before and After the Faint: Classical vs. Christian Temperance,' 41–64. Though Hamilton (*The Structure of Allegory* 1961) argues that Spenser's temperance departs from Aristotle's in a Christian (and Platonic) direction (49–50), he is not prepared (1977) to accord the virtue so transcendent a status as that which attaches to holiness: 'While the Book of Holiness reveals man's spiritual life through his right relationship to God in the vertical perspective of heaven and hell, the Book of Temperance analyses man's natural life through his right relationship to his own nature in a horizontal perspective of the world in which he lives' (163).

10 Hume, *Edmund Spenser: Protestant Poet,* 67 (italics added). For Hume's rejection of Woodhouse, see her chapter four, 'Nature and Grace Reconsidered,' 59–71.

11 See especially A.C. Hamilton, '"Like race to runne": The Parallel Structure of *The Faerie Queene,* Books I and II,' *PMLA,* 73 (1958), 327–34.

12 A.C. Hamilton, 'A Theological Reading of *The Faerie Queene,* Book II,' *ELH,* 25 (1958), 156

13 Berger, *The Allegorical Temper* (1957), 120–60. Maureen Quilligan, 'The Comedy of Female Authority in *The Faerie Queene,*' *ELR,* 17 (1987), 156–71; passage quoted, 163

14 Hamilton, *The Structure of Allegory* (1961), 136–7

15 Berger, *The Allegorical Temper* (1957), 144, 149, 146–7

16 Acts 5:15, 19:12

17 See above, chapter 5, 101, note 17.

18 See above, chapter 5, 106, note 38.

19 Hamilton (1977), 195

20 Tuve, *Allegorical Imagery* (1966), 363

21 Stephen Fallon, 'Belphoebe, Braggadochio, and the Education of Guyon,' *Spenser at Kalamazoo, 1983*, ed. Francis G. Greco (Clarion University of Pennsylvania 1983), 152

22 Ibid., 153

23 This interpretation of Belphoebe in Book Two pertains only to Book Two and to the account of her miraculous birth in Three. In her dealings with Timias in Books Three and Four she emerges in a somewhat different light. Her virginity in these episodes seems less attractive, and her jealousy of Amoret in Book Four destroys the illusion of impassibility. Since, however, these developments are subsequent to her original, emblematic presentation and since they are to be accounted for by the pressures of the political allegory, they do not in my judgment invalidate my reading of her role in Two. Belphoebe is not the only figure whose significance alters in the course of the poem, and I believe all agree that Books Four through Six develop under different impulses.

24 Stephen Greenblatt, *Renaissance Self-Fashioning from More to Shakespeare* (Chicago: University of Chicago Press 1980), 172

25 Ibid., 172

26 Ibid., 173

Chapter Seven

1 Paul J. Alpers, *The Poetry of 'The Faerie Queene'* (Columbia: University of Missouri Press 1982), 255

2 Berger, *The Allegorical Temper* (1957), chapter 1, 'The Hero Faints: A Critical Misadventure,' 3–38; Hume, *Edmund Spenser: Protestant Poet*, 120; the following articles present still other variations on Berger's thesis: Maurice Evans, 'The Fall of Guyon,' *ELH*, 28 (1961), 215–24; Humphrey Tonkin, 'Discussing Spenser's Cave of Mammon,' *SEL*, 13 (1973), 1–13; Geoffrey A. Moore, 'The Cave of Mammon: Ethics and Metaphysics in Secular and Christian Perspective,' *ELH*, 42 (1975), 157–70; Roger C. Swearingen, 'Guyon's Faint,' *SP*, 74 (1977), 165–85. Frank Kermode argues to the contrary (and he is almost alone in doing so) that 'Guyon's openly encountering Mammon is parallel' to Christ's wishing 'to be tempted "that he might strengthen us against temptations" (*Summa Theologica*, III, 41, 1); this was, as St. Gregory said, "not unworthy in him" ...' nor is Guyon's conduct unworthy either. 'The Cave of Mammon' in Kermode, *Shakespeare, Spenser, Donne* (1971), 77; Kermode stops short of arguing as I shall in this chapter

that Guyon like Red Crosse becomes, to use Kermode's own phrase, 'Christ himself.'

3 Patrick Cullen, 'Guyon *Microchristus*,' in *Infernal Triad: The Flesh, the World, and the Devil in Spenser and Milton* (Princeton: Princeton University Press 1974), 89

4 See A. Kent Hieatt, *Chaucer, Spenser, Milton: Mythopoeic Continuities and Transformations* (Montreal: McGill-Queens University Press 1975), 196

5 Nohrnberg, *The Analogy of 'The Faerie Queene,'* 187

6 A. Kent Hieatt, 'Three Fearful Symmetries and the Meaning of *Faerie Queene* II,' in *A Theatre for Spenserians*, ed. Judith M. Kennedy and James A. Reither (Toronto: University of Toronto Press 1973), 39, 43

7 Patrick Cullen, 'Guyon *Microchristus*,' 88–9

8 Ibid., 85, 89, 92

9 Ibid., 92, 90

10 Ibid., 89

11 Ibid., 91–2

12 New York (1947), II, 2116

13 *De Fide Orthodoxa*, III, iii–iv: Schaff & Wace, IX, 48–9; Basel (1548), 183–4, 190; Paris (1577), fols 246^v and 250^r

14 *Homily on the Transfiguration*, III: Weatherby (1987), 4; Paris (1577), fol 358^r

15 *De Fide Orthodoxa*, III, iii: Schaff & Wace IX, 48; Basel (1548), 184; Paris (1577), fol 246^v

16 *Paracletice* (Athens 1979), 357

17 The best known of these are the *Historia Monachorum in Aegypto* in a Latin version probably by Rufinus of Aquileia (J.-P. Migne *Patrologiae cursus completus ... series Latina* (Paris 1844–1902) 221 vols, 21, 387–462 – series cited hereafter as *PL*.) and the *Apophthegmata Patrum* (*PG*, 65, 71–440). For contemporary studies see Derwas J. Chitty, *The Desert a City* (Oxford: Basil Blackwell 1966) and Philip Rousseau, *Ascetics, Authority, and the Church in the Age of Jerome and Cassian* (Oxford: Oxford University Press 1978).

18 Cassian visited the desert monks, and his accounts of their lives and teachings were principal sources for knowledge of them in the West. For Renaissance editions dating back to 1481 see *PL*, 49, 11–26. A likely source for Spenser would have been the 1578 edition by Christophorus Plantinus of Antwerp, publisher, as we have seen, of both Chrysostom's and Gregory of Nyssa's treatises on virginity (1575 and 1574).

19 *The Golden Legend or Lives of the Saints* as Englished by William Caxton (1483) (London: J.M. Dent 1900), III, 108

20 *Triodion*: Athens (1987), 124, 126, 125

21 *Homilies on Matthew*, XIII, 1: Prevost, I, 174; Basel (1530), III, 81

22 *Vita Antonii*, VIII–X: Paris (1581), V, 636–7

23 *Triodion*: Athens (1987), 59

24 Alpers, *Poetry of the 'Faerie Queene,'* 248

25 Berger, *The Allegorical Temper,* 16

26 The following hymn for the dead from the *Triodion* is characteristic: 'Free *among the dead,* as Lord (lit. "author") of life and death, do Thou grant rest to those whom Thou hast taken and cause them to dwell in Thy courts, O lover of mankind' (Athens 1987), 226

27 *Paracletice*: Athens (1979), 296

28 *Golden Legend*: London (1900), III, 130

29 *Triodion*: Athens (1987), 349, 268–9, 133, 347, 226

30 *Vita Antonii,* VI: Paris (1581), V, 636

31 *Homilies on Matthew,* XIII, 3, 4: Prevost, I, 177, 179; Basel (1530), III, 83

32 Ibid., XIII, 4, 6; Prevost, I, 178, 181; Basel (1530), III, 83, 85

33 For this stool, many critics, beginning with Upton, have suggested ingenious interpretations. For some of these see Hamilton's gloss on II, vii, 63, 9, in 1977, 236

34 Cullen, 'Guyon *Microchristus,'* 80–1

35 Berger (*The Allegorical Temper,* 1957) develops this interpretation at length (19ff). That Guyon's 'greedy vew' is not culpable and not a manifestation of desire seems evident from the fact that the fiend which follows Guyon could have seized him 'If euer couetous hand, *or lustfull eye,* / Or lips he layd on thing, that likt him best' (II, vii, 27; italics added).

36 Alpers' commentary on this matter is especially good (*The Poetry of 'The Faerie Queene,'* 262 ff.).

37 Kathleen Williams comes very close to such an interpretation: Guyon's 'collapse when he reaches the vital air again is a sign not of failure but of the magnitude of his success, what he has taken upon himself is the limit of what frail flesh can stand. He faints because he has conquered at the necessary cost of going without the food and sleep which would have committed him to Mammon, a risk taken in order to learn the utmost man can know and see the utmost man can have from Mammon and to reject it.' *Spenser's World of Glass: A Reading of 'The Faerie Queene'* (Berkeley: University of California Press 1966), 61–2

38 Judith Anderson, *The Growth of a Personal Voice: 'Piers Plowman' and 'The Faerie Queene'* (New Haven: Yale University Press 1976), 64

39 Passus xviii, 159–61. I quote from *'The Vision of Pierce Plowman,* nowe the seconde tyme imprinted by Roberte Crowlye' (London 1550), STC 19907, fol lxxxxix^r (Crowley's edition does not have numbered lines).

40 Passus xx, 164–5. I quote from the edition of the C-text by Derek Pearsall (Berkeley: University of California Press 1978), 326.

41 Ibid., xviii, 292; Crowley, fol cii^v

42 Ibid., xviii, 339–40; Crowley, fol cii^r

43 Ibid., xviii, 355–61; Crowley, fol ciii^v

44 A.C. Hamilton, 'Spenser and Langland,' *SP*, 55 (1958), 533–48, and 'The Visions of *Piers Plowman* and *The Faerie Queene*,' in *Form and Convention in the Poetry of Edmund Spenser*, ed. William Nelson (New York: Columbia 1961), 1–34

45 Hamilton argues persuasively for resemblances between Red Crosse as Harrower and the role of Piers-Christ.

46 *Canterbury Tales*, I, 4321: 'A gylour shal hymself bigyled be.'

47 Ephesians 4:8

48 *Triodion*: Athens (1987), 479

49 54, 7–8 in *The Oxford Book of Medieval Latin Verse* (Oxford: Clarendon Press 1970). My translation. Is it possible that another famous hymn by Fortunatus, which also deals with the Harrowing, the *Vexilla Regis*, exerted an influence on the end of canto seven?

> *Beata cuius bracchiis*
> *pretium pependit saeculi,*
> *statera facta est corporis*
> *praedam tulitque tartari.*   (55, 21–4); Oxford (1970).

> Blest [tree] upon whose branches
> hung the price of the world!
> The price of the body is paid, and
> He bore away the prey of Tartarus.

There, perhaps, is the source of Spenser's *prey.* But of more interest: Christ being the 'price of the world' hanging on the tree is by metaphoric extension a monetary fruit, of which Mammon's golden apples may be a fallen, materialist's parody – just as the entire Garden of Proserpina is a fallen, materialist's parody of the Paradise of I, xi in which the Tree of Life (by typological association, the Cross) gives 'happie life to all' (I, xi, 46). Christ was able to pay Adam's price and thus bear away the prey of Tartarus because he was 'not tempted' by Satan. Guyon as Christ, refusing to taste – not tempted to taste – Mammon's golden fruit, releases himself, the prey, from the fallen garden. In that context of associations, Pilate's presence, which has continued to resist convincing interpretation, makes both theological and poetic sense. The man who was instrumental in hanging the 'price of the world' upon the tree is a fitting companion to Tantalus who wishes to pick the fruit which made the payment of that price necessary. Tantalus, like Adam and Eve, craves fruit which can satisfy neither body nor soul while Pilate has 'Deliuered vp ... to die' (II, vii, 62) and ironically made available to Adam and Eve, the only fruit which can. Pilate so conceived is an inverse symbol of the Passion and Harrowing, which Guyon, by not desiring what Adam and Eve desired, has participated in.

50 See above, chapter 5, 107, note 41.

51 Rothmagi (1514), fol lxxv^v

52 *Paracletice*: Athens (1979), 411

Chapter Eight

1 I quote the translations by Peter Holmes and Robert E. Wallis in *A Select Library of The Nicene and Post-Nicene Fathers of The Christian Church*, ed. Philip Schaff (New York: Christian Literature Company 1887), V, i, 20, 253. There is a vast literature on the subject. For contemporary discussions see Norman P. Williams, *The Ideas of the Fall and of Original Sin* (London: Longmans Green 1927); Kelly, 344–74; Pelikan, I, 278–331; Henri Rondet, SJ, *Orginal Sin: The Patristic and Theological Background*, trans. Cajetan Finegan, OP (Staten Island: Alba House 1972). The best concise studies of the subject are the entries for 'Péché originel' by A. Gaudel and 'Péché originel dans l'église grecque après saint Jean Damascène' by M. Jugie (cols 275–606, 606–24) in *Dictionnaire de Théologie Catholique* (Paris: Librairie Letouzey et Ane 1933), XII. Cols 387–402 contain an excellent explanation of Saint Augustine's position.

2 New York (1947), I, 952–3

3 Luther: 'What, then, is original sin?' Not a mere 'privation or lack of original righteousness' but the 'loss of all uprightness ... the proneness toward evil; the loathing of the good; the disdain for light and wisdom but fondness for error and darkness ... an eagerness for doing evil' (from *Lectures on Romans*, trans. & ed. Wilhelm Pauck, in The Library of Christian Classics [Philadelphia: Westminster Press 1961], XV, 167–8). Calvin: 'In the person of the first man we are fallen from our original condition'; Adam's 'guilt being the origin of that curse which extends to every part of the world, it is reasonable to conclude its propagation to all his offspring'; 'this is that hereditary corruption which the fathers called *original sin*.' Calvin admits that nothing is 'more remote from natural reason, than that all should be criminated on account of the guilt of one' and believes that for that reason 'the most ancient doctors of the Church did but obscurely glance at this point, or at least explained it with less perspicuity than it required.' (He probably alludes to what is in fact rejection of 'this point' before Augustine.) But in response to Pelagius 'good men, and beyond all others Augustine, have laboured to demonstrate that we are not corrupted by any adventitious means, but that we derive an innate depravity from our very

birth' (*Inst.*, II, i, 1, 5; I, 266, 270–1). Perkins: Original sin is 'corruption engendered in our first conception, whereby every faculty of soul and body is prone and disposed to evil'; 'the propagation of sin from the parents to the children is either because the soul is infected by the contagion of the body ... or because God, in the very moment of creation and infusion of souls into infants, doth utterly forsake them. For as Adam received the image of God both for himself and for others, so did he lose it for himself and others' (191–2). On the Protestant understanding of original sin see Gaudel, cols 511–13. For literary applications of Protestant teaching, see Barbara K. Lewalski, *Protestant Poetics and the Seventeenth-Century Religious Lyric* (Princeton University Press 1979), especially chapter one, 'The Protestant Paradigm of Salvation,' 13–27: despite 'justification' and 'imputed righteousness,' 'the Christian remains radically sinful in himself' (17). See also Grant, *The Transformation of Sin* (1974) and Richard Strier, *Love Known: Theology and Experience in George Herbert's Poetry* (Chicago: University of Chicago Press 1983).

4 *PG*, 74, 785C, 788A, 788C–D, 789A–B
5 Ibid., 789A
6 David Weaver's three-part article provides a thorough discussion of differences between Eastern and Western understandings of the Fall and its consequence: 'From Paul to Augustine: Romans 5:12 in Early Christian Exegesis,' *St. Vladimir's Theological Quarterly*, 27 (1983), 187–206; 29 (1985), 133–59, 231–57; for passage quoted see 29 (1985), 149. I have relied heavily upon Weaver for direction to pertinent patristic texts, but I have examined all of them in sixteenth-century versions and produced my own translations (some of his are faulty).
7 See *PG*, 68, 105–6.
8 I translate from Theodoret's commentary on Romans 5:12 in Cologne (1573), II, 18; see bibliography.
9 *Contra Haereses*, V, i, 3: *LF* (1872) XLII, 451; Paris (1545), 437
10 Grant, *The Transformation of Sin* (1974)
11 *De Baptismo Liber*, XVIII: Evans, 39; Paris (1545), fol 273^v
12 *Exhortatio ad Castitatem*, II: Paris (1545), fol 199^r
13 Pelikan, *The Christian Tradition*, I, 290
14 *Adversus Marcionem*, I, 22, 8: Paris (1545), fol 58^r
15 *Contra Arianos*, III, xxvi, 33: Schaff & Wace, IV, 411; Paris (1581), I, 163 (in this edition, *Sermo Qvartus*)
16 *De Infantibus Qui Praemature Abripiuntur*: Basel (1571), 136
17 *De Oratione Dominica*, V: Basel (1571), 27
18 *De Vita Moysis*, II, 32; *In Psalmos*, VI: Basel (1571), 499, 82. The Greek text of *De Vita Moysis* was published at Leyden by Davidus Hoeschelius in 1586. I

have not been able to see the edition, but it is reproduced by Migne (*PG*, 44, 297–430) in Fronton du Duc's version. For this passage, see col 336B; for *In Psalmos* VI see *PG*, 44 609 D.

19 *Homilies on Romans*, X: Verona (1529), I, fol 39ᵛ; Basel (1536), I, 69

20 Weaver, 'From Paul to Augustine,' 29 (1985), 142

21 Johannes Quasten, *Patrology* (Utrecht/Antwerp: Spectrum Publishers 1960), III, 478

22 For references to Pelikan and Kelly, see note 1 of this chapter. John S. Romanides, 'Original Sin According to St. Paul,' *St. Vladimir's Seminary Quarterly*, 4 (1955–6), 5–28; also see Meyendorff (1974), 143–6. I have relied heavily upon these studies for the interpretation of original sin in this chapter but not upon any secondhand quotation of patristic material.

23 The first edition of Erasmus' New Testament appeared in March, 1516. In a short note on Romans, 5:12, he explained his grammatical reasons for revising the Vulgate translation. He expanded the note slightly in editions of 1519 and 1527. It became a full-scale commentary with copious patristic citation in 1535. For discussions of the *adnotatio* and its consequences see John B. Payne, 'Erasmus: Interpreter of Romans,' *Sixteenth Century Essays and Studies*, ed. Carl S. Meyer (St. Louis: The Foundation for Reformation Research 1971), II, 1–15; Jerry H. Bentley, *Humanists and Holy Writ* (Princeton: Princeton University Press 1983), 170–3; and Robert Coogan, 'The Pharisee Against the Hellenist: Edward Lee Versus Erasmus,' *Renaissance Quarterly*, 39 (1986), 476–506. For a recent discussion of the dating of Erasmus' translation, see Andrew J. Brown, 'The Date Of Erasmus' Latin Translation of the New Testament,' *Transactions of the Cambridge Bibliographical Society*, 8 (1984), 351–80. For a recent and learned commentary on Romans 5:12 and the meaning of ἐφ' ᾧ see C.E.B. Cranfield, 'Introduction and Commentary on Romans I–VIII,' which is Volume I of *A Critical and Exegetical Commentary on 'The Epistle to the Romans'* (Edinburgh: T. & T. Clark, Ltd. 1975), 274–9. Cranfield makes no mention of Erasmus, but he relies as Erasmus did on patristic exegesis. Since I completed this study, Robert Coogan has published *Erasmus, Lee and the Correction of the Vulgate: The Shaking of the Foundations* (Geneva: Librairie Droz 1992). Coogan's first chapter, 'Pelagianism and original sin' (pp. 25–51), deals in detail with Erasmus' annotation on Romans 5:12 and contemporary responses to it.

24 *On Forgiveness of Sins and Baptism*, Schaff, V, 19

25 And a faulty text, which omitted *death* in the second half of the verse. See Rondet, *Original Sin*, 128–9.

26 See Bentley, 172–3 and Payne, 13.

27 For the text of Erasmus' *adnotatio* I rely upon a 1555 edition of the *Annotationes* from Froben in Basel. For Erasmus' translation I use a 1542 edition of his *Novum Testamentum* also from Froben (see bibliography). The University

of Toronto Press will publish the *Annotations on Romans* in the spring or summer of 1994 as part of its *Collected Works of Erasmus*.

28 Bentley, 173

29 Tyndale (1525): 'In so moche that all men synned'; Great Bible (1539): 'In so moch as all we have synned'; Geneva Bible (1560): 'For asmuche as all men have sinned'; Bishops' Bible (1568): 'In so much as all have sinned'; King James (1611): 'For that all have sinned.' Rheims (1582) adopts Augustine's second reading of *in quo*, that all have sinned in Adam's *sin*: 'In which al sinned.'

30 *Most Learned and Fruitful Commentaries of D. Peter Martir Vermilius ... vpon the Epistle of S. Paul to the Romanes* (London: Iohn Daye 1568), STC 24672

31 *Annotationes*: Basel (1555), 389

32 Ibid., 391

33 Ibid., 391–2

34 If Osgood's *Concordance* is to be trusted, the phrase, 'original sin,' does not occur in Spenser's canon – a notable absence in theological poety written in a milieu influenced by Augustine, Luther, and Calvin.

35 *De Vita Moysis*, II, 59–60: PG, 44, 341D–344A; Basel (1571), 501

36 Homily, IV: Weatherby (1987), 6–7; Paris (1577), 359^V

37 Lampe fills half a column with patristic citations of $\varphi\theta o\rho\dot{\alpha}$ signifying the 'corruptible state of present life' and gives only one citation signifying 'defilement, i.e. sin.'

38 R. Ellrodt, *Neoplatonism in the Poetry of Spenser*, 39–45

39 If any asserts that Adam 'has transfused only death and the pains of the body into the whole human race, but not sin also ... let him be anathema.' The sin of Adam is 'transfused into all' 'by propagation, not by imitation.' 'Fifth Session'in *Canons and Decrees of the Council of Trent*, trans. H.J. Schroeder (St. Louis: B. Herder Book Co. 1941), 22. For extensive quotations from the Council's decrees and a full discussion, see Gaudel, cols 513–527.

Chapter Nine

1 Lilian Winstanley, ed. *The Faerie Queene, Book II* (Cambridge: Cambridge University Press 1914), 243. I quote from Hamilton (1977), 165.

2 A.C. Hamilton, 'A Theological Reading,' 156. Hamilton's interpretation has established itself as standard. Kellogg's and Steele's gloss is characteristic; they take for granted that 'Ruddymane's bloodstained hands are ... best interpreted as the effects of original sin' (*Books I and II of 'The Faerie Queene,'* 57). James Nohrnberg offers the same interpretation: 'Ruddymane is a child of wrath, and his hands are indelibly stained with the "deep sanguine" of an inherited "bloud-guiltinesse" ... This guilt, baptism cannot remove' (*The Analogy of 'The Faerie Queene,'* 355).

3 Hamilton (1977), 177

4 Alastair Fowler, 'The Image of Mortality: *The Faerie Queene*, II, i–ii,' *Hunting-ton Library Quarterly*, 24 (1961), 91–110; I quote here from the reprint of the article in *Essential Articles*, 144.

5 Fowler quotes from Ficino's *De religione christiana* (Paris, 1559), fol 105^v; Fowler, 147.

6 Hamilton (1977), 182 (gloss on II, ii, 3)

7 Ibid., 182 (gloss on II, ii, 1)

8 Fowler, 143

9 Ibid., 144

10 From private correspondence, quoted with Professor Kaske's permission. She has not published a discussion of this matter.

11 See chapter 8, 159, note 6.

12 *Faerie Queene*, II, ii, 5–10

13 As Kellogg and Steele show, Spenser may initially have conceived of two springs or streams, for in the 'Letter to Raleigh' the Palmer is said to have brought the bloody-handed babe to Gloriana's court and *there* to have secured Guyon's services, presumably 'after the burial of Mordant and Amavia and before the washing episode. In that case, the two wells ... may not originally have been the same well' (*Books I and II of 'The Faerie Queene,'* 57). That they are, however, the same in the completed poem seems reason enough to build an interpretation on their identity. Spenser's revision of his (perhaps) original conception may have been motivated for all we know by a desire to ascribe Mordant's death and the babe's abortive washing to the same cause.

14 Fowler, 143

15 Ibid., 145

16 Ibid., 141. Kellogg and Steele (58) say that 'in the washing episode the nymph's spring strongly suggests the Old Law,' but they go on (rather inconsistently) to say that 'Mordant must die to sin (in baptism) ...' Nohrn-berg suggests that same curious fusion of motifs (288–9).

17 Carole V. Kaske, who also identifies the stream as the Mosaic law, is persua-sive in applying to the passage Augustine's idea of 'negative suggestibility.' See her 'Augustinian Psychology in *The Faerie Queene* Book II,' *University of Hartford Studies in Literature*, 15 (3), 16 (1) (1984), 93–8.

18 Fowler, 141

19 See chapter eight, 166–7.

20 There is no contradiction between those two significations, for, as Origen and other Fathers teach, all men were in Adam when he became subject to death.

21 Woodhouse, 194–228; I quote from the reprint in *Essential Articles*, 78. Charles G. Osgood in 'Comments on the Moral Allegory of *The Faerie Queene*,' *MLN*, 46 (1931), 502–7, had argued that Maleger is physical disease

(505–6), and the *Variorum* editors give Osgood's reading their apparent
imprimatur (II, 343). Rosemond Tuve in *Allegorical Imagery* (1966) calls
Woodhouse's interpretation 'brilliant' (131) and 'of an unequaled brilliance'
(137, note 50).
22 Ibid., 78
23 Hamilton, *The Structure of Allegory* (1961), 103
24 Hamilton (1977), 276 (gloss on II, xi, 22)
25 Ibid., 276 (gloss on II, xi, 22) and Woodhouse, 78
26 *The Works of John Ruskin*, ed. E.T. Cook and Alexander Wedderburn (London: George Allen and New York: Longmans 1903–12), X, 383. Quoted by Hamilton (1977), 167
27 *Menaion of January*: Athens (1960), 148, 149
28 When the passions renew their attack on Alma after Guyon's departure for the Bower (II, xi, 1–16), they seem to put her in greater danger than before. The bulwarks of her house (the body) 'threaten neare decay' (stanza fourteen), and Alma is 'dismayed with that dreadful sight: / For neuer was she in so euill cace' (stanza sixteen).
29 Hume, *Edmund Spenser: Protestant Poet*, 125
30 Ibid., 125–6

Chapter Ten

1 Hamilton (1977), 702
2 Ibid., 299
3 Thomas P. Roche, Jr, *The Kindly Flame: A Study of the Third and Fourth Books of Spenser's 'Faerie Queene'* (Princeton: Princeton University Press 1964), 104–6
4 Richard Berleth, 'Heavens Favorable and Free: Belphoebe's Nativity in *The Faerie Queene*,' *ELH*, 40 (1973), 479–500
5 *De Civ. Dei*, XIV, xxi (Penguin 1972), 583. For commentary on Augustine's development of the idea, see Peter Brown, *Augustine and Sexuality*, which is Colloquy 46 of the Center for Hermeneutical Studies in Hellenistic and Modern Culture (Berkeley: Center for Hermeneutical Studies 1983). See also Peter Brown's recent and monumental study, *The Body and Society: Men, Women and Sexual Renunciation in Early Christianity* (New York: Columbia University Press 1988). Brown offers further evidence for the contrasts I draw in the following pages between Augustine's position and that of the earlier and contemporary Greek Fathers. My discussion is not, however, indebted to Brown's, which appeared after mine was written. Augustine's teaching prevailed among most Protestants, so Spenser could have encountered it in various contexts. Milton scholars, not surprisingly, have explored the tradition fully. For a recent study, see James Grantham Turner, *One Flesh*:

Paradisal Marriage and Sexual Relations in the Age of Milton (Oxford: Clarendon Press 1987).

6 *De Civ. Dei*, XIV, xxiii; 585
7 Ibid., XIV, xxvi; 591
8 Ellrodt, *Neoplatonism in The Poetry of Spenser*, 85
9 *Stromateis*, III, xvii, 102–3
10 See chapter 5, 102; notes 18, 19.
11 *De Virginitate Liber*, XIII: Schaff & Wace, V, 360; Antwerp (1574), 120, 121
12 'Various Texts on Theology, the Divine Economy, and Virtue and Vice,' I, 14; *The Philokalia*, II, 168. I have found no sixteenth-century edition of the *Various Texts*.
13 *Paracletice*: Athens (1979), 355
14 New York (1947), I, 493–4
15 Richard Helgerson, 'The New Poet Presents Himself,' in *Self-Crowned Laureates: Spenser, Johnson, Milton and the Literary System* (Berkeley: University of California Press 1983), 97

Bibliography

Renaissance patristic and liturgical editions
and other sixteenth-century works
quoted in this book

Patristic:

Omnia qvotqvot extant D. Ambrosii Episcopi Mediolanensis *Opera*, Primvm per Des. Erasmvm Roterodamvm, mox per Sig. Gelenium, deinde per alios eruditos uiros diligenter castigata ... [Froben], Basileae M. D. LV. Cited as 'Basel (1555).'

Divi Athanasii Magni Alexandrini Archiepiscopi, Scriptoris Gravissimi, et Sanctissimi Christi Martyris, *omnia quae extant Opera* ... Parisiis, Apud Michaelem Sonnivm ... M. D. LXXXI. (This is Peter Nannius' translation, published originally in 1556.) Cited as 'Paris (1581).'

Divi Basilii Magni *Opera* Graeca quae ad nos extant *omnia*, Froben, Basileae, M D LI. Cited as 'Basel (1551).'

Opera D. Basilii Magni Caesariae Cappadociae Episcopi *Omnia*: Iam recens per Wolfgangvm Mvscvlvm partim locis aliquot castigata, partim luculentis accessionibus aucta ... Basileae, Per Ioan. Oporinvm, et Haeredes Ioannis Heruagii. 1565. (Latin text.) Cited as 'Basel (1565).'

ΚΛΗΜΕΝΤΟΣ ΑΛΕΞΑΝΔΡΕΩΣ ΤΑ ΕΥΡΙΣΚΟΜΕΝΑ ἅπαντα ... Cudebat Florentiae Laurentius Torrentinus Cum Iulii. III. Pont. Max. Caroli V. Imperatoris, Henrici Gallorum Regis II. Cosmi Medicis Florent. Ducis II. Priuilegiis. M D L. (Greek text.) Cited as 'Florence (1550).'

Clementis Alexandrini *Omnia* Qvae Qvidem extant *opera*, nunc primum è tenebris eruta Latinitateque donata, Gentiano Herueto Aurelio interprete ... Laur. Torrentinus Ducalis typographus excudebat. Florentiae, M D LI. Cited as 'Florence (1551).'

Sancti Cyrilli Hierosolymorum Archiepiscopi *Catecheses* ex Bibliotheca Henrici Memmii libellorum supplicum in Regia Magistri ... Parisiis M. D. LXIIII, Apud Guil. Morelium in Graecis typographum Regium. Cited as 'Paris (1564).'

Sancti Patris Nostri Cyrilli Archiepiscopi Hierosolymorvm, *Catecheses* Illvminatorvm Hierosolymis XVIII & quinque Mystagogicae ... nunc primùm Latinitate donatae in lucem prodeunt. Ioanne Grodecio ... interprete ... Coloniae, Apud Maternum Cholinum, M. D. LXIIII. Cited as 'Cologne (1564).'

D. Dionysii Areopagitae Atheniensium Episcopi *ad Timotheum de ecclesiastica hierarchia*, Oratio ... Adiuncta sunt fini Graeca Scholia in hanc orationem ... Basileae in Officina Heruagiana, Anno M. D. XXXIX. (Greek and Latin texts.) Cited as 'Basel (1539).'

S. Dionysii Areopagitae Martyris, Episcopi Athenien. et Gallorvm Apostoli, *Opera* (quae quidem extent) *omnia*, quintuplici translatione versa, & Commentariis D. Dionysii A Rikel Carthvsiani ... Coloniae ex officina Haeredum Ioannis Quentel, anno CHRISTI nati 1556. mense Ianuario. Cited as 'Cologne (1556).'

Dionysii Areopagitae, *Opera quae extant*. In eadem Maximi Scholia. Georgii Pachymerae Paraphrasis ... Parisiis, M.D.LXII, Apud Guil. Morelium, in Graecis typographum Regium. Cited as 'Paris (1562).'

ΓΡΗΓΟΡΙΟΥ ΤΟΥ ΝΑΖΙΑΝΖΗΝΟΥ ΤΟΥ ΘΕΟΛΟΓΟΥ ΑΠΑΝΤΑ, *τὰ μέχρι νῦν μὲν εὑρισκόμενα* ... 'Εν βασιλείᾳ, ἀναλώμασι Ιοάννου τοῦ ἐρβαγίου, (1550). Cited as 'Basel (1550).'

Divi Gregorii Nazianzeni, Cognomento Theologi, *Opera Omnia*, qvae qvidem extant, nova translatione donata ... Quae omnia nunc primùm Latina facta sunt, IACOBI BILLII Prunaei ... Addita sunt etiam ubique breuia quaedam Scholia, eodem Abbate auctore ... Parisiis, apud Ioannem Bene natum. 1569. Cited as 'Paris (1569).'

D. Gregorii Nyssae Pontificis, Magni Basilii Fratris, Doctissimvs in *Hexaemeron* Commentarivs ... Petro Francisco Zino, Veronensi, Interprete. Aldi Filii, Venetiis, M. D. LIII. Cited as 'Venice (1553).'

Opvs Admirandvm Gregorii Nysseni Antistitis, *De Hominis Opificio*: Interprete Iohanne Lewenklaio: Annotationibus etiam necessariis additis ... Basileae, per Ioannem Oporinum ... Anno Salutis M.D.LXVII, Mense Augusto. (Date appears at the end of the volume.) Cited as 'Basel (1567).'

Opera D. Gregorii, Nysseni Episcopi, Fratris Basilii Magni, de Graeco in Latinvm Sermonem conuersa, studio potissimùm atque opera Lavrentii Sifani I.V.D. & Ioannis Lewenklaii ... Basileae, per Evsebivm Episcopivm, et Nicolai fratres haeredes, M.D. LXXI. Cited as 'Basel (1571).'

D. Patris Gregorii Nysseni Antistitis *De Virginitate Liber*: Graecè & Latinè nunc primùm editus, Interprete Iohanne Livineio Gandensi ... Antverpiae, Ex officina Christophori Plantini, Architypographi Regii. CIƆ IƆ LXXIIII. (1574). Cited as 'Antwerp (1574).'

Contra Haereses. Divi Irenaei Episcopi Lvgdvnensis in quinque libros digestum ... Erasmi Roterodami ... Parisiis apud Maturinum Dupuys ... 1545. Cited as 'Paris (1545).'

Diui Ioannis Chrysostomi *in omnes Pauli apostoli epistolas* accuratissima, uereque aurea, & diuina interpretatio ... Veronae typis aereis excusum per Stephanum, & fratres a Sabio quarto kalendas Iulias, MDXXIX. (Greek text.) Cited as 'Verona (1529).'

D. Ioannis Chrysostomi ... *opera*, quae hactenus uersa sunt *omnia*, ad Graecorum codicum collationem multis in locis per utriusque linguae peritos emendata ... Basileae, in Officina Frobeniana, Mense Avgvsto, Anno M. D. XXX. (Edited and partly translated by Erasmus.) Cited as 'Basel (1530).'

D. Ioannis Chrysostomi Archiepiscopi Constantinopolitani *in omnes D. Pauli epistolas* commentarii, quotquot apud Graecos extant latinitate donati ... recens a D. Wolfgango Musculo traducta est ... Basileae ex officina Ioan. Hervag. Anno M.D. XXXVI. Cited as 'Basel (1536).'

Divi Patris Ioannis Chrysostomi Archiepisc. Constantinopolitani *De virginitate liber*, Graecè & Latinè nunc primùm editus; Interprete Ioanne Liuineio Gandensi ... Antverpiae, Ex officina Christophori Plantini, Architypographi Regii. M. D. LXXV. Cited as 'Antwerp (1575).'

An Exposition Vpon the Epistle of S. Paule the Apostle to the Ephesians: By S. Iohn Chrysostome, Archbishop of Constantinople. Truely and faithfully translated out of Greeke ... At London: Printed by Henry Binneman and Ralph Newberie ... 24.Decembris. 1581. Cited as 'London (1581).' *STC* 14632, 14632a.

Beati Ioannis Damasceni *Orthodoxae Fidei* accvrata Explicatio, iiii libris distincta, nuncque primùm Graecè & Latinè simul ... edita: Iacobo Fabro Stapulensi interprete ... Basileae, per Henrichum Petri, 1548. Cited as 'Basel (1548).'

Sancti Ioannis Damasceni *Opera*, Mvlto qvam vnqvam antehac auctiora, magnáque ex parte nunc de integro conuersa. Per D. Iacobvm Billivm Prunaeum, S. Michaëlis in eremo Coenobiarcham ... Parisiis. Apud Guillelmum Chaudiere ... M. D. LXXVII. Cited as 'Paris (1577).'

B. Maximi Monachi, *Capitum Theologicorum Centuriae quinque* ... Parisiis, M. D. LX. Apud Guil. Morelium in Graecis typographum Regiũ. Cited as 'Paris (1560).'

Opera Q. Septimiiflorentis Tertvlliani Carthaginensis, Inter Latinos Ecclesiae scriptores primi ... Nunc verò denuo ad fidem veterũ exemplarium manu descriptorũ collata & restituta ... Parisiis. Apud Carolam Guillard ... M. D. XLV. Cited as 'Paris (1545).'

Beati Theodoreti, Cyrensis Episcopi, Theologi Vetvstissimi, *Opera*, in dvos tomos distincta ... Coloniae Agrippinae, apvd Ioannem Birckmannvm, Anno Salvtis M.D.LXXIII. Cited as 'Cologne (1573).'

Liturgical:
MIssale ad vsũ insignis ac preclare ecclesie Sar. nuper accuratissime castigatũ ...

Magister Martinus Morin ... recētissime Impressum Rothomagi ... Anno dñi. m. ccccc. et. xiiii. die vero. xv. mensis Februarii. Cited as 'Rothomagi (1514).' *STC* 16192, 16194.

MAnuale ad vsum percelebris ecclesie Sarisberieñ. nouissime, et non antea tali volumine, cum latine tum anglice Impressum, Parrisiis Per Desideriū maheu ... Anno dñi, M.ccccccxxvi. Cited as 'Paris (1526).' *STC* 16147.

ΤΡΙΩΔΙΟΝ. Τὸ παρὸν βιβλίον τετύπωται, Παρὰ 'Αντωνίῳ τῷ Πινέλλῳ. Ἀναλώμασι μὲν τοῖς αὐτοῦ ... 'ΕΝΕΤΙΉΣΙΝ, Ἔτει ἀπὸ τῆς ἐν σάρκου οἰκονομίας. ,α χ ι δ' Cited as 'Venice (1641).'

ΠΕΝΤΗΚΟΣΤΑΡΙΟΝ ... Venetiis per Ioan. Ant. et Petrum de Nicolinis de Sabio, sumptu & requisitione D. Damiani de sancta Maria da Spici. Anno dni. M.D.XLIIII. Cited as 'Venice (1544).'

ΜΗΝ ΙΑΝΟΥΑΡΙΟΣ ΟΥΤΟΣΙ. Τὸ παρὸν μηναῖον τετύπωται, 'Ενετίησιν, παρὰ Πέτρου, υἱοῦ τοῦ ποτὲ. Χριστοφόρου τοῦ τζανέτου ... Ἔτει ἀπὸ τῆς ἐνσάρκου οἰκονομίας ,α φ ῃ ε'. Cited as 'Venice (1595).'

ΒΙΒΛΙΟΝ ΤΟΥ ΑΠΡΙΛΛΙΟΥ ΜΗΝΟΣ. ... Τὸ παρὸν μηναῖον ἐτυπώθη ἐνετίησιν ἐν οἰκίᾳ κυρίου 'Ιακώβου τοῦ Λεογγίνου ... Ἔτει τῷ ἀπὸ τῆς ἐνσάρκου οἰκονομίας τοῦ χύ ἡμῶν 'Ιῦ Χῦ, ,α φ ξ θ'. Cited as 'Venice (1569).'

ΒΙΒΛΙΟΝ ΤΟΥ 'ΑΥΓΟΥΣΤΟΣ ΜΗΝΟΣ ... 'ΕΝΕΤΙΉΣΙΝ. Παρὰ Πέτρου υἱοῦ τοῦ ποτὲ. χριστοφόρου, τοῦ τζανέτου. μ φ ῃ α'. Cited as 'Venice (1591).'

Other:

NOVVM TESTAMENTVM Iam qvintvm ac postremvm accvratissima cvra recognitvm à Des. Erasmo Roterodamo cum Annotationibus eiusdem ita locupletatis, ut propémodum opus nouum uideri possit. Froben, Basileae, Anno M D XLI. Cited as 'Basel (1542).'

Des. Erasmi Rot. *IN NOVVM TESTAMENTVM ANNOTATIONES,* ex Postrema Ipsivs Avthoris recognitione, addito Indice plus tertia parte superioribus editionibus locupletiore. Froben ... Basileae, MDLV. Cited as 'Basel (1555).'

THESAVRVS GRAECAE LINGUAE, ab Henrico Stephano constructus, IN QVO PRAETER ALIA PLVRIMA Quae Primus Praestitit ... Vocabula in Certas Classes Distribuit, Multiplici Deriuatorum Serie Ad Primigenia, Tanquam Ad Radices Vnde Pullulant, Reuocata ... ANNO M.D.LXXII, Excudebat Henr. Stephanus. CVM PRIVILEGIO CAES. MAIESTATIS, ET CHRISTIANISS. GALLIARVM REGIS.

General Index

Aaron, as type of Christ, 39
Acidale, Mount, 205, 206
Acrasia: symbolism of, 109, 117, 144, 193–4, 206; and Mordant, 111, 116, 118, 119, 128, 155, 172, 173, 177, 178
Acrates, 109
Adam: legacy of, 156, 159–62, 165–71, 172, 174–5, 177, 181, 198, 203, 206; the second, 35, 71–2
Adam and Eve: in Hades, 27, 49; restoration of, 34, 55, 200–1, 205; symbols of, 57, 245–6
Adonis, Garden of, 129, 199–202, 203, 205–6
alabaster box, 20
Alan, 92–4, 110
Alcyone, 57
Allegory of Love (Lewis), 3
Alma, 180, 182, 183, 184–5, 251
Amavia: allegory of the Fall, 122, 172, 173, 175–7, 180; grief of, 117–18, 119; mention, 128
Ambrose: accessibility of, 4–5, 6, 7, 11, 27, 223; on deification, 39; on the eucharist, 62, 64, 65; on temperance, 110; on unfallen eros, 202; mention, 33, 115

Ambrosiaster, 158
Amoret, 19–20, 192, 194–6, 198, 200, 205–6, 207
Amoretti and Epithalamion, 194, 206, 207
Andrewes, Lancelot, 7, 8, 47, 217–18, 229, 230
angel, and Guyon, 151–2
Anglican. *See* Church of England
Annunciation, the, 198–9
Anselm of Canterbury, 35–6
Anthony, asceticism of, 100–1, 104–5, 111, 119, 121, 124, 134, 137, 139, 142, 143
anti-Catholic polemic, 3
apathy [ἀπάθεια], concept of in patristic theology, 106–8, 110, 120, 123, 125, 131, 138, 144, 145–6
Aquinas, Thomas: accessibility of, 7; on baptism, 40; on nature of Christ, 136; on original sin, 157; on the passions, 98, 108, 236; on temperance, 99–100, 108, 109; on unfallen eros, 204; mention, 115, 118–19, 120
Archimago, 69, 74
Aristotle, 98, 99, 108–13, 114, 115, 118

Author Index

This index is devoted to modern authors and Spenserian scholars. Patristic Fathers are in the General Index.

Alpers, Paul J., 132, 139, 140
Anderson, Judith, 147-8

Bennett, Josephine Waters: on St. George, 230; on Transfiguration symbolism, 93; on Una's betrothal, 63, 64–5, 66, 67–8
Bentley, Jerome, 164
Berger, Harry, Jr.: on Belphoebe, 122, 123; on Guyon's faint, 132, 140, 147, 244; on temperance in *FQ*, 118, 121
Berleth, Richard, 198–9
Bieman, Elizabeth, 15–19, 20–1, 42
Bromiley, G. W., 32
Brown, Peter, 251

Cain, Thomas, 72–3
Cullen, Patrick, 132–7, 144–5

Danielou, Jean, 62, 211

Ellrodt, Robert, 170, 200–1

Fallon, Stephen, 126–7
Fowler, Alastair: on numerology in *FQ*, 89; on Ruddymane, 172–3, 174, 175, 176; on the spring, 177

Grant, Patrick, 54, 57–8, 59–60
Greenblatt, Stephen, 130–1
Greenslade, S.L., 6

Hamilton, A.C.: on Acrasia, 193; on Belphoebe, 123, 124, 125, 126; on 'image in the glass,' 76; on images in *FQ*, 13–14; on the 'liquor pure,' 18–19; on Maleger, 179–80, 181, 182, 184; on New Jerusalem, 55–6; on Pastorella, 192; on Red Crosse as dissolute, 9–10; on Ruddymane, 172–3, 175, 249; on the spring, 177; on the standing lake, 186; on temperance 115–16, 121, 122, 241; on the Well, 230; mention, 20, 35, 148
Hankins, John Erskine, 14, 26, 81, 220
Helgerson, Richard, 207

Index of References to
The Faerie Queene

Index of Scripture References